II049660

OTHER TITLES OF INTEREST FROM ST. LUCIE PRESS

The 90-Day ISO 9000 Manual and Implementation Guide

The Executive Guide to Implementing Quality Systems

Focused Quality: Managing for Results

Improving Service Quality: Achieving High Performance in the Public and Private Sectors

Introduction to Modern Statistical Quality Control and Management

ISO 9000: Implementation Guide for Small to Mid-Sized Businesses

Organization Teams: Continuous Quality Improvement

Organization Teams: Facilitator's Guide

Principles of Total Quality

Quality Improvement Handbook: Team Guide to Tools and Techniques

The Textbook of Total Quality in Healthcare

Total Quality in Higher Education

Total Quality in Managing Human Resources

Total Quality in Marketing

Total Quality in Purchasing and Supplier Management

Total Quality in Radiology: A Guide to Implementation

Total Quality in Research and Development

Total Quality Management for Custodial Operations

Total Quality Management: Text, Cases, and Readings, 2nd Edition

Total Quality Service

For more information about these titles call, fax or write:

St. Lucie Press
100 E. Linton Blvd., Suite 403B
Delray Beach, FL 33483
TEL (407) 274-9906 • FAX (407) 274-9927

S_L^t

Total Quality in
RESEARCH
AND
DEVELOPMENT

The St. Lucie Press
Total Quality Series™

BOOKS IN THE SERIES:

Total Quality in HIGHER EDUCATION

Total Quality in PURCHASING and SUPPLIER MANAGEMENT

Total Quality in INFORMATION SYSTEMS

Total Quality in RESEARCH and DEVELOPMENT

Total Quality in MANAGING HUMAN RESOURCES

Total Quality in ORGANIZATIONAL DEVELOPMENT

Total Quality in MARKETING

MACROLOGISTICS IN STRATEGIC MANAGEMENT

For more information about these books call St. Lucie Press at (407) 274-9906

Series Editor • Frank Voehl
Series Development Editor • Sandy Pearlman

Total Quality in

RESEARCH
AND
DEVELOPMENT

By
Gregory C. McLaughlin, DBA
President
Inthesis, Inc.
Palm Beach Gardens, Florida

St. Lucie Press
Delray Beach, Florida

$S{^t_L}$

Published by
St. Lucie Press
100 E. Linton Blvd., Suite 403B
Delray Beach, FL 33483

CONTENTS

SERIES PREFACE

The St. Lucie Press Series on Total Quality originated in 1993 when some of us realized that the rapidly expanding field of quality management was neither well defined nor well focused. This realization, coupled with America's hunger for specific, how-to examples, led to the formulation of a plan to publish a series of subject-specific books on total quality, a new direction for books in the field to follow.

The essence of this series consists of a core nucleus of seven new direction books, around which the remaining books in the series will revolve over a three-year period:

- Education Transformation: *Total Quality in Higher Education*

- Respect for People: *Total Quality in Managing Human Resources*

- Speak with Facts: *Total Quality in Information Systems*

- Customer Satisfaction: *Total Quality in Marketing*

- Continuous Improvement: *Total Quality in Research and Development*

- Supplier Partnerships: *Total Quality in Purchasing and Supplier Management*

- Cost-Effective, Value-Added Services: *Measuring Total Quality*

We at St. Lucie Press have been privileged to contribute to the convergence of philosophy and underlying principles of total quality, leading to a common set of assumptions. One of the most important deals with the challenges facing the transformation of the R&D community for the 21st century. This is a particularly exciting and turbulent time in this field, both domestically and globally, and change may be viewed as either an opportunity or a threat. As such, the principles and practices of total quality can aid in this transformation or, by flawed implementation approaches, can bring an organization to its knees.

As the author explains, the total quality orientation to R&D redefines line managerial roles and identifies new responsibilities for the traditional function to come to grips with. The R&D practitioner's role now includes strategic input and continual development of strategic planning as well as the operational planning system to increase customer satisfaction both now and in the future. The full meaning of these changes is explored in light of the driving forces reshaping the R&D environment.

As Series Editor, I am pleased with the manner in which the series is coming together. Its premise is that excellence can be achieved through a singular focus on customers and their interests as a number one priority, a focus that requires a high degree of commitment, flexibility, and resolve. The new definition of the degree of satisfaction will be the total experience of the interaction—which will be the determinant of whether the customer stays a customer. However, no book or series can tell an organization how to achieve total quality; only the customers and stakeholders can tell you when you have it and when you do not. High-quality goods and services can give an organization a competitive edge while reducing costs due to rework, returns, and scrap. Most importantly, outstanding R&D quality performance generates satisfied customers, who reward the organization with continued patronage and free word-of-mouth advertising.

In the area of abstracts, we are indebted to Richard Frantzreb, President of Advanced Personnel Systems, who has granted permission to incorporate selected abstracts from their collection, which they independently publish in a quarterly magazine called *Quality Abstracts*. This feature is a sister publication to *Training and Development Alert*. These journals are designed to keep readers abreast of literature in the field of quality and to help readers benefit from the insights and experience of experts and practitioners who are implementing total quality in their organizations. Each journal runs between 28 and 36 pages and contains about 100 carefully selected abstracts of articles and books in the field. For further information, contact Richard Frantzreb (916-781-2900).

We trust that you will find this book both usable and beneficial and wish you maximum success on the quality journey. If it in some way makes a contribution, then we can say, as Dr. Deming often did at the end of his seminars, "I have done my best."

Frank Voehl
Series Editor

AUTHOR'S PREFACE

Research and its subsequent development into profitable products and services continues to serve our technologically driven economy. Without these critical activities, the advancement of technology would stagnate. Therefore, given its importance, the application of total quality principles and practices supports technological advances and ensures continued growth. This text serves to define those total quality principles and practices that can be directly applied to R&D.

Total Quality in Research and Development provides the management methods and social and technological skills to achieve total quality. Total quality is achieved when there is an equal interaction between a management system that provides leadership, a social system that empowers people, and a technical system that provides for innovation and creativity. Each system is explored in detail, along with strategies for implementing total quality. Systems are assessed through survey instruments that highlight total quality elements such as strategy, communication skills and systems, values and principles, process control, and customer satisfaction. The result of completing these instruments is a better understanding of present practices and identification of opportunities for improvement. A systematic plan, designed specifically for R&D, to implement total quality practices is presented in detail. Benchmarks that yield success are highlighted. ISO 9000, an international quality standard, is examined for applicability and use in R&D to improve quality, efficiency, and effectiveness. A case study, tracking the progress of an internationally recognized R&D facility, is presented as a model for implementing total quality principles within a R&D facility/department.

The importance of implementing total quality principles in R&D cannot be overstated. Too often, the literature has focused solely on manufacturing applications without incorporating the critical link between design/development and product quality. This text attempts to bridge that gap and provides the R&D department or facility with a road map for success. The R&D organization that can use total quality principles to improve systems and empower employees will surely benefit today and well into the next century.

The author would like to acknowledge the assistance of the St. Lucie Press staff and Mr. Frank Voehl for their helpful comments and suggestions. In addition, the author wishes to thank the Quality First staff at Palm Beach Community College (David Locke, Gene Hope, and Dr. Ottis Smith) for their assistance, patience, and diligence in preparing this text. Finally, all those individuals, co-workers, and friends who have influenced and taught the author the true meaning of total quality are acknowledged. This especially applies to my family (Eleanor and Joseph Rodgers and Dr. Tim McLaughlin and family). Without the love and support of these fine people, I would not have accomplished this dream.

THE SERIES EDITOR

Frank Voehl has had a twenty-year career in quality management, productivity improvement, and related fields. He has written more than 200 articles, papers, and books for international business journals, publications, and conferences worldwide on the subject of quality. Mr. Voehl has consulted on quality and productivity issues, as well as measurement system implementation, for hundreds of companies (many Fortune 500 corporations). As general manager of FPL Qualtec, he was influential in the FPL Deming Prize process, which led to the formation of the Malcolm Baldrige Award, as well as the National Quality Award in the Bahamas. He is a member of Strategic Planning committees with the ASQC and AQP and has assisted the IRS in quality planning as a member of the Commissioner's Advisory Group.

An industrial engineering graduate from St. John's University in New York City, Mr. Voehl has been a visiting professor and lecturer at NYU and the University of Miami, where he helped establish the framework for the Quality Institute. He is currently president and CEO of Strategy Associates, Inc. and a visiting professor at Florida International University.

On the local level, Mr. Voehl served for ten years as vice chairman of the Margate/Broward County Advisory Committee for the Handicapped. In 1983, he was awarded the Partners in Productivity award by Florida Governor Graham for his efforts to streamline and improve the Utilities Forced Relocation Process, which saved the state some $200 million over a seven-year period.

THE AUTHOR

Gregory C. McLaughlin, DBA, is Director of Quality First, Palm Beach Community College, Florida and has over fifteen years of extensive experience in the field of quality engineering, quality management, team building, and statistical analyses. Dr. McLaughlin has been employed with Eastman Kodak Company, Baxter Healthcare, Reynolds Metals Company, and QualPro, Inc. He has consulted with over fifty companies, both large and small, and is credited with assisting Milliken and Company in achieving the 1989 National Quality Award. He has worked directly with Dr. W. Edwards Deming and has attained the achievement of "Deming Master." His experience extends to R&D, service, and manufacturing. He is a recognized expert in the field of continuous quality improvement, customer satisfaction, and organizational communications.

Dr. McLaughlin received his doctoral degree in business administration from Nova Southeastern University and both his master's degree in statistics and his bachelor's degree in atmospheric physics from Florida State University. He has published numerous articles and technical papers in all aspects of quality assurance and continuous quality improvement and organizational communication effectiveness.

He received his Certified Quality Engineer Certificate from the American Society for Quality Control and has served ASQC as chairman of the Greater Palm Beach Section. Dr. McLaughlin is an IQA-certified ISO 9000 Quality Systems Provisional Assessor.

CHAPTER 1

TOTAL QUALITY IN R&D

OVERVIEW

Those individuals who perform research and development (R&D) functions in organizations and corporations face an unparalleled challenge within the workplace. As competitive pressures grow and the search for new products and processes accelerates, the need for a total quality systematic approach becomes evident. Companies face the prospect of introducing new products at a frightening pace. Those organizations and businesses unable to maintain an effective R&D organization must face the challenge posed by larger organizations that can move products to market rapidly. Executives often expect that the R&D function will perform successfully with reduced resources and unrealistic objectives. Cycle times within the R&D function must improve dramatically given that companies now employ fewer individuals in the R&D function.[1] Fewer people are doing more work in shorter times with increased pressure. The need for teamwork, efficient and effective management systems, and appropriate technologies has become critical. R&D personnel must experience the benefits of working in a positive environment that supports the goals of total quality. These goals include team accomplishments, searching collectively for improved productivity, redesigning management systems to promote a total quality approach, and

1

eliminating variation in research design and implementation. These goals are reason enough for implementing some sort of total quality improvement effort within a facility or department.

Many researchers feel that a total quality system stifles inventiveness, ingenuity, and individual accomplishment. In reality, total quality promotes collaborative accomplishments, rewards both team and individual performance, and initiates and maintains an environment conducive to creativity. Present practices in many organizations often stifle creativity and inventiveness because the environment (managerial and social systems) creates fear and mistrust. No individual can achieve his or her best in a work environment that creates excess stress and demands that the individual operate in a vacuum.[1] If organizational objectives are unclear, then the norm is generally to outperform others through a system that rewards values that are not fully conducive to organizational goals. Often the research environment is more like that of an academic institution, where a philosophy of "sink or swim" prevails. This "academic" philosophy is in contradiction to established total quality principles. Researchers, like academicians, often prosper by participating in a system that rewards individual achievement and discourages alliance building and cooperation. Researchers form teams that function like a small department and may erect barriers to outsiders by discouraging interaction outside the "team." Like corporations and organizations preparing to do business in the 1990s, the R&D function must build alliances and partnerships in order to survive and prosper. Total quality produces the optimal environment for research. Total quality is not just a system, method, or philosophy but rather is a working model for daily operations. This working model includes actual daily work practices, guideposts and measurements for success, and management practices that stress creativity and group accomplishments which support company goals.

As the 21st century approaches, the need for total quality in R&D becomes increasingly important. The total quality philosophy prepares the work force for positive change through continuous improvement, by motivating and energizing employees and empowering all within the system. The result of these efforts is products and services that meet customer needs and expectations through systems that are both effective and efficient in meeting shareholder needs and management priorities.

CRITICAL FACTORS AFFECTING THE R&D ENVIRONMENT

The present environment for R&D can be characterized in two simple words: **inconsistent horizons**. The rapid development of technology and the number of new scientific discoveries have led to tremendous change. Information is increasing exponentially. Markets are opening at a frantic pace. Businesses are modifying their entire corporate structure, downsizing and "right-sizing." The result (or cause) of this change causes the organization to operate in a constant state of flux. Rapid change in an uncontrolled environment can best be described as inconsistent. Additionally, the future of R&D is at best clouded by this inconsistency. Traditional approaches to R&D continue to fail. Given that the success of R&D is dependent on its ability to develop and produce new products that customers want, the R&D organization and its culture must change. Thus, the future horizon is a large unknown variable, which makes R&D a risky venture.

Four factors that influence the environment which affects R&D are described in this section. These four factors have a pronounced effect on R&D. They speak to the statement of need for a total quality approach in R&D.

Global Economy

Recent political events, which began in the 1980s, have entirely revised the world marketplace. A large and fairly underdeveloped marketplace exists. New markets (new customers) create the need for new products. Growing demands should bode well for increased research dollars. However, the number and diversity of "players" have also dramatically increased. Successful R&D needs an environment that promotes innovation and creativity. Efficient and effective systems must drive the research organization. New markets and new "competition" require a new philosophy. Total quality provides the mechanism for revitalizing R&D.

Many underdeveloped economies are grasping for scant resources. The unavailability of capital needed for research is also a pressing problem. Capital creation and growth continue to expand; however, the growing number of markets causes a competitive environment. Many U.S. organizations that have traditionally supported numerous R&D projects are currently reevaluating their research budgets. The environment that exists seems to be one of retrenchment, with companies trying to protect their products and markets. Yet new products are needed at a frantic pace. The Japanese continue to demonstrate that R&D can prosper in a total quality environment.

As Japan increases its research budget to over 2.9% of total gross national product (GNP),[2] other countries view R&D as a way to increase market share. There is a competitive aspect to R&D in the 1990s. International firms are emphasizing R&D to gain a competitive advantage. Scientific progress and inventiveness are not the sole property of the industrialized nations. Research as a percent of GNP has fallen to less than 2.5% in the United States.[2] Competitive and marketplace pressures require new and innovative products and processes.

Lack of new government research is also a potential problem for U.S. firms. Political realities have caused a decrease in the U.S. defense budget, with a corresponding reduction in new R&D. Nearly 50% of all research in the United States is solely for military purposes,[2] yet over one-third of all U.S. profits come from new products. Lack of funding, either from government or industry sources, signals a reduction in R&D when the opposite should be true. Funding alone will not solve the problem of sluggish R&D results. Ineffective practices and inflexible corporate R&D cultures need to be changed through the practice of total quality.

Finally, the movement in the United States to a service economy has hurt R&D. Services need R&D at a reduced pace and funding level. The service economy (and its resulting mentality) downplays the need for new products and processes, relying on traditional managerial and operational paradigms.

Reengineering the Organization

The corporate (and organizational) stampede to reengineering, downsizing, right-sizing, etc. affects R&D in both spirit and impact. Although organizational "fat" needs to be trimmed, the method by which it is accomplished is crucial. By restructuring the organization through attrition, job elimination, forced retirement, etc., the spirit of the organization (esprit de corps) suffers tremendously. Trust, security, and positive communications are replaced with anxiety, back-stabbing, and "rumor mills." The corporate culture becomes protective and fearful, with little creativity or innovation. Costs, budgets, and the bottom line are managed rather than people. Unfortunately, an examination of the curriculum at many business schools will confirm the presence of financial and cost management as the critical core of knowledge. The key resource (employees) is set adrift to survive the storm. The environment stifles creativity and innovation—the keys to successful research. R&D personnel may view the downsizing procedure as a method to increase their productivity with reduced resources and manpower. The damage caused by such malicious actions is unknown and may remain unknowable.[3]

Before downsizing or reengineering the organization, formal and informal networks need to be mapped and identified.[4] A **network** is an information chain that is established between two or more individuals. Networks are linchpin strategies, developed within organizations, which permit individuals to access and respond to information within and about the firm.[4] Formal networks define the organizational structure whereas informal networks define the human interaction with the organizational structure. Krackhardt and Hanson define three such informal networks that employees use:

1. **Advice networks**—technical and problem-solving information

2. **Trust networks**—exchange of human and political information

3. **Communication networks**—employee and organizational communications[4]

According to Krackhardt and Hanson,[4] managers must identify these networks, and their efficiency and effectiveness, before attempting reengineering. Within R&D, these networks serve to accomplish tasks, improve morale, and contribute significantly to the bottom line. Failure to identify informal networks may significantly decrease productivity and creativity within the organization.[4] Informal networks become a linchpin to understanding the information exchange system in R&D.

In practice, restructuring the organization may be a natural evolution. If the restructuring strengthens the organization through employee empowerment (participatory management–power sharing), improved management facilitation, and efficient systems, then the effort can be successful. Integrating management, technical, and social systems into a synergistic balance yields the largest benefit. Restructuring through the implementation of total quality principles will ensure that employees participate in the change. Reengineering principles need a total quality approach to successfully change the organization. (For additional information, see Abstract 1.1 at the end of this chapter.)

Improved Cycle Time

Given the constraints of a global economy and restructured businesses, R&D facilities need to improve turnaround time to remain competitive. **Cycle time** refers to the amount of time required to design, produce, and test a new product. By increasing cycle time, R&D facilities accomplish their primary objective more rapidly. Cycle time, however, is an internal factor to R&D that is often driven by external influences such as corporate decision making, customer needs, and organizational goals. Many of these external influences are outside the control of the R&D department and therefore limit its ability to effectively control these variables. Often, the success of a R&D project is highly dependent on uncontrolled factors which may ultimately be responsible for affecting the effectiveness of the organization. This "Catch-22" situation may be one reason for reduced funding and department downsizing.

In the near future, products and processes will require shorter cycle times from initial design to customer purchase. The drive to invent, test, produce, and ensure the safety of the product and satisfy a customer need grows shorter every year. In order to accomplish this task, new and innovative systems that address all critical needs must be established. Traditional academic-based research management paradigms fall short of producing the necessary results. Individual performance and rewards, common in many R&D organizations, need to be replaced with systems that reward team accomplishments. New products (as well as modifications to existing products) require a process that minimizes waste, rework, and inefficiency. New measures, such as benchmarking, are needed to determine the success of introducing a new or modified product. Included in this measure of success is an examination of the efficiency and effectiveness of the process used to design and prototype the product. Total quality provides such a mechanism to ensure effective designs, built from a customer satisfaction perspective, which meet all required needs in the shortest possible time.

Emergence of New Technology

Finally, the influence of new discoveries and improved technology greatly impacts the R&D environment. The speed at which technology is introduced, accepted, and then modified to meet unfulfilled needs continues to increase. Technologies change so rapidly that today's market leader is tomorrow's market loser.

Responsiveness to changing customer needs must drive the R&D organization. R&D must view technology and scientific advances as tools to assist the organization in meeting company goals. Technology is a means to an end rather than an end in itself. Technology both threatens and safeguards R&D. The need exists to place technology within the larger framework of total quality, balancing it with the managerial and social systems.

R&D organizations that rely solely on technology as a strategy for growth and expansion[5] may experience increasing failure in the 21st century. Unfortunately, the dependence on technology as a sufficient strategy[5] is faulty because the demands on the entire marketplace continue to change so rapidly. Inevitably, technology must be managed within the R&D organization to benefit all employees/shareholders. The ability to manage effectively can best be achieved through the implementation of total quality principles.

HISTORY OF R&D

The single most important factor in the industrial success of the United States in this century has been the systematic exploitation of science and technology.[6] R&D provided the impetus by which this transformation occurred. The history of R&D from its beginnings after 1870 up to the present is traced in this section.

Prior to 1870, most technological advances were the result of the discovery process. That is, product advances were singular in nature, without the benefit of the resulting processes needed to incorporate them into mass production. Eli Whitney's cotton gin is one example of a technological advance that revolutionized the entire world. After 1870, however, the beginnings of mass production and modern business practices can be seen. Consequently, some authors have referred to this period of numerous inventions as the "Second American Revolution."[6] Men such as Thomas Edison (more than 1000 patents) dominated the research field.[6] Inventors used science and scientific principles combined with an entrepreneurial spirit to perform research and advance technology.

By 1900, this "period of invention" was quickly supplemented by a move from the independent inventor to organized research facilities operated by large manufacturing firms.[6] Business executives realized the potential for capitalizing on new technology and began to assimilate the expertise of scientists and engineers into a formalized research organization. General Electric (GE) was the first such organization to benefit from this partnership of research and business.[6] Other large organizations, such as AT&T, Eastman Kodak, RCA, and DuPont, took on a similar appearance. These laboratories concerned themselves with internal inventive activities but also monitored the environment for technological threats and opportunities.[7] Research organizations developed a strategic posture to introduce new products and maintain market dominance.[7] DuPont's research approach was originally designed to develop and exploit "monumental breakthroughs."[6] This strategic direction, practiced by organizations such as GE, led to both dramatic success and disastrous failure.

The development of corporate research laboratories reflected the structure of the organization.[7] The development of industrial research was associated with expansion and diversification in the activities and products of manufacturing firms.[7] "Research facilities developed their own internal organizations, culture, and agendas...seeking advice both from the scientific as well as business communities."[6] At GE's lab, Willis Whitney created a laboratory with an academic environment coupled with a defined system of seminars and collegial meetings for the benefit of researchers. GE's model became the normative method of operation and management for industrial research facilities well into the 1980s. In reality, the corporate research organization became detached from the strategic posturing and planning of the organization.[8]

Strong antitrust policies in the United States (Sherman Antitrust Act) resulted in the establishment of multiple research facilities or significant expansion of central research facilities.[7] These strong antitrust activities, unknown in Europe, increased the reliance on industrial research.[7] Antitrust litigation in the early 20th century produced research labs such as

AT&T's famous Bell Labs through superior technological advances that promoted market domination. This research also led to broadened activities for AT&T, such as research into transmission and communications.[7] Unlike GE and DuPont, AT&T Bell Labs remained more tightly concentrated on telecommunications and is now recognized as the leading research organization of its kind in the United States.

Contract and industrial research firms grew rapidly in the first half of this century.[7] R&D grew at an outstanding rate from 1900 to 1940, with nearly 350 independent laboratories established. R&D established a dualistic structure in this period, with firms that supported internal research competing with R&D firms designed to provide research services.[7] By the 1930s, "science was becoming widely regarded as the driving force behind the process of innovation."[6] Those firms that could not or would not invest in R&D faced "significant handicaps in the innovation process."[7]

Between 1921 and 1946, 200 of the largest American firms invested in R&D. The significant investment in R&D during the 1930s paid off for these companies by ensuring their survival. During this period, academic institutions pursued a parallel effort to U.S. industries, stressing a decentralized structure by developing products and services geared for commercial use.[7] These efforts linked higher education (especially state-funded public universities) and industrial research. State contributions to academic R&D exceeded those of the federal government during the 1930s.[7] Curriculum and research activities in public universities aligned themselves with commercial opportunities.[7] During World War II, the federal government invested heavily in research, and the effect of this partnership with business is one reason for the outcome of the war.[6] This partnership expanded the scope of research and technology and contributed greatly to the U.S. industrial and marketplace dominance in later years.

Concurrent with the change in emphasis of R&D, the basic idea of total quality was born during the first half of this century. Walter A. Shewhart described his concept of quality in his 1931 pioneering work entitled *The Economic Control of Quality of Manufactured Product.* Shewhart defined the notion that product quality was a critical element for sustained economic growth. Quality was the result of a consistent process that operated with controlled variability. Dr. Shewhart, a physicist, was a member of AT&T's prestigious Bell Labs and worked with Western Electric Company at the famous Chicago Hawthorne Plant. Dr. Shewhart's work enabled AT&T to reliably mass produce telecommunication equipment both efficiently and effectively. More importantly, he defined the concept and scope of quality control/assurance up to the present day. Contemporary researchers of Dr. Shewhart, such as Dr. W. Edwards Deming, have extended and redefined the concepts of total quality. Yet today, total quality is often considered a foreign concept—the product of manufacturers and businesses. The truth lies in the fact that total quality is a philosophy and method born and developed from R&D. Total quality exemplifies the best efforts of R&D that contributes to modern life.

After the war, R&D expanded rapidly, with many organizations creating a "campus"-type environment for their researchers. Management, however, grew tired of large research budgets that frequently produced little if any tangible results.[6] During the 1960s and 1970s, companies moved many of their research efforts into basic, if not mundane, research.[6] The golden age of research, however, occurred during the 1970s, before the restructuring of corporate strategic policies.[8] The 1980s was characterized by rapid changes in both the organization and the mission of R&D. At present, a definite lack of strategy and vision has severely hampered R&D.[8] Yet the United States continues to lead the world in basic research and has a research-driven university system that is unequaled.[9]

As in the 1940s, an upsurge of spending in public universities is occurring at present and may be a forerunner of increased product innovation for the future. Many U.S. executives have been disillusioned by the slow pace of product development and basic research and have come to see their expectations unfulfilled. In contrast to past successes, the outlook for the 1990s and beyond remains uncertain.

Research budgets have steadily deteriorated in the United States to less than 2.5% of GNP.[2] In contrast, the Japanese have increased their R&D budget to over 2.9%.[2] The Japanese have continued to maintain a strong emphasis on basic and product research. Three such government organizations have sponsored and guided research activities in Japan:[2]

1. MITI (Ministry of International Trade and Industry)

2. The Ministry of Education, Science and Culture

3. STA (Science and Technology Agency)

After the war, Japan focused its efforts on producing competent scientists and engineers capable of improving Western technology. Unlike Americans, the Japanese easily apply R&D to the factory floor and are capitalizing on their successes.[9] Now their efforts are centered on creating new technology through innovation and basic (breakthrough) research.[2] A fourfold increase in basic (fundamental) technology is occurring in Japan, with organizations such as Hitachi building an AT&T-style research facility to compete worldwide.[2] In contrast to the United States, the Japanese have used the principles of total quality to adapt and expand the horizons of research.[9] Too often the administration of total quality is seen as incompatible with the present structure of many U.S. R&D organizations.[10]

International R&D cooperation continues to gain acceptance. In addition, U.S. firms are collaborating and cooperating worldwide with organizations to improve their products and services.[7] Cooperation and collaboration have not been easy for R&D. Cooperation among and between R&D organizations is seen as one method of improving the product development cycle. *Techno-globalism*, a term to describe cooperative R&D ventures between international organizations, has become a buzzword in many facilities.[11] By sharing research and technical information, R&D organizations form alliances and partnerships necessary for future growth and expansion.

TOTAL QUALITY MODEL FOR R&D

The result of implementing a total quality approach in any organization is a firm that continuously serves the needs of its customers (both internal and external) in an efficient and effective manner. Therefore, in order for total quality to function as designed (*plan*), systems must be instituted (*do*), studied (*study*), measured, and reviewed (*act*) for effectiveness.[12] Accomplishing this cycle of improvement requires an interacting set of systems that operate in tandem. The first such system—the **management system**—provides those policies/strategies/operations/processes that affect the business on a daily basis. The second such system—the **social system**—details the human dynamics present in any business or organization. Human dynamics include personal interactions, employee growth/development, teamwork, communications, rewards, performance, and productivity. The third system—the **technical system**—includes those tools and methods used by employees to accomplish tasks and responsibilities. The interactions of the three systems is illustrated in Figure 1.1.

In an ideal situation, all three circles are of equal weight, with an overlap in the center demonstrating synergy. Synergistic balance of all three systems is the result of implementing a total quality approach. The idealized total quality model is a goal for all R&D organizations, bringing into balance those elements that become distorted or displaced.

Figure 1.2 represents a conceptual framework of the present state of R&D when compared with the idealized total quality model. Shapes of the three interlocking systems (Figure 1.2) are distorted to show their present relative importance. Deviations from the idealized model indicate opportunities for improvement.

The dominant system at present is the social system. A large social system indicates that individual accomplishments receive the greatest reward. At present, most R&D organizations have a unique social structure that more closely represents an academic institution than a business. A protective, closed environment prevails. Interpersonal skills are limited to those needed only in interacting with the group. The social group is fairly

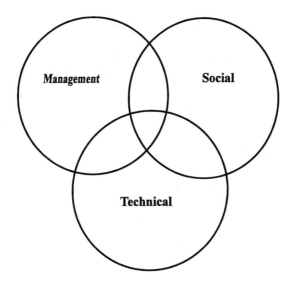

Figure 1.1 Total Quality Systematic Structure.

colloquial and often seems to outsiders as "elitist." (For additional informa-tion, see Abstract 1.2 at the end of this chapter.)

The technical system is considered by some as the dominant force in R&D. The technical system is critical to R&D due to its unique mission. Technology and scientific advances are the backbone of the R&D organiza-tion. Yet technology is a tool and in and of itself cannot drive a human-designed organization. As illustrated in Figure 1.2, the overlap between technical systems and social (human) systems often becomes blurred. The social system is often interwoven into the technical system through train-

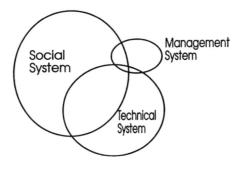

Figure 1.2 Present R&D Systematic Structure.

ing, social encounters (seminars, colloquia), and symposia. Unfortunately, technology may become a driving force in R&D organizations even if it remains at odds with company goals and objectives. This forced separation may further alienate R&D from the goals and objectives of the organization. An inflated technical system may be seen as incompatible with business and financial objectives. Finally, many R&D personnel consider new technology as a reward mechanism and not as a tool, further distorting the two closely related systems. (For additional information, see Abstract 1.3 at the end of this chapter.)

The management system is often disjointed and quite removed from daily operations. The R&D organization is usually managed by a senior researcher skilled in defending and protecting his or her department. Many R&D organizations are detached from their business centers in both physical and emotional terms. Operational systems reflect this detachment. Management structure is limited in scope and often hierarchical. Managerial skills are uncommon, with the overlap between systems amorphous.

The overall present structure does not maximize the efforts and talents of persons involved within the system. The unbalanced management system may prevent teamwork and collaboration (cooperation). Additionally, the management system may offer little protection against downsizing through misinformation or unstructured procedures. The social/technical driver for the system remains strictly individualistic. Systems that remain unbalanced become dysfunctional (i.e., prevent positive change by maintaining the status quo). Table 1.1 compares traditional R&D practices with those that accompany the implementation of total quality. Implementing total quality within the R&D organization will bring balance and synergy.

BARRIERS TO TOTAL QUALITY

Although implementing total quality may appear simple on the surface, there are numerous barriers to overcome. Most barriers protect the status quo or a person benefiting from the present paradigm. Unless total quality is designed to benefit all employees rather than a select few, the amount of support and commitment will vary widely. Many total quality management (TQM) programs begun in the 1980s have failed because management redirected human benefits to the bottom line. Financial and cost reduction issues, while important, did not directly affect employees. Interest quickly waned, and the amount of management support and commitment eroded over time.

The barriers to total quality prevent continuous improvement. Each of the seven barriers discussed in this section presents a unique management challenge. By overcoming or, more importantly, preventing each barrier,

Table 1.1 Traditional R&D Practices Compared with Total Quality

Categories	Traditional R&D	Total quality
Management practices		
Command structure	Hierarchical, dominated by "chief researcher"	Participatory—improve the system
Interactions with management	Limited	Frequent, management accepts "coaching"/ facilitator role
Environment	Clandestine, academic, protective	"Mentor" environment, supportive, highly inter-active, creative, innovative
Rewards and recognition	Individual performance or achievement	Benefits are highly publi-cized and support goals; frequent recognition
Strategic input	Minimal, most researchers unaware of organizational goals/objectives	Employees contribute to and support company goals and objectives
Customer orientation	Competitive focus, protective	Customer focus (both internal and external)
Human resources	"Personnel" function main emphasis on policies and procedures	"Holistic" approach, where employees are seen as most critical resource
Employee development	Limited managerial, supervisory, or human skills training; heavy emphasis on "technical" aspects	Training in human and job skills is frequent and promotes employee and team development
Technology	Heavy emphasis—proficiency stressed	Accepted as a tool for gaining markets and not as a replacement for human potential
Systems		
Operational	Loose control, highly unstructured	Process oriented, systematic
Organizational	Differentiated by discipline	Team oriented
Communication	Closed, top-down, informal	Open, two way, positive

the pathway to total quality becomes more pronounced. These barriers also serve as warning signs for possible breakdowns. Failure to address these barriers prior to implementing a total quality effort will certainly impede substantial progress.

Barrier 1: Strategic

Strategic barriers occur when management and executives focus corporate energies toward a goal other than complete (internal and external) customer satisfaction. Directing company or organizational efforts toward financial or cost containment performance (including shareholder value) minimizes the importance of growth factors such as meeting customer needs. In addition, other strategic factors act as barriers to total quality. These factors include:

1. Lack of vision and purpose (mission)

2. Inconsistent or unethical values

3. Poor leadership (decision making)

4. Lack of corporate or organizational planning

5. Reliance on short-term goals[3]

6. Lack of control

7. Inconsistent strategies (e.g., bottom-line performance rather the customer satisfaction)

8. Failure to involve employees in corporate policy and goals

Strategic barriers prevent the organization from focusing on what is truly important. Lack of vision, leadership, and planning results in poor commitment (buy-in) from employees. This buy-in is necessary to effect positive change.

Barrier 2: Structural

Structural barriers consist of internal and external policies, procedures, and regulations that prevent the realization of total quality. Structural issues arise when designing and framing organizational policies and procedures. Policies that obstruct employee participation, teamwork, customer satisfaction, creative problem solving, or problem prevention raise barriers to total quality. Some regulations may be imposed (e.g., union rules) or mandated. Policies that impose rigid controls on human ingenuity and participation limit the system from experiencing positive change. Mandated rules, set by a regulatory organization, that limit scientific discovery or human innovation prevent the full benefits of total quality. The policies and procedures designed by employees should form the "foundation" or building blocks for total quality. Leadership and commitment alone cannot effect permanent change if the structure that supports the philosophy is faulty. The design of organizational systems (or the redesign of existing systems) to permit the total quality philosophy to flourish must be of primary importance. Otherwise, structural issues will limit the potential or defeat the positive effects of total quality. Many organizations have failed to implement total quality because structural issues were never given priority or addressed.

Barrier 3: Systems

System barriers are common when a process is permitted to operate outside a state of statistical control. Systems involve the interaction of a process (people, machines, methods, materials, and measurements) with its environment. Systems that produce inconsistent products or services will not satisfy customers. Any operation, policy, or procedure that affects the process or its output raises a potential barrier to total quality. A central principle of total quality is the control of systems through measurements that indicate inconsistent variations in performance. Operational decisions by employees or managers that intentionally permit faulty products or services violate total quality principles. Systems that permit scrap and rework, inefficient performance, or reduced human productivity do not produce quality. System barriers create operations that oppose total quality principles.

Barrier 4: Social

Social barriers exert a powerful influence on human decision making. Social pressures, peer groups, role models, individual behaviors, and expectations of performance all exert a powerful barrier to change. Self-image and self-worth, formed through group interaction, drive the individual and affect both behavior and decisions. If natural leaders perceive that total quality is of little benefit to them individually, they can have a strong effect on the emotional reactions/decisions of the entire group. Human, rather than technical or managerial, barriers to change are the most difficult to surmount. A positive method of reducing or eliminating social barriers is to individualize the benefits gained from accepting the new paradigm. Social benefits, such as employee empowerment, employee development, productivity, and creativity, are achievable when strategies are formulated early in the design and development process. Employees who see little or no benefit can bring "social warfare" tactics to eliminate the opposing philosophy. Peer pressure, disenfranchisement, "blackballing," and threats are tactics available to defeat the opposition.

Researchers committed to supporting total quality implementation should recognize **power grids** that exist throughout the organization. Similar to networks, power grids describe the organizational control structure exerted by managers and employees. If the power grid opposes total quality, then implementation can be difficult and dangerous. Circumventing the power grid is equally disastrous. Support should flow freely from established power conduits (channels) to ensure success. For total quality to succeed, managers and employees must address all social barriers and develop strategies to install a "win–win" environment for all organizational members. (For additional information, see Abstract 1.4 at the end of this chapter.)

Barrier 5: Communication

Communication barriers exist internally and externally. Barriers to internal communication arise when:

1. Management and employees do not communicate effectively[13]

2. Communications are not objective, timely, thorough, credible, open, honest, consistent, trustworthy, and coordinated[14,15]

3. Information is not regularly or freely exchanged[16] or does not convey a specific message[17] without blame[18]

4. Organizational goals, policies, procedures, and expectations are not clearly stated[19–21]

Employee dissatisfaction with lateral and vertical communications creates barriers to improvement. Dysfunctional information exchange occurs when two-way communication becomes ineffective, sending various mixed messages. The result of poor listening or feedback skills inhibits the organization in promoting its goals and objectives.[22] In effect, internal communication barriers limit improvement and creativity by distorting information. This misinformation leads to mistrust and the loss of commitment and support from employees.

External communication barriers occur when the customer (external environment) is removed from the information-gathering cycle. Without this information, decision making is severely hampered. External communication must demonstrate and reinforce the values and social responsibility of the organization.[23,24] It must be consistent with internal communication[15] and must avoid becoming reactive.[25] By increasing or maintaining external communication barriers, the customers remain unserved and total quality becomes a distant goal.

Improving communication begins with examining the message, transmission, comprehension, and receptivity. Assessing the organization's communication effectiveness is one method of determining successful communication. The Organizational Communication Effectiveness Survey (Exercise 1.1)[26] at the end of this chapter evaluates employee perceptions of communication satisfaction. The 29 statements in the survey yield five key dimensions of quality and satisfaction:

1. Information exchange (Statements 1, 2, 4, and 5)

2. Personal/individual aspects of communication (Statements 6 through 10)

3. Organizational response and receptivity (Statements 11 through 19)

4. Message clarity (Statements 21 through 28)

5. Measures of ineffectiveness (Statements 3, 20, and 29)[26]

This validated survey instrument provides a global view of communication effectiveness and reveals potential problems in the communication system. Evaluating the organization's communication system is only one aspect of the entire information exchange process. Individuals can improve their process of communicating by applying four simple principles (elements):

1. Provide a benefit for the listener (for example, present something of interest such as a common goal)

2. Involve the individual in the information exchange

3. Control the quality of the information by focusing on the structure, meaning, content, method, and consistency

4. Obtain feedback to measure the success of the exchange

By assessing the system and actively training individuals to achieve successful information exchange, the communication barrier can be significantly minimized.

Barrier 6: Cultural

Cultural barriers affect the organization's environment and values (principles).[27] That is, the culture sets the tone of daily human interactions and focuses attention on what is important. If the culture of the organization is aggressive or reactive, then the environment is usually confrontational and controlled. The Japanese culture, which supports *kaizen* principles, views human resources and group achievement as critical to their society.[9] Americans, on the other hand, cling to "rugged individualism," which views achievement as a self-initiated venture. This recognition of "self" has led the American culture to reject certain management theories (Y and Z) which stress a collective perspective to success.[9] Individualism, according to Kelley and Caplan,[28] is an ideal for most researchers since they fear becoming clones. Therefore, traditional cultural practices such as pay for performance have flourished. Although the culture has produced significant scientific and technical advances, changing economic and world political situations favor a more collaborative effort. (For additional information, see Abstract 1.5 at the end of this chapter.)

Cultural influences also affect the organization internally. Certain traditional business activities, such as marketing and R&D, have developed a distinctive cultural pattern. Marketing organizations, for instance, are often dominated by a high-pressure environment, where sales and market position are the key measures of success. Cultural barriers, often set to maintain a given environmental paradigm, can be difficult to hurdle. The individual or group must often risk reputation and position to challenge the existing paradigm.

Total quality as a cultural issue challenges the prevailing wisdom of traditional business practices by focusing on the customer. Although the philosophy was born in the United States, its "Japanese" flavor has discouraged many business executives. Implementing total quality requires that identified cultural barriers be surmounted by stressing the positive benefits of the change.

Barrier 7: Attitudinal

The final barrier is closely aligned with the social and cultural influences encountered on a daily basis. Changing attitudes requires that beliefs (perceptions) be brought into alignment with expectations. Positive attitudes are the result of perceptions that meet or exceed an individual's expectations.[29] Attitudes are cultivated over time and result from experiences that have left a permanent set of expectations from which the individual judges future encounters.[29] Attitudinal barriers arise when an individual has experienced a negative encounter or his or her expectations have been unfulfilled. Preventing attitudinal barriers requires that an individual's beliefs and needs be assessed. By understanding these needs (or past negative experiences), negative attitudes can be modified or eliminated.

Attitudinal barriers that surround total quality usually result from negative expectations or experiences. These negative experiences were the result of nonexistent leadership, little or no identification of benefits (rewards), unclear strategies or plans, or a negative focus on achievement. Considering attitudinal barriers prior to implementing total quality is a requirement for success. Creating realistic expectations, considering the beliefs and anxieties of others, and establishing a clear path for success is one way of eliminating the harsh effects of attitudinal barriers.

Summary

In summary, employees hurdle barriers not only by examining the consequences of change, but by examining the method used to bring about change as well. Successful implementation of total quality can never be fully realized until the major barriers are identified. Developing a strategy to counter any type of barrier is one method of achieving success. (For additional information, see Abstract 1.6 at the end of this chapter.)

ENDNOTES

1. Freundlich, Naomi and Schroeder, Michael. *Business Week/Quality*, pp. 149–152, 1991.

2. "Can Japan Make Einsteins Too?" *The Economist*, pp. 81–83, August 11, 1990.

3. Deming, W. Edwards. *Out of the Crisis*, Cambridge, MA: Massachusetts Institute of Technology, 1986.

4. Krackhardt, David and Hanson, Jeffrey R. "Informal Networks: The Company." *Harvard Business Review*, pp. 105–111, July–August 1993.

5. Maccoby, Michael. "Move from Hierarchy to Heterarchy." *Research Technology Magazine*, pp. 46–47, September–October 1991.

6. "The Rise and Fall of Industrial Research." *Financial World*, pp. 64–68, June 25, 1991.

7. Mowery, David C. "The Development of Industrial Research in U.S. Manufacturing." *The Economic History of Technology*, 80(2), pp. 345–349, 1990.

8. Stumpe, Warren R. "R&D: It Ain't What It Used to Be!" *Research Technology Magazine*, pp. 7–8, September–October 1989.

9. Rogers, Rolf E. "Managing for Quality: Current Differences between Japanese and American Approaches," *National Productivity Review*, pp. 503–517, Autumn 1993.

10. Place, Geoffrey. "IRI's First 100 Years." *Research Technology Magazine*, pp. 21–26, January–February 1989.

11. Dodgson, Mark. "The Future for Technological Collaboration." *Futures*, 24(5), p. 459, June 1992.

12. Deming, W. Edwards. personal correspondence with the author, 1990.

13. Pincus, J.D., Rayfield, R.E., and Debonnis, J.N. "Transforming CEO's into Chief Communication Officers." *Public Relations Journal*, 47(11), pp. 22–27, 1991.

14. Sonneberg, F. "Internal Communication: Turning Talk into Action." *Supervisory Management*, 37(9), pp. 8–9, 1992.

15. Finkin, E.F. "Effective External Communications in Downsizing." *Journal of Business Strategy*, XX, pp. 62–64, 1992.

16. McCathrin, E.Z. "Beyond Employee Publications." *Public Relations Journal*, 45(7), pp. 14–20, 1989.

17. O'Connor, S.J. *Service Quality, Services Marketing, and the Health Care Consumer: A Study Assessing the Dimensions of Service Quality and Their Influence on Patient Satisfaction and Intentions to Return*, Ann Arbor, MI: University Microfilms International, 1988.

18. McClelland, V. and Wilmont, R. "Lateral Communication." *IABC Communication World*, 9(12), pp. 32–35, 1992.

19. O'Connor, J.V. "Building Internal Communications." *Public Relations Journal*, 46(6), pp. 29–33, 1990.

20. Zeithaml, V.A., Berry, L.L., and Parasuraman, A. "Communication and Control Processes in the Delivery of Service Quality." *Journal of Marketing*, 52(2), pp. 35-48, 1988.

21. Cunningham, B. and Lischeron, J. "Improving Internal Communications. Issues Facing Managers." *Optimum*, 21(3), pp. 53–70, 1991.

22. Davis, D.C. "QA in the R&D Environment." *Defense Electronics*, 26(2), pp. 30–31, 1994.

23. Shaffer, J.C. "Customers and Commitment." *IABC Communication World*, 7(12), pp. 23–27, 1990.

24. Strenski, J.B. "Quality and Communication: Keys to Leadership in the Service Industry." *Public Relations Quarterly*, 34(4), pp. 17–18, 1989–90.

25. McClelland, V. and Wilmont, R. "Lateral Communication." *IABC Communication World*, 9(12), pp. 32–35, 1992.

26. McLaughlin, Gregory C. "The Role of Organizational Communication Effectiveness in the Development of Service Quality Satisfaction," Dissertation, Nova Southeastern University, 1994.

27. Covey, Stephen R. *Principle-Centered Leadership*, New York: Simon & Shuster, 1991.

28. Kelley, Robert and Caplan, Janet. "How Bell Labs Creates Star Performers." *Harvard Business Review*, pp. 128–139, July–August 1993.

29. Oliver, R.L. "Measurement and Evaluation of Satisfaction Processes in Retail Settings." *Journal of Retailing*, 57(3), pp. 25–48, 1981.

ABSTRACTS

ABSTRACT 1.1
"IF IT ISN'T PERFECT, MAKE IT BETTER"

Montana, Anthony J.
Research-Technology Management, July–August 1992, pp. 38–41

Too often, says the author, R&D functions are the last groups to fully accept the quality process. He highlights some of the reasons for lack of acceptance: (a) lack of an empirical model, (b) misunderstanding of the definition of quality as "perfection," (c) difficulty in establishing objective measures of performance, and (d) resistance to the people side of quality. Next, the author looks at how the Japanese have incorporated quality into their R&D enterprise, and he concludes by outlining a process to implement a quality program within R&D:

1. Develop a clear understanding of the R&D function, i.e., to develop and transfer technology between marketing and manufacturing, as well as within R&D.

2. Establish a definition for quality that the R&D scientist can relate to, such as "doing it the right way the first time."

3. Develop a vision statement which represents a desired future state of the R&D organization.

4. Construct a list of productivity indices that can be effectively measured against the expectations of the vision statement.

5. Flowchart the R&D process to clarify it.

6. Develop a total team approach for R&D.

7. Adopt a customer focus and customer mindset.   (©*Quality Abstracts*)

ABSTRACT 1.2
PUTTING QUALITY INTO THE R&D PROCESS

Francis, Philip H.
Research-Technology Management, July–August 1992, pp. 16–23

"As in all other operations," says the author, "R&D must be subject to effectiveness measurements, or payoff assessments." Though some have questioned whether quantitative measurements can be made with enough fidelity to be meaningful, the author offers a framework for measurement of six aspects of R&D:

- **Project completed.** Determine the present value (payback of the product or process that is to incorporate this technology, compared to the present value in the absence of the technology, and subtract cost investment, to calculate a net present value or payback.

- **Project begun or still in process.** This involves a similar payback calculation based on expected probabilities of both commercial and technical success.

- **Specific cost avoidance realized.** Calculate the difference between the cost avoidance discounted over time and the R&D investment that enabled the cost avoidance.

- **Institutionalized new practice.** Enhanced technological practice, such as process simulation or CASE tools, may be quantified by estimating the value of results shown to have resulted from such practice.

- **Maintained technology awareness.** Annual net present value (or payback) of time spent staying abreast of a technological field may be quantified by estimating the size of the current and expected future markets to which these technical awareness foci apply.

- **General internal consulting.** Determine the magnitude of the cost issue that drove the internal customer to ask for help from R&D.

The author offers several caveats to this approach to measurement: (a) avoid overstating the claimed value of R&D, (b) be rigorous in the process of measurement, (c) use existing staff to make measurements, and (d) have customers sign off as to the reasonableness of the calculation system for their project. Finally, the author briefly notes how this measurement system for R&D worked at Square D Company. The article also includes an introductory discussion of the quality movement and a table of how eight quality axioms compare to similar tenets expressed in R&D terminology. (©*Quality Abstracts*)

ABSTRACT 1.3
APPLYING QUALITY TO R&D MEANS "LEARN-AS-YOU-GO"

Eidt, Clarence M. Jr.
Research–Technology Management, July–August 1992, pp. 24–31

While the application of quality principles to R&D may not be as straight-forward as for a manufacturing function, says the author, there is no doubt that the basic principles are applicable. He examines how the customer focus, work process, and supportive work environment themes of TQM differ in R&D, but he contends that R&D is a "natural" for quality in terms of customer involvement, analyzing work processes ("a paraphrased version of the scientific method"), empowerment of researchers, and cultivating teamwork. Then the author describes some lessons learned at Exxon Research and Engineering Company about incorporating quality principles into its R&D:

- Translate TQM jargon into the language of R&D, and illustrate it with examples to which researchers can readily relate.

- Do not position quality as a new and revolutionary concept, since that suggests that previous work was not of high quality.

- Look forward to change throughout the entire organization, rather than castigating management as scapegoats.

The author reports that minimizing the quality administrative superstructure has been effective, as has been steadily pushing decision making down into the organization. Moreover, an employee-designed reward and recognition system has achieved "overwhelmingly positive" results. While a variety of performance indicators have been more effective than a "universal gauge," progress up the "S" curve toward ultimate potential of a given technology is carefully monitored as a function of time or cumulative R&D efforts. Finally, the author describes some of the training classes offered in areas of customer focus and work process training, as well as leadership, team building, and facilitation. (©*Quality Abstracts*)

ABSTRACT 1.4
BUILDING A VISION COMMUNITY

Ferris, Gregory, L.
Journal for Quality and Participation, October–November 1992, pp. 18–20

A new CEO took over at Batesville Casket Co. of Batesville, Indiana, where the previous leadership style had been one of mandates. The CEO asked all employees to view Joel Barker's video "Discovering the Future—The Business of Paradigms" and then discuss it in small groups. As a result of feedback, the CEO dethroned the MBO system which was not soliciting ideas or innovation from employees. What emerged was a vision-driven process, which involved two steps:

1. In an overview presentation, vision was characterized as a means to drive the business plan and as a performance management system. The specifics of the plan were presented to managers through numerous department focus groups, and feedback showed that managers needed training to understand the system.

2. Vision training involved two workshops. (1) The first workshop increased awareness through the CEO's presentation of his vision for the organization, a discussion of issues, and Barker's video "The Power of Vision." Then each employee was asked to begin developing a draft of an individual vision. (2) Four months later, a second session provided structural aids to help employees write their vision statements, and the session concluded with the comment: "Vision without action is merely a dream; action without vision just passes time; vision with action can change the world."

The shift from MBO to vision was difficult for many employees during the first year, says the author. However, after introduction of a vision/risk leadership profile and a vision workbook—both of which the author describes—two years of visioning has brought excellent results: creative ideas, proactivity, frequent reviews for adjustment, and improvement in organizational communication. *(©Quality Abstracts)*

ABSTRACT 1.5
MAKING TOTAL QUALITY WORK: ALIGNING ORGANIZATIONAL PROCESSES, PERFORMANCE MEASURES, AND STAKEHOLDERS

Olian, Judy D. and Rynes, Sara L.
Human Resources Management, Fall 1991, Vol. 30 Issue 3, pp. 303–333

Throughout this article, four survey sources are used: the KPMG survey of 62 companies, two Conference Board surveys of 149 firms and 158 Fortune 1000 companies, and the AQF/Ernst & Young study of 500 international organizations. The cornerstone of this 30-page article revolves around the authors' statement: "The goals of total quality can be achieved only if organizations entirely reform their cultures. Total quality (TQ) is increasingly used by companies as an organization-wide system to achieve fully satisfied customers through the delivery of the highest quality in products and services. In fact, TQ is the most important single strategic tool available to leaders to effect the transformation of their organizations. Traditional management, operations, finance and accounting systems are reviewed against changes that are needed in organizational processes, measurement systems, and the values and behaviors of key stakeholders to transform the status quo and shift to a total quality culture that permeates every facet of the organization."

Total quality must reflect a system-wide commitment to the goal of serving the strategic needs of the organization's customer bases, through internal and external measurement systems, information and authority sharing, and committed leadership. In this sense, the objectives are very similar to ISO 9000 readiness for registration. Therefore, the concepts presented by the authors are also valid for those sales-based TQM organizations that are seeking ISO 9000 certification. The article contains the following pertinent data: (1) organizational synergies critical to achieving a pervasive culture, whether it be for TQM, ISO 9000, or other types of quality assurance; (2) the essentials of TQ; (3) organizational processes that support TQ; (4) establishing quality goals, including a look at Six Sigma and benchmarking; (5) training for TQ; (6) recognition and rewards; (7) measuring customer reactions and satisfaction; (8) developing four areas of measurement: operation, financial, breakthrough, and employee contributions; and (9) getting stakeholder support. Of significant added value are over 60 references on the subjects discussed, which are reason enough to obtain a copy of this extremely worthwhile article, in spite of its formidable length. It is highly recommended reading for staff organizations seeking to implement total quality.

ABSTRACT 1.6
RETURN ON QUALITY

Rust, Roland, Zahorik, Anthony, and Keiningham, Timothy
Probus Publishing, New York, 1994

The premise of this book is that very few companies can accurately translate subjective goals relating to quality and customer satisfaction into hard numbers which can be linked to specific improvement programs. This book describes a methodology to measure corporate quality efforts and to quantify "their return on investment." The authors stress that it is undeniable that organizations desperately need such a system; the question is how to provide one that works. The ability to accurately measure results provides the basis for accurate forecasting, as well as providing for the logical deployment of resources. The key problem, as the authors point out, is that placing a value on feelings such as satisfaction proves to be a difficult assignment under even the best conditions.

The authors attempt to solve this dilemma by first analyzing the decision paths where quality leads to profits. These paths, which can include product performance as well as both process and service features, lead to customer satisfaction, which leads to increased market share, which leads to improved profitability and competitive advantage. The book contains surveys, user studies, quality tools, and instructions for conducting focus groups, as well as numerous other techniques for gathering data at each step of the process. It also shows how to use statistical analysis to translate findings into hard numbers, which are then applied to the model to rationalize decision making and help in the strategic quality planning process. The promise of the book is the creation of the "high-performance business."

A unique addition to the book is an added value return-on-quality software system which computerizes the decision-making and planning process. The reader can use a demonstration disk (available from the publisher for an additional fee) to process the statistics gathered from customers into the proper screens, from which the software generates models. According to reviewer Ted Kinni, about 25% of the book describes this software, and several case studies illustrate this illusive concept of "return on quality" in action.

This book is an impressive work, although it has some weaknesses. The concept of translating customer values into numbers is a difficult task "fraught with peril and the values generated by the model are only as good as its assumptions and data fed into it." In bold print, the authors issue this caution: "Remember this warning: decision support systems supply input to a manager's decision. They don't make the decision." In other words, *caveat emptor*—let the buyer–reader beware. All in all, this is a must read for the R&D professional.

EXERCISE

EXERCISE 1.1
ORGANIZATIONAL COMMUNICATION EFFECTIVENESS SURVEY

Rate the statements below as to how well XYZ Department communicates with you and other employees. The purpose of this questionnaire is to get your opinion on how XYZ Department as a whole is communicating with you. When answering this questionnaire, think about your entire experience with XYZ Department and not just your business or organization. All responses will be kept in the strictest confidence. Please do not place your name on this document.

DEFINITIONS
Communications: Giving or receiving information to or from someone. Communicated messages can be spoken, written, or broadcast.
XYZ Department: Your R&D Department.
Manager: Any person (employee) who holds a position that is responsible for evaluating one or more employees within their business, department, or division.
Employee: Any person who is employed by XYZ.

DIRECTIONS
Place a number from 1 to 7 in the space to the right of each statement. "1" indicates that you strongly disagree with the statement. "7" indicates that you strongly agree with the statement. You may record any number from 1 to 7 to indicate how strong your feelings are. There are no right or wrong answers; simply indicate the number that best shows how you feel about communications with XYZ Department.

RESPONSE

	Strongly Disagree						Strongly Agree	
	1	2	3	4	5	6	7	

1. Information that I receive from XYZ Department is complete. _____

2. Information that I receive from XYZ Department is useful. _____

3. Information that I receive from XYZ Department sends mixed messages. _____

4. Information that I receive from XYZ Department is straightforward. _____

	Strongly Disagree						Strongly Agree
	1	2	3	4	5	6	7

5. Information that I receive from XYZ Department is timely. _____

6. XYZ Department meets individual needs when communicating with me. _____

7. XYZ Department listens to me. _____

8. XYZ Department uses the information I provide. _____

9. XYZ Department discusses problems with me. _____

10. XYZ Department discusses complaints with me. _____

11. XYZ Department uses communication to solve problems. _____

12. XYZ Department is receptive to my suggestions. _____

13. XYZ Department communicates ideas and thoughts with me in my area. _____

14. XYZ Department acts responsibly for its communications. _____

15. XYZ Department communicates goals or objectives with employees in my area. _____

16. XYZ Department understands me when I speak or write. _____

17. XYZ Department discusses strategic issues and policies with employees. _____

18. XYZ Department communicates its values to employees. _____

19. XYZ Department communicates honestly with me. _____

20. XYZ Department limits (restricts) some communications. _____

21. Communications from XYZ Department are accurate. _____

22. Written communications from XYZ Department are clear and understandable. _____

23. Spoken communications from XYZ Department are clear and understandable. _____

24. When XYZ Department communicates with me, the message is understandable. _____

	Strongly Disagree					Strongly Agree	
	1	2	3	4	5	6	7

25. When I speak, XYZ Department clearly understands my message. _____

26. I trust what XYZ Department communicates to me. _____

27. Employees understand the message that XYZ Department communicates. _____

28. Employees of XYZ Department communicate well with each other when needed. _____

29. Employee communications with each other are often haphazard. _____

CHAPTER 2

OVERVIEW of TOTAL QUALITY

Frank Voehl

WHAT IS TOTAL QUALITY?

Introduction

During the past five years, there has been an explosion of books in the field of total quality. Yet in all of the thousands of books and billions of words written on the subject, there is an absence of three essential ingredients: a good working definition, a comprehensive yet concise history, and a clear and simple systems model of total quality. This overview of total quality is intended to fill that void and provide some interesting reading at the same time.

Understanding the Concept of Total

Total quality is total in three senses: it covers every process, every job, and every person. First, it covers *every process*, rather than just manufacturing or production. Design, construction, R&D, accounting, marketing, repair, and every other function must also be involved in quality improvement. Second, total quality is total in that it covers *every job*, as opposed to only those involved in making the product. Secretaries are expected not to make typing errors, accountants not to make posting errors, and presidents not to make strategic errors. Third, total quality recognizes that *each person* is responsible for the quality of his or her work and for the work of the group.

Total quality also goes beyond the traditional idea of quality, which has been expressed as the degree of conformance to a standard or the product of workmanship. Enlightened organizations accept and apply the concept that quality is the degree of user satisfaction or the fitness of the product for use. In other words, *the customer determines whether or not quality has been achieved in its totality.*

This same measure—total customer satisfaction—applies throughout the entire operation of an organization. Only the outer edges of the company actually have contact with customers in the traditional sense, but each department can treat the other departments as its customers. The main judge of the quality of work is the customer, for if the customer is not satisfied, the work does not have quality. This, coupled with the achievement of corporate objectives, is the bottom line of total quality.

In that regard, it is important, as the Japanese say, to "talk with facts and data." Total quality emphasizes the use of fact-oriented discussions and statistical quality control techniques by everyone in the company. Everyone in the company is exposed to basic quality control ideas and techniques and is expected to use them. Thus, total quality becomes a common language and improves "objective" communication.

Total quality also radically alters the nature and basic operating philosophy of organizations. The specialized, separated system developed early in the 20th century is replaced by a system of *mutual feedback and close interaction of departments*. Engineers, for example, work closely with construction crews and storekeepers to ensure that their knowledge is passed on to workers. Workers, in turn, feed their practical experience directly back to the engineers. The information interchange and shared commitment to product quality is what makes total quality work. Teaching all employees how to apply process control and improvement techniques makes them party to their own destiny and enables them to achieve their fullest potential.

However, total quality is more than an attempt to make better products; it is also a search for better ways to make better products. Adopting the total quality philosophy commits the company to the belief that there is always a better way of doing things, a way to make better use of the company's resources, and a way to be more productive. In this sense, total quality relies heavily upon value analysis as a method of developing better products and operations in order to maximize value to the stakeholder, whether customers, employees, or shareholders.

Total quality also implies a different type of worker and a different attitude toward the worker from management. Under total quality, workers are generalists rather than specialists. *Both workers and managers are expected to move from job to job, gaining experience in many areas of the company.*

Defining Total Quality

First and foremost, total quality is a set of philosophies by which management systems can direct the efficient achievement of the objectives of the organization to ensure customer satisfaction and maximize stakeholder value. This is accomplished through the continuous improvement of the quality system, which consists of the social system, the technical system, and the management system. Thus, it becomes a way of life for doing business for the entire organization.

Central to the concept is the idea that a company should *design quality into its products,* rather than inspect for it afterward. Only by a devotion to quality throughout the organization can the best possible products be made. Or, as stated by Noriaki Kano, "Quality is too important to be left to inspectors."[1]

Total quality is too important to take second place to any other company goals. Specifically, it should not be subsidiary to profit or productivity. Concentrating on quality will ultimately build and improve both profitability and productivity. Failure to concentrate on quality will quickly erode profits, as customers resent paying for products they perceive as low quality.

The main focus of total quality is on *why.* It goes beyond the *how to* to include the *why to.* It is an attempt to identify the causes of defects in order to eliminate them. It is a continuous cycle of detecting defects, identifying their causes, and improving the process so as to totally eliminate the causes of defects.

Accepting the idea that the customer of a process can be defined as the next process is essential to the real practice of total quality. According to total quality, control charts should be developed for each process, and any errors identified within a process should be disclosed to those involved in the next process in order to raise quality. However, it has been said that it seems contrary to human nature to seek out one's own mistakes. People tend to find the errors caused by others and to neglect their own. Unfortunately, exactly that kind of self-disclosure is what is really needed.[2]

Instead, management too often tends to blame and then take punitive action. This attitude prevails from frontline supervisors all the way up to top management. In effect, we are encouraged to hide the real problems we cause; instead of looking for the real causes of problems, as required by total quality, we look the other way.

The Concept of Control

The Japanese notion of *control* differs radically from the American; that difference of meaning does much to explain the failure of U.S. management to adopt total quality. In the United States, control connotes someone or something that limits an operation, process, or person. It has overtones of a "police force" in the industrial engineering setting and is often resented.

In Japan, as pointed out by Union of Japanese Scientists and Engineers counselor and Japanese quality control scholar Noriaki Kano, *control* means "all necessary activities for achieving objectives in the long-term, efficiently and economically. Control, therefore, is doing whatever is needed to accomplish what we want to do as an organization."[1]

The difference can be seen very graphically in the Plan, Do, Check, Act (P-D-C-A) continuous improvement chart, which is widely used in Japan to describe the cycle of control (Figure 2.1). Proper control starts with planning, does what is planned, checks the results, and then applies any necessary corrective action. The cycle represents these four stages—Plan, Do, Check, Act—arranged in circular fashion to show that they are continuous.

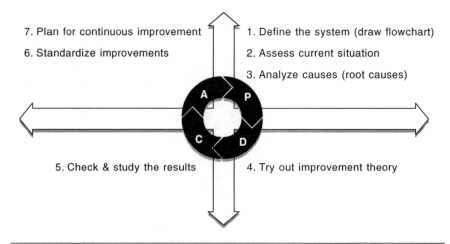

Figure 2.1 P-D-C-A Chart. System improvement is the application of the Plan-Do-Check-Act cycle to an improvement project.

In the United States, where specialization and division of labor are emphasized, the cycle is more likely to look like Fight, Plan, Do, Check. Instead of working together to solve any deviations from the plan, time is spent arguing about who is responsible for the deviations.

This sectionalism, as the Japanese refer to it, in the United States hinders collective efforts to improve the way things are done and lowers national productivity and the standard of living. *There need be nothing threatening about control if it is perceived as exercised in order to gather the facts necessary to make plans and take action toward making improvements.*

Total quality includes the control principle as part of the set of philosophies directed toward the efficient achievement of the objectives of the organization. Many of the individual components of total quality are practiced by American companies, but few practice total quality as a whole.

TOTAL QUALITY AS A SYSTEM

Introduction

Total quality begins with the redefinition of management, inspired by W. Edwards Deming:

> *The people work in a system. The job of the manager is to work on the system, to improve it continuously, with their help.*

One of the most frequent reasons for failed total quality efforts is that many managers are unable to carry out their responsibilities because they have not been trained in how to improve the quality system. They do not have a well-defined process to follow—a process founded on the principles of customer satisfaction, respect for people, continuous improvement, and speaking with facts. Deming's teachings, as amplified by Tribus,[3] focus on the following ten management actions:

1. Recognize quality improvement as a system.

2. Define it so that others can recognize it too.

3. Analyze its behavior.

4. Work with subordinates in improving the system.

5. Measure the quality of the system.

6. Develop improvements in the quality of the system.

7. Measure the gains in quality, if any, and link them to customer delight and quality improvement.

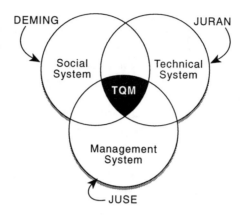

Figure 2.2 Implementing TQM—System Model.

8. Take steps to guarantee holding the gains.

9. Attempt to replicate the improvements in other areas of the system.

10. Tell others about the lessons learned.

Discussions with Tribus to cross-examine these points have revealed that the manager must deal with total quality as *three* separate systems: a social system, a technical system, and a management system. These systems are depicted as three interlocking circles of a ballantine,[4] as shown in Figure 2.2.

Overview of the Social System

Management is solely responsible for the transformation of the social system, which is basically the culture of the organization. It is the social system that has the greatest impact on teamwork, motivation, creativity, and risk taking. How people react to one another and to the work depends on how they are managed. If they enter the organization with poor attitudes, managers have to re-educate, redirect, or remove them. The social system includes the reward structure, the symbols of power, the relationships between people and among groups, the privileges, the skills and style, the politics, the power structure, the shaping of the norms and values, and the "human side of enterprise," as defined by Douglas McGregor.

If a lasting culture is to be achieved, where continuous improvement and customer focus are a natural pattern, the social system must be rede-

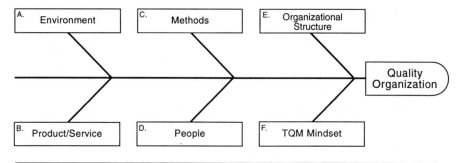

Figure 2.3   Strategic Areas for Cultural Transformation.

signed so as to be consistent with the vision and values of the organization. Unfortunately, the social system is always in a state of flux due to pressure from ever-changing influences from the external political and technological environments. The situation in most organizations is that the impact of total quality is not thought through in any organized manner. Change occurs when the pain of remaining as the same dysfunctional unit becomes too great and a remedy for relief is sought.

As shown in Figure 2.3, six areas of strategy must be addressed in order to change and transform the culture to that of a quality organization:

- Environment
- Product/service
- Methods
- People
- Organizational structure
- Total quality management mindset

Each of these areas will be covered in some detail in the chapters in this book. Of the six, however, structure is key in that total quality is about empowerment and making decisions at lower levels in the organization. Self-managing teams are a way to bring this about quickly.

The Technical System

According to Tribus,[5] "The technical system includes all the tools and machinery, the practice of quality science and the quantitative aspects of quality. If you can measure it, you can probably describe and perhaps improve it using the technical systems approach." The technical system thus is concerned with the flow of work through the organization to the ultimate customer. Included are all the work steps performed, whether by equipment, computers, or people; whether manual labor or decision making; or whether factory worker or office worker.

The technical system in most organizations contains the following core elements:

- Scientific accumulation of technology

- Pursuit of standardization

- Workflow, materials, and specifications

- Job definitions and responsibility

- Machine/person interface

- Number and type of work steps

- Availability and use of information

- Decision-making processes

- Problem-solving tools and process

- Physical arrangement of equipment, tools, and people

The expected benefits from analyzing and improving the technical system are to (1) improve customer satisfaction, (2) eliminate waste and rework, (3) eliminate variation, (4) increase learning, (5) save time and money, (6) increase employee control, (7) reduce bottlenecks and frustration, (8) eliminate interruptions and idle time, (9) increase speed and responsiveness, and (10) improve safety and quality of work life.

The three basic elements of every system are (1) suppliers who provide input, (2) work processes which add value, and (3) output to the customer. High-performing units and teams eliminate the barriers and walls between these three elements. A standard problem-solving process is often used by teams, such as the quality control story, business process analysis, etc.[6]

The Management System

The third system is the managerial system, which becomes the integrator. Only senior managers can authorize changes to this system. This is the system by which the other two systems are influenced. It is the way that practices, procedures, protocols, and policies are established and maintained.

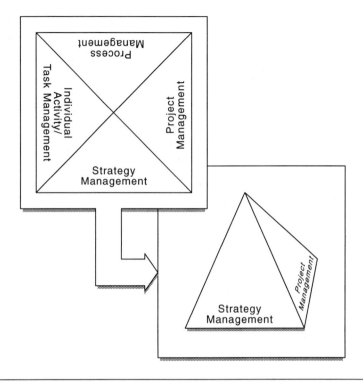

Figure 2.4   Management System Pyramid.

It is the leadership system of the organization, and it is the measurement system of indicators that tell management and the employees how things are going.

The actual deployment of the management system can be visualized in the shape of a pyramid. As shown in Figure 2.4, there are four aspects or intervention points of deployment: strategy management, process management, project management, and individual activity management. A brief overview of these four aspects is as follows:

- **Strategy management:** Purpose is to establish the mission, vision, and guiding principles and deployment infrastructure which encourage all employees to focus on and move in a common direction. Objectives, strategies, and actions are considered on a three- to five-year time line.

- **Process management:** Purpose is to assure that all key processes are working in harmony to guarantee customer satisfaction and maximize operational effectiveness. Continuous improvement/problem-solving efforts are often cross-functional, so that process owners and indicator owners need to be assigned.

- **Project management:** Purpose is to establish a system to effectively plan, organize, implement, and control all the resources and activities needed for successful completion of the project. Various types of project teams are often formed to solve and implement both process-related as well as policy-related initiatives. Team activities should be linked to business objectives and improvement targets.

- **Individual activity management:** Purpose is to provide all employees with a method of implementing continuous improvement of processes and systems within each employee's work function and control. Flow-charting key processes and individual mission statements are important linkages with which all employees can identify. A quality journal is often used to identify and document improvements.

Various types of assessment surveys are used to "audit" the quality management system. Examples include the Malcolm Baldrige assessment, the Deming Prize audit, and the ISO 9000 audit, among others. Basic core elements are common to all of these assessments. Their usefulness is as a yardstick and benchmark by which to measure improvement and focus the problem-solving effort. Recent efforts using integrated quality and productivity systems have met with some success.[7]

The House of Total Quality

The House of Total Quality (Figure 2.5) is a model which depicts the integration of all of these concepts in a logical fashion. Supporting the three systems of total quality described in the preceding section are the four principles of total quality: customer satisfaction, continuous improvement, speaking with facts, and respect for people. These four principles are inter-related, with customer satisfaction at the core or the hub.

As with any house, the model and plans must first be drawn, usually with some outside help. Once the design has been approved, construction can begin. It usually begins with the mission, vision, values, and objectives which form the cornerstones upon which to build for the future. The pillars representing the four principles must be carefully constructed, well positioned, and thoroughly understood, because the success of the total quality system is in the balance. As previously mentioned, many of the individual components of total quality are practiced by American companies, but few practice total quality as a whole.

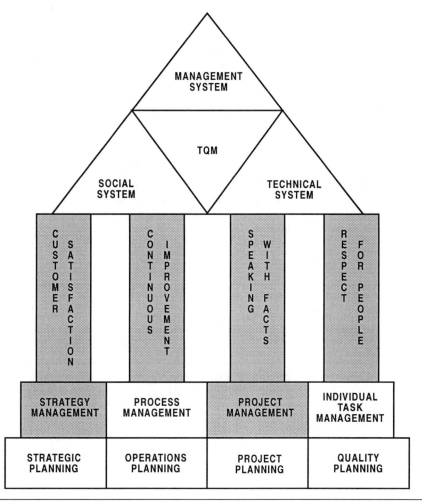

Figure 2.5 House of Quality.

HISTORY OF TOTAL QUALITY

In the Beginning

About the year one million B.C., give or take a few centuries, man first began to fashion stone tools for hunting and survival.[8] Up until 8000 B.C., however, very little progress was made in the quality control of these tools. It was at this time that man began assembling instruments with fitting holes, which suggests the use of interchangeable parts on a very limited basis. Throughout this long period, each man made his own tools. The evidence of quality control was measured to some extent by how long he stayed alive. If the tools were well made, his chances of survival increased. A broken axe handle usually spelled doom.

Introduction of Interchangeable Parts and Division of Labor

A little over 200 years ago, in 1787, the concepts of interchangeable parts and division of labor were first introduced in the United States. Eli Whitney, inventor of the cotton gin, applied these concepts to the production of 10,000 flintlock rifles for the U.S. military arsenal. However, Whitney had considerable difficulty in making all the parts exactly the same. It took him ten years to complete the 10,000 muskets that he promised to deliver in two years.

Three factors impacted Whitney's inability to deliver the 10,000 muskets in two years as promised. First, there was a dramatic shortage of qualified craftsmen needed to build the muskets. Consequently, Whitney correctly identified the solution to the problem—machines must do what men previously did. If individual machines were assembled to create each individual part needed, then men could be taught to operate these machines. Thus, Whitney's application of division of labor to a highly technical process was born. Whitney called this a *manufactory.*

Next, it took almost one full year to build the manufactory, rather than two months as Whitney originally thought. Not only did the weather inflict havoc on the schedule, but epidemics of yellow fever slowed progress considerably.

Third, obtaining the raw materials in a timely, usable manner was a hit-or-miss proposition. The metal ore used was often defective, flawed, and pitted. In addition, training the workers to perform the actual assembly took much longer than Whitney imagined and required a considerable amount of his personal attention, often fifteen to twenty hours a day. Also, once the men were trained, some left to work for competing armories.[9]

To compound these factors, his ongoing cotton gin patent lawsuits consumed a considerable amount of his highly leveraged attention and time. Fortunately for Whitney, his credibility in Washington granted him considerable laxity in letting target dates slip. War with France was no longer imminent. Thus, a quality product and the associated manufacturing expertise were deemed more important than schedule. What was promised in 28 months took almost 120 months to deliver.

Luckily for Whitney, the requirement of "on time and within budget" was not yet in vogue. What happened to Whitney was a classic study in the problems of trying to achieve a real breakthrough in operations. Out of this experience, Whitney and others realized that creating parts exactly the same was not possible and, if tried, would prove to be very expensive. This concept of interchangeable parts would eventually lead to statistical methods of control, while division of labor would lead to the factory assembly line.

The First Control Limits

The experiences of Whitney and others who followed led to a relaxation of the requirements for exactness and the use of tolerances. This allowed for a less-than-perfect fit between two (or more) parts, and the concept of "go–no-go" tolerance was introduced between 1840 and 1870.[10]

This idea was a major advancement in that it created the concept of upper and lower tolerance limits, thus allowing the production worker more freedom to do his job with an accompanying lowering of cost. All he had to do was stay within the tolerance limits, instead of trying to achieve unnecessary or unattainable perfection.

Defective Parts Inspection

The next advancement centered around expanding the notion of tolerance and using specifications, where variation is classified as either meeting or not meeting requirements. For those pieces of product that every now and then fell outside the specified tolerance range (or limits), the question arose as to what to do with them. To discard or modify these pieces added significantly to the cost of production. However, to search for the unknown causes of defects and then eliminate them also cost money. The heart of the problem was as follows: how to reduce the percentage of defects to the point where (1) the rate of increase in the *cost of control* equals the rate of *increase* in *savings*, which is (2) brought about by *decreasing the number of parts rejected.*

In other words, inspection/prevention had to be cost effective. Minimizing the percent of defects in a cost-effective manner was not the only problem to be solved. Tests for many quality characteristics require destructive testing, such as tests for strength, chemical composition, fuse blowing time, etc. Because not every piece can be tested, use of the statistical sample was initiated around the turn of the century.

Statistical Theory

During the early part of the 20th century, a tremendous increase in quality consciousness occurred. What were the forces at work that caused this sudden acceleration of interest in the application of statistical quality control? There were at least three key factors.

The first was a rapid growth in standardization, beginning in 1900. Until 1915, Great Britain was the only country in the world with some type of national standardization movement. The rate of growth in the number of industrial standardization organizations throughout the world, especially between 1916 and 1932, rose dramatically.[11] During that 15-year period, the movement grew from one country (Great Britain) to 25, with the United States coming on line about 1917, just at the time of World War I.

The second major factor ushering in the new era was a radical shift in ideology which occurred in about 1900. This ideological shift was away from the notion of exactness of science (which existed in 1787 when inter-changeability of parts was introduced) to probability and statistical concepts, which developed in almost every field of science around 1900.

The third factor was the evolution of division of labor into the factory system and the first assembly line systems of the early 20th century. These systems proved to be ideal for employing an immigrant work force quickly.

Scientific Management and Taylorism

Frederick Winslow Taylor was born in 1856 and entered industry as an apprentice in the Enterprise Hydraulics Shop in 1874. According to popular legend, the old-timers in the shop told him: "Now young man, here's about how much work you should do each morning and each afternoon. Don't do any more than that—that's the limit."[12]

It was obvious to Taylor that the men were producing below their capacity, and he soon found out why. The short-sighted management of that day would set standards, often paying per-piece rates for the work. Then, when a worker discovered how to produce more, management cut the rate. In turn, management realized that the workers were deliberately restricting output but could not do anything about it.

It was Taylor's viewpoint that the whole system was wrong. Having studied the writings and innovations of Whitney, he came to realize that the concept of division of labor had to be revamped if greater productivity and efficiency were to be realized. His vision included a super-efficient assembly line as part of a management system of operations. He, more than anyone at the time, understood the inability of management to increase individual productivity, and he understood the reluctance of the workers to produce at a high rate. Because he had been a working man, it was apparent to him that there was a tremendous difference between *actual* output and *potential* output. Taylor thought that if such practices applied throughout the world and throughout all industry, the potential production capacity was at least three or four times what was actually being produced.

When he became a foreman, Taylor set out to find ways to eliminate this waste and increase production.

For more than 25 years, Taylor and his associates explored ways to increase productivity and build the model factory of the future. The techniques they developed were finally formalized in writing and communicated to other people. During the early years of this experimentation, most who knew about it were associated with Taylor at the Midvale Steel Company and Bethlehem Steel.

Other famous names began to enter the picture and contribute to the body of science of the new management thinking. Among them were Carl G. L. Barth, a mathematician and statistician who assisted Taylor in analytical work, and Henry L. Gantt (famous for the Gantt chart), who invented the slide rule. Another associate of Taylor's, Sanford E. Thompson, developed the first decimal stopwatch.[12] Finally, there was young Walter Shewhart, who was to transform industry with his statistical concepts and thinking and his ability to bridge technical tools with a management system.

At the turn of the century, Taylor wrote a collection of reports and papers that were published by the American Society of Mechanical Engineers. One of the most famous was *On the Art of Cutting Metals*, which had worldwide impact. With Maunsel White, Taylor developed the first high-speed steel. Taylor was also instrumental in the development of one of the first industrial cost accounting systems, even though, according to legend, he previously knew nothing about accounting.

Frank G. and Lillian Gilbreth, aware of Taylor's work in measurement and analysis, turned their attention to mechanizing and commercializing Taylorism. For their experimental model, they chose the ancient craft of bricklaying. It had been assumed that production in bricklaying certainly should have reached its zenith thousands of years ago, with nothing more to be done to increase production. Yet Frank Gilbreth was able to show that by following his techniques and with proper management planning, production could be raised from an average of 120 bricks per hour to 350 bricks per hour, and the worker would be less tired than he had been under the old system.

The Gilbreths refined some of the studies and techniques developed by Taylor. They used the motion picture camera to record work steps for analyses and broke them down into minute elements called "therbligs" (Gilbreth spelled backwards). Their results were eventually codified into the use of predetermined motion–time measures which were used by industrial engineers and efficiency experts of the day.

By 1912, the efficiency movement was gaining momentum. Taylor was called before a special committee of the House of Representatives which was investigating scientific management and its impact on the railroad industry. He tried to explain scientific management to the somewhat hostile railroad hearings committee, whose members regarded it as "speeding up" work. He said:

> Scientific management involves a complete mental revolution on the part of the *working man* engaged in any particular establishment or industry...a complete mental revolution on the part of these men as to their duties toward their work, toward their fellowman, and toward their employers.
>
> And scientific management involves an equally complete mental revolution on the part of those on *management's side*...the foreman, the superintendent, the owner of the business, and the board of directors. Here we must have a mental revolution on their part as to their duties toward their fellow workers in management, toward their workmen, and toward all of their daily problems. Without this complete mental revolution on both sides, scientific management does not exist!
>
> I want to sweep the deck, sweep away a good deal of the rubbish first by pointing out what scientific management is not— it is not an efficiency device, nor is it any bunch or group of efficiency devices. It is not a new system of figuring costs. It is not a new scheme of paying men. It is not holding a stopwatch on a man and writing things down about him. It is not time study. It is not motion study, nor an analysis of the movements of a man. Nor is scientific management the printing and ruling and unloading of a ton or two of blank forms on a set of men and saying, "Here's your system—go to it."
>
> It is not divided foremanship, nor functional foremanship. It is not any of these devices which the average man calls to mind when he hears the words "scientific management." I am not sneering at cost-keeping systems—at time-study, at functional foremanship, nor at any of the new and improved schemes of paying men. Nor am I sneering at efficiency devices, if they are really devices which make for efficiency. I believe in them. What I am emphasizing is that these devices in whole or part are *not* scientific management; they are useful adjuncts to scientific management, but they are also useful adjuncts to other systems of management.[12]

Taylor found out, the hard way, the importance of the cooperative spirit. He was strictly the engineer at first. Only after painful experiences did he realize that the human factor, the social system, and mental attitude of people in both management and labor had to be adjusted and changed completely before greater productivity could result.

Referring to his early experiences in seeking greater output, Taylor described the strained feelings between himself and his workmen as "miserable." Yet he was determined to improve production. He continued his experiments until three years before his death in 1915, when he found that human motivation, not just engineered improvements, could alone increase output.

Unfortunately, the human factor was ignored by many. Shortly after the railroad hearings, self-proclaimed "efficiency experts" did untold damage to scientific management. Time studies and the new efficiency techniques were used by incompetent "consultants" who sold managers on the idea of increasing profit by "speeding up" employees. Consequently, many labor unions, just beginning to feel their strength, worked against the new science and all efficiency approaches. With the passing of Taylor in 1915, the scientific management movement lost, for the moment, any chance of reaching its true potential as the catalyst for the future total quality management system. Still, the foundation was laid for the management system that was soon to become a key ingredient of organizations of the future.

Walter Shewhart—The Founding Father

Walter Shewhart was an engineer, scientist, and philosopher. He was a very deep thinker, and his ideas, although profound and technically perfect, were difficult to fathom. His style of writing followed his style of thinking—very obtuse. Still, he was brilliant, and his works on variation and sampling, coupled with his teachings on the need for documentation, influenced forever the course of industrial history.

Shewhart was familiar with the scientific management movement and its evolution from Whitney's innovation of division of labor. Although he was concerned about its evolution into sweatshop factory environments, his major focus was on the other of Whitney's great innovations—interchangeable parts—for this encompassed variation, rejects, and waste.

To deal with the issue of variation, Shewhart developed the control chart in 1924. He realized that the traditional use of tolerance limits was short-sighted, because they only provided a method for judging the quality of a product that had already been made.[13]

The control limits on Shewhart's control charts, however, provided a ready guide for acting on the process in order to eliminate what he called *assignable causes*[8] of variation, thus preventing inferior products from being produced in the future. This allowed management to focus on the future, through the use of statistical probability—a prediction of future production based upon historical data. Thus, the emphasis shifted from costly correction of problems to prevention of problems and improvement of processes.[14]

Like Taylor, Shewhart's focus shifted from individual parts to a systems approach. The notion of zero defects of individual parts was replaced with zero variability of system operations.

Shewhart's Control System

Shewhart identified the traditional act of control as consisting of three elements: the act of specifying what is required, the act of producing what is specified, and the act of judging whether the requirements have been met. This simple picture of the control of quality would work well if production could be viewed in the context of an exact science, where all products are made exactly the same. Shewhart knew, however, that because variation is pervasive, the control of quality characteristics must be a matter of probability. He envisioned a statistician helping an engineer to understanding variation and arriving at the economic control of quality.[15]

Shewhart's Concept of Variation

Determining the *state of statistical control* in terms of degree of variation is the first step in the Shewhart control system. Rather than specifying what is required in terms of tolerance requirements, Shewhart viewed variation as being present in everything and identified two types of variation: *controlled* and *uncontrolled*.

This is fundamentally different from the traditional way of classifying variation as either acceptable or unacceptable (go–no-go tolerance). Viewing variation as controlled or uncontrolled enables one to focus on the causes of variation in order to improve a process (before the fact) as opposed to focusing on the output of a process in order to judge whether or not the product is acceptable (after the fact).

Shewhart taught that controlled variation is a consistent pattern of variation over time that is due to random or *chance causes*. He recognized that there may be many chance causes of variation, but the effect of any one of these is relatively small; therefore, which cause or causes are responsible for observed variation is a matter of chance. Shewhart stated that a process that is being affected only by *chance* causes of variation is said to be *in a state of statistical control*.

All processes contain chance causes of variation, and Shewhart taught that it is possible to reduce the chance causes of variation, but it is not realistic or cost effective to try to remove them all. The control limits on Shewhart's control charts represent the boundaries of the occurrence of chance causes of variation operating within the system.

The second type of variation—uncontrolled variation—is an inconsistent or changing pattern of variation that occurs over time and is due to what Shewhart classified as *assignable causes*. Because the effects of assignable causes of variation are relatively major compared to chance causes, they can and must be identified and removed.[16] According to Shewhart, a process is *out of statistical control* when it is being affected by assignable causes.

One of Shewhart's main problems was how to communicate this newfound theory without overwhelming the average businessman or engineer. The answer came in the form of staged experiments using models which demonstrated variation. His *ideal bowl experiment*[17] with poker chips was modeled by his protege, W. Edwards Deming, some 20 years later with his famous *red bead experiment*.

Another major contribution of Shewhart's first principle of control was recognition of the need for operational definitions that can be communicated to operators, inspectors, and scientists alike. He was fond of asking, "How can an operator carry out his job tasks if he does not understand what the job is? And how can he know what the job is if what was produced yesterday was O.K., but today the same product is wrong?" He believed that inspection, whether the operator inspects his own work or relies on someone else to do it for him, must have operational definitions. Extending specifications beyond product and into the realm of operator performance was the first attempt to define the "extended system of operations" which would greatly facilitate the production process.

The Shewhart System of Production

Shewhart's second principle—the act of producing what is specified—consists of five important steps (Shewhart's teachings are in italics):

1. **Outline the data collection framework:** *Specify in a general way how an observed sequence of data is to be examined for clues as to the existence of assignable causes of variability.*

2. **Develop the sampling plan:** *Specify how the original data are to be taken and how they are to be broken up into subsamples upon the basis of human judgments about whether the conditions under which the data were taken were essentially the same or not.*

3. **Identify the formulas and control limits for each sample:** *Specify the criterion of control that is to be used, indicating what statistics are to be computed for each subsample and how these are to be used in computing action or control limits for each statistic for which the control criterion is to be constructed.*

4. **Outline the corrective actions/improvement thesis:** *Specify the action that is to be taken when an observed statistic falls outside its control limits.*

5. **Determine the size of the database:** *Specify the quantity of data that must be available and found to satisfy the criterion of control before the engineer is to act as though he had attained a state of statistical control.*[8]

The Shewhart system became a key component of the technical system of total quality. The works of Deming, Juran, Feigenbaum, Sarasohn, Ishikawa, and others who followed would amplify Shewhart's concept of quality as a *technical system* into its many dimensions, which eventually led to the body of knowledge known as total quality.

The Shewhart Cycle: When Control Meets Scientific Management

From the "exact science" days of the 1800s to the 1920s, *specification, production,* and *inspection* were considered to be independent of each other when viewed in a straight line manner. They take on an entirely different picture in an inexact science. When the production process is viewed from the standpoint of the control of quality as a matter of probability, then specification, production, and inspection are linked together as represented in a circular diagram or wheel. *Specification and production* are linked because it is important to know how well the tolerance limits are being satisfied by the existing process and what improvements are necessary. Shewhart compared this process (which he called the Scientific Method) to the dynamic process of acquiring knowledge, which is similar to an experiment. Step 1 was formulating the hypothesis. Step 2 was conducting the experiment. Step 3 was testing the hypothesis.[18] In the Shewhart wheel, the successful completion of each interlocking component led to a cycle of continuous improvement. (Years later Deming was to popularize this cycle of improvement in his famous Deming wheel.)

Shewhart Meets Deming

It was at the Bell Laboratories in New Jersey where Shewhart, who was leading the telephone reliability efforts during the 1930s, first met Deming. Shewhart, as discussed earlier, was developing his system for improving worker performance and productivity by measuring variation using control charts and statistical methods. Deming was impressed and liked what he saw, especially Shewhart's intellect and the *wheel*—the Shewhart cycle of control. He realized that with training, workers could retain control over their work processes by monitoring the quality of the items produced.

Deming also believed that once workers were trained and educated and were empowered to manage their work processes, quality would be increased and costly inspections could once and for all be eliminated. He presented the idea that higher quality would cost less, not more. Deming studied Shewhart's teachings and techniques and learned well, even if at times he was lost and said that his genius was in knowing when to act and when to leave a process alone. At times he was frustrated by Shewhart's obtuse style of thinking and writing.[19]

In 1938, Shewhart delivered four lectures to the U.S. Department of Agriculture (USDA) Graduate School at the invitation of Deming. In addition to being in charge of the mathematics and statistics courses at the USDA Graduate School, Deming was responsible for inviting guest lecturers. He invited Shewhart to present a series of lectures on how statistical methods of control were being used in industry to economically control the quality of manufactured products. Shewhart spent an entire year developing the lectures, titled them *Statistical Method from the Viewpoint of Quality Control*, and delivered them in March of 1938. They were subsequently edited into book format by Deming and published in 1939.

In a couple of years, both Deming and Shewhart were called upon by the U.S. government to aid the war effort. As David Halberstam recounted, the War Department, impressed by Shewhart's theories and work, brought together a small group of experts on statistical process control (SPC) to establish better quality guidelines for defense contractors.[20] Deming was a member of that group and he came to love the work.

Origins of Deming

Who was Dr. W. Edwards Deming, the man who was to take Shewhart's teachings, popularize them, and even go beyond? He was born on October 14, 1900 and earned his Ph.D. in physics at Yale University in the summer of 1927, which is where he learned to use statistical theory. As a graduate student in the late 1920s, he did part-time summer work at the famous Western Electric Hawthorne plant in Chicago. It was at this plant that Elton Mayo some ten years later would perform his experiments later known as the Hawthorne Experiments. While working at Hawthorne, Deming could not help noticing the poor working conditions of this sweatshop environment, which employed predominantly female laborers to produce telephones. Deming was both fascinated and appalled by what he saw and learned. It was at Hawthorne where he saw the full effects of the abuses of the Taylor system of scientific management. He also saw the full effect of Whitney's second great innovation—division of labor—when carried to extreme by ivory tower management uncaring about the state of the social system of the organization. So what if the work environment was a sweatshop—the workers were paid well enough! "The women should be happy just to have a job" seemed to be the unspoken attitude.

When Deming Met Taylor(ism)

A couple of years before meeting Shewhart, when Deming encountered Taylorism at Hawthorne, he found a scientific management system with the following objectives:

- Develop a science for each element of work.

- Scientifically select a workman and train and develop him.

- Secure whole-hearted cooperation between management and labor to ensure that all work is done in accordance with the principles developed.

- Divide the work between management and labor. The manager takes over all work for which he is better suited than the workman.

It was the fourth point, which evolved out of the division of labor concept, that Deming found to be the real villain. In practice, this meant removing from the worker basic responsibility for the quality of the work. What Deming disliked was that workers should not be hired to think about their work. That was management's job. Errors will occur, but the worker need not worry—the inspector will catch any mistakes *before* they leave the plant. In addition, management could always reduce the per-piece pay to reflect scrap and rework. Any worker who produced too many inferior quality pieces would be fired.

The problem with Taylorism is that it views the production process mechanistically instead of holistically, as a system which includes the human elements of motivation and respect. Taylorism taught American industry to view the worker as "a cog in the giant industrial machine, whose job could be defined and directed by educated managers administering a set of rules."[21] Work on the assembly lines of America and at Hawthorne was simple, repetitive, and boring. Management was top-down. Pay per piece meant that higher output equals higher take-home pay. Quality of work for the most part was not a factor for the average, everyday worker.

This system found a friend in the assembly line process developed by Henry Ford and was widely incorporated into America's private and public sectors. Taylor's management system made it possible for waves of immigrants, many of whom could not read, write, or speak English (and at times not even communicate with one another), to find employment in American factories. Taylor's ideas were even introduced into the nation's schools.[22]

Edwards Deming had various colleagues at the time, one of whom was

Joseph Juran, another famous quality "guru." They rebelled at the scientific management movement. They felt that the authoritarian Taylorism method of management was degrading to the human spirit and counterproductive to the interests of employees, management, the company, and society as a whole.[23] Mayo and his Hawthorne research team confirmed these feelings with their findings: good leadership leads to high morale and motivation, which in turn leads to higher production. Good leadership was defined as democratic, rather than autocratic, and people centered, as opposed to production centered. Thus began the human relations era.

Post-World War II

When the war ended, American industry converted to peacetime production of goods and services. People were hungry for possessions and an appetite developed worldwide for products "made in the U.S.A." The focus in the United States returned to quantity over quality, and a gradual deterioration of market share occurred, with billions of dollars in international business lost to Japanese and European competitors. These were the modern-day phoenixes rising from the ashes of war. America became preoccupied with the mechanics of mass production and its role as world provider to a hungry people. What followed was an imbalance between satisfying the needs of the worker and a lack of appreciation for and recognition of the external customer. America moved away from what had made it great!

The Japanese Resurrection

Japan first began to apply statistical control concepts in the early 1920s, but moved away from them when the war began.[24] In 1946, under General Douglas MacArthur's leadership, the Supreme Command for the Allied Powers (SCAP) established quality control tools and techniques as the approach to affect the turnaround of Japanese industry. Japan had sacrificed its industry, and eventually its food supply, to support its war effort. Subsequently, there was little left in post-war Japan to occupy. The country was a shambles. Only one major city, Kyoto, had escaped wide-scale destruction; food was scarce and industry was negligible.[24]

Against a backdrop of devastation and military defeat, a group of Japanese scientists and engineers—organized appropriately as the Union of Japanese Scientists and Engineers (JUSE)—dedicated themselves to working with American and Allied experts to help rebuild the country. Reconstruction was a daunting and monumental task. With few natural resources available or any immediate means of producing them, export of manufactured goods was essential. However, Japanese industry—or what was left of it—was producing inferior goods, a fact which was recognized worldwide. JUSE was faced with the task of drastically improving the quality of Japan's industrial output as an essential exchange commodity for survival.

W.S. Magill and Homer Sarasohn, among others, assisted with the dramatic transformation of the electronics industry and telecommunications. Magill is regarded by some as the father of statistical quality control in Japan. He was the first to advocate its use in a 1945 lecture series and successfully applied SPC techniques to vacuum tube production in 1946 at NEC.[25]

Sarasohn worked with supervisors and managers to improve reliability and yields in the electronics field from 40% in 1946 to 80 to 90% in 1949; he documented his findings for SCAP, and MacArthur took notice. He ordered Sarasohn to instruct Japanese businessmen how to get things done. The Japanese listened, but the Americans forgot. In 1950, Sarasohn's attention was directed toward Korea, and Walter Shewhart was asked to come to Japan. He was unable to at the time, and Deming was eventually tapped to direct the transformation.

In July 1950, Deming began a series of day-long lectures to Japanese management in which he taught the basic "Elementary Principles of Statistical Control of Quality." The Japanese embraced the man and his principles and named their most prestigious award for quality The Deming Prize. During the 1970s, Deming turned his attention back to the United States. He died at the age of 93, still going strong. His Fourteen Points go far beyond statistical methods and address the management system as well as the social system or culture of the organization. In many ways, he began to sound more and more like Frederick Taylor, whose major emphasis in later years was on the need for a *mental revolution*—a transformation. Deming's Theory of Profound Knowledge brings together all three systems of total quality.

The Other "Gurus" Arrive

What began in Japan in the 1950s became a worldwide quality movement, albeit on a limited basis, within 20 years. During this period, the era of the "gurus" evolved (Deming, Juran, Ishikawa, Feigenbaum, and Crosby). Beginning with Deming in 1948 and Juran in 1954, the movement was eventually carried back to the United States by Feigenbaum in the 1960s and Crosby in the 1970s. Meanwhile, Ishikawa and his associates at JUSE kept the movement alive in Japan. By 1980, the bell began to toll loud and clear in the West with the NBC White Paper entitled "If Japan Can Do It, Why Can't We?" The following are thumbnail sketches of the teachings of the other gurus.

Joseph Juran

Joseph Juran was the son of an immigrant shoemaker from Romania and began his industrial career at Western Electric's Hawthorne plant before World War II. He later worked at Bell Laboratories in the area of quality assurance. He worked as a government administrator, university professor, labor arbitrator, and corporate director before establishing his own consulting firm, the Juran Institute, in Wilton, Connecticut. In the 1950s, he was invited to Japan by JUSE to help rebuilding Japanese corporations develop management concepts. Juran based some of his principles on the work of Walter Shewhart and, like Deming and the other quality gurus, believed that management and the system are responsible for quality. Juran is the creator of statistical quality control and the author of *The Quality Control Handbook*, which has become an international standard reference for the quality movement.

Juran's definition of quality is described as "fitness for use as perceived by the customer." If a product is produced and the customer perceives it as fit for use, then the quality mission has been accomplished. Juran also believed that every person in the organization must be involved in the effort to make products or services that are fit for use.

Juran described a perpetual spiral of progress or continuous striving toward quality. Steps on this spiral are, in ascending order, research, development, design, specification, planning, purchasing, instrumentation, production, process control, inspection, testing, sale, service, and then back to research again. The idea behind the spiral is that each time the steps are completed, products or services would increase in quality. Juran explained that chronic problems should be solved by following this spiral; he formulated a breakthrough sequence to increase the standard of performance so that problems are eliminated. To alleviate sporadic problems, which he finds are often solved with temporary solutions, he suggests carefully examining the system causing the problem and adjusting it to solve the difficulty. Once operating at this improved standard of performance, with the sporadic problem solved, the process of analyzing chronic and sporadic problems should start over again.

Juran pointed out that companies often overlook the cost of producing low-quality products. He suggested that by implementing his theories of quality improvement, not only would higher quality products be produced, but the actual costs would be lower. His Cost of Quality principle was known as "Gold in the Mine."

Juran is known for his work with statistics, and he relied on the quantification of standards and statistical quality control techniques. He is credited with implementing use of the Pareto diagram to improve business systems as well.

Juran's concept of quality included the managerial dimensions of planning, organizing, and controlling (known as the Juran Trilogy) and focused on the responsibility of management to achieve quality and the need to set goals. His ten steps to quality are as follows:

1. Build awareness of opportunities to improve.

2. Set goals for improvement.

3. Organize to reach goals.

4. Provide training.

5. Carry out projects to solve problems.

6. Report progress.

7. Give recognition.

8. Communicate results.

9. Keep score.

10. Maintain momentum by making annual improvement part of the regular systems and processes of the company.

Ishikawa and the Japanese Experts

Kaoru Ishikawa studied under both Homer Sarasohn and Edwards Deming during the late 1940s and early 1950s. As President of JUSE, he was instrumental in developing a unique Japanese strategy for total quality: the broad involvement of the entire organization in its *total* sense—every worker, every process, and every job. This also included the complete life cycle of the product, from start to finish.

Some of his accomplishments include the success of the quality circle in Japan, in part due to innovative tools such as the cause-and-effect diagram (often called the Ishikawa fishbone diagram because it resembles a fish skeleton). His approach was to provide easy-to-use analytical tools that could be used by all workers, including those on the line, to analyze and solve problems.

Ishikawa identified seven critical success factors that were essential for the success of total quality control in Japan:

1. Company-wide total quality control and participation by *all* members of the organization

2. Education and training in all aspects of total quality, which often amounts to 30 days per year per employee

3. Use of quality circles to update standards and regulations, which are in constant need of improvement

4. Quality audits by the president and quality council members (senior executives) twice a year

5. Widespread use of statistical methods and a focus on problem prevention

6. Nationwide quality control promotion activities, with the national imperative of keeping Japanese quality number one in the world

7. Revolutionary *mental* attitude on the part of both management and workers toward one another and toward the customer, including welcoming complaints, encouraging risk, and a wider span of control

Ishikawa believed that Japanese management practices should be democratic, with management providing the guidelines. Mission statements were used extensively and operating policies derived from them. Top management, he taught, must assume a leadership position to implement the policies so that they are followed by all.

The impact on Japanese industry was startling. In seven to ten years, the electronics and telecommunications industries were transformed, with the entire nation revitalized by the end of the 1960s.

Armand Feigenbaum

Unlike Deming and Juran, Feigenbaum did not work with the Japanese. He was Vice President of Worldwide Quality for General Electric until the late 1960s, when he set up his own consulting firm, General Systems, Inc. He is best known for coining the term *total quality control* and for his 850-page book on the subject. His teachings center around the integration of people–machine–information structures in order to economically and effectively control quality and achieve full customer satisfaction.

Feigenbaum taught that there are two requirements to establishing quality as a business strategy: establishing customer satisfaction must be central and quality/cost objectives must drive the total quality system. His systems theory of total quality control includes four fundamental principles:

- Total quality is a continuous work process, starting with customer requirements and ending with customer satisfaction.

- Documentation allows visualization and communication of work assignments.

- The quality system provides for greater flexibility because of a greater use of alternatives provided.

- Systematic reengineering of major quality activities leads to greater levels of continuous improvement.

Like Juran and Deming, Feigenbaum used a visual concept to capture the idea of waste and rework—the so-called Hidden Plant. Based upon studies, he taught that this "Hidden Plant" can account for between 15 and 40% of the production capacity of a company. In his book, he used the concept of the "9 M's" to describe the factors which affect quality: (1) markets, (2) money, (3) management, (4) men, (5) motivation, (6) materials, (7) machines and mechanization, (8) modern information methods, and (9) mounting product requirements.

According to Andrea Gabor in "The Man Who Discovered Quality," Feigenbaum took a nut-and-bolts approach to quality, while Deming is often viewed as a visionary. Nuts and bolts led him to focus on the benefits and outcomes of total quality, rather than only the process to follow. His methods led to increased quantification of total quality program improvements during the 1970s and 1980s.

Philip Crosby

Unlike the other quality gurus, who were scientists, engineers, and statisticians, Philip Crosby is known for his motivational talks and style of presentation. His emergence began in 1961, when he first developed the concept of zero defects while working as a quality manager at Martin Marietta Corporation in Orlando, Florida. He believed that "zero defects" motivated line workers to turn out perfect products. He soon joined ITT, where he quickly moved up the ranks to Vice President of Quality Control Operations, covering 192 manufacturing facilities in 46 countries. He held the position until 1979, when he opened his own consulting company, which became one of the largest of its kind with over 250 people worldwide.

He established the Quality College in 1980 and used that concept to promote his teachings and writings in 18 languages. It has been estimated that over five million people have attended its courses, and his trilogy of books are popular and easy to read. It is in these works where he introduces the four absolutes of his total quality management philosophy:

1. The definition of quality is conformance to requirements.

2. The system of quality is prevention of problems.

3. The performance standard of quality is zero defects.

4. The measurement of quality is the price of nonconformance, or the cost of quality.

The fourth principle, the Cost of Quality, is similar to Feigenbaum's Hidden Plant and Juran's Gold in the Mine. Like Deming, he has 14 steps to quality improvement. Also like Deming, he has been very critical of the Malcolm Baldrige National Quality Award, although his influence (like Deming's) can be seen in virtually all seven categories.

He departs from the other gurus in his emphasis on performance standards instead of statistical data to achieve zero defects. He believes that identifying goals to be achieved, setting standards for the final product, removing all error-causing situations, and complete organizational commitment comprise the foundation for excellence.

ISO 9000 and the Quality Movement

At the turn of the century, England was the most advanced nation in the world in terms of quality standards. During World War I, England led the charge and during World War II was at least the equal of the United States—with one exception. England did not have Shewhart, Deming, and the other American quality gurus. It was not until the Common Market accepted the firm touch of Prime Minister Margaret Thatcher that the European movement was galvanized in 1979 with the forerunner of ISO 9000. It was Thatcher who orchestrated the transformance of the British ISO 9000 series for the European community. In less than 20 years, it has become the worldwide quality standard.

ENDNOTES

1. During the course of the Deming Prize examination at Florida Power & Light in 1988 and 1989, Dr. Kano consistently emphasized this point during site visits to various power plants and district customer service operations. The concept of worker self-inspection, while new in the United States, has been a practiced art in Japan over the past 20 years.

2. Whethan, C.D. *A History of Science* (4th edition), New York: Macmillan, 1980.

3. Tribus, Myron. *The Systems of Total Quality*, 1990, published by the author.

4. The total quality ballantine was developed by Frank Voehl to illustrate the three-dimensional and interlocking aspects of the quality system. It is loosely based on the military concept of three interlocking bullet holes representing a perfect hit.

5. Tribus, Myron. *The Three Systems of Total Quality*, 1990, published by the author; referenced in Voehl, Frank. *Total Quality: Principles and Practices within Organizations*, Coral Springs, FL: Strategy Associates, 1992, pp. IV, 20.

6. The use of a storyboard to document the various phases of project development was introduced by Dr. Kume in his work on total quality control and was pioneered in the United States by Disney Studios, where it was used to bring new movies to production sooner.

7. For details, see Voehl, F.W. *The Integrated Quality System*, Coral Springs, FL: Strategy Associates, 1992.

8. Shewhart, W.A. *Economic Control of Quality of Manufactured Product*, New York: Van Nostrand, 1931.

9. Olmstead, Denison. *Memoir of Eli Whitney, Esq.*, New York: Arno Press, 1972.

10. Walter Shewhart on the "go–no-go" concept: If, for example, a design involving the use of a cylindrical shaft in a bearing is examined, interchangeability might be ensured simply by using a suitable "go" plug gauge on the bearing and a suitable "go" ring gauge on the shaft. In this case, the difference between the dimensions of the two "go" gauges gives the minimum clearance. Such a method of gauging, however, does not fix the maximum clearance. The production worker soon realized that a slack fit between a part and its "go" gauge might result in enough play between the shaft and its bearing to cause the product to be rejected; therefore, he tried to keep the fit between the part and its "go" gauge as close as possible, thus encountering some of the difficulties that had been experienced in trying to make the parts exactly alike.

11. Walter Shewhart was the first to realize that, with the development of the atomic structure of matter and electricity, it became necessary to regard laws as being statistical in nature. According to Shewhart, the importance of the law of large numbers in the interpretation of physical phenomena will become apparent to anyone who even hastily surveys any one or more of the following works: Darrow, K.K. "Statistical Theories of Matter, Radiation, and Electricity." *The Physical Review Supplement*, Vol. I No. I, July 1992 (also published in the series of Bell Telephone Laboratories reprints, No. 435); Rice, J. *Introduction to Statistical Mechanics for Students of Physics and Physical Chemistry*, London: Constable & Company, 1930; Tolman, R.E. *Statistical Mechanics with Applications to Physics and Chemistry*, New York: Chemical Catalog Company, 1927; Loeb, L.B. *Kinetic Theory of Gases*, New York: McGraw-Hill, 1927; Bloch, E. *The Kinetic Theory of Bases*, London: Methuen & Company, 1924; Richtmeyer, F.K. *Introduction to Modern Physics*, New York: McGraw-Hill, 1928; Wilson, H.A. *Modern Physics*, London: Blackie & Son, 1928; Darrow, K.K. *Introduction to Contemporary Physics*, New York: D. Van Nostrand, 1926; Ruark, A.E. and Urey, H.C. *Atoms, Molecules and Quanta*, New York: McGraw-Hill, 1930.

12. Matthies, Leslie. "The Beginning of Modern Scientific Management." *The Office*, April 1960.

13. Walter Shewhart on the use of the control chart: Whereas the concept of mass production of 1787 was born of an *exact* science, the concept underlying the quality control chart technique of 1924 was born of a *probable*

science, which has empirically derived control limits. These limits are to be set so that when the observed quality of a piece of product falls outside of them, even though the observation is still within the limits L_1 and L_2 (tolerance limits), it is desirable to look at the manufacturing process in order to discover and remove, if possible, one or more causes of variation that need not be left to chance.

14. Shewhart noted that it is essential, however, in industry and in science to understand the distinction between a stable system and an unstable system and how to plot points and conclude by rational methods whether they indicate a stable system. To quote Shewhart, "This conclusion is consistent with that so admirably presented in a recent paper by S.L. Andrew in the *Bell Telephone Quarterly*, Jan., 1931, and also with conclusions set forth in the recent book *Business Adrift*, by W. B. Donham, Dean of the Harvard Business School. Such reading cannot do other than strengthen our belief in the fact that control of quality will come only through the weeding out of assignable causes of variation—particularly those that introduce lack of constancy in the chance cause system."

15. As the statistician enters the scene, the three traditional elements of control take on a new meaning, as Shewhart summarized: "Corresponding to these three steps there are three senses in which statistical control may play an important part in attaining uniformity in the quality of a manufactured product: (a) as a concept of a statistical state constituting a limit to which one may hope to go in improving the uniformity of quality; (b) as an operation or technique of attaining uniformity; and (c) as a judgment."

16. Deming refers to assignable causes as being "specific to some ephemeral (brief) event that can usually be discovered to the satisfaction of the expert on the job, and removed."

17. Shewhart used what he called the *Ideal Bowl Experiment* to physically characterize a state of statistical control. A number of physically similar poker chips with numbers written on them are placed in a bowl. Successive samples (Shewhart seems to prefer a sample size of four) are taken from the bowl, each time mixing the remaining chips. The chips removed from the bowl are drawn by chance—there are only chance causes of variation. In speaking of chance causes of variation, Shewhart proves, contrary to popular belief, that the statistician can have a sense of humor. "If someone were shooting at a mark and failed to hit the bull's-eye and was then asked why, the answer would likely be *chance*. Had someone asked the same question of one of man's earliest known ancestors, he might have attributed his lack of success to the dictates of fate or to the will of the gods. I am inclined to think that in many ways one of these excuses is about as good as another. The Ideal Bowl Experiment is an abstract means of characterizing the physical state of statistical control." A sequence of samples of any process can be compared mathematically to the bowl experiment and, if found similar, the process can be said to be affected only by random or chance causes of variation or

can be characterized as being in a *state of statistical control*. Shewhart states: "It seems to me that it is far safer to take some one physical operation such as drawing from a bowl as a physical model for an act that may be repeated at random, and then to require that any other repetitive operation believed to be random shall in addition produce results similar in certain respects to the results of drawing from a bowl before we act as though the operation in question were random."

18. It may be helpful to think of the three steps in the mass production process as steps in the Scientific Method. In this sense, specification, production, and inspection correspond, respectively, to formulating a hypothesis, conducting an experiment, and testing the hypothesis. The three steps constitute the dynamic scientific process of acquiring knowledge.

19. The following story was related at one of Deming's now-famous four-day quality seminars: I remember him (Shewhart) pacing the floor in his room at the Hotel Washington before the third lecture. He was explaining something to me. I remarked that these great thoughts should be in his lectures. He said that they were already written up in his third and fourth lectures. I remarked that if he wrote up these lectures in the same way that he had just explained them to me, they would be clearer. He said that his writing had to be foolproof. I thereupon remarked that he had written his thoughts to be so darn foolproof that no one could understand them.

20. Halberstam, David. The War Effort during WWII, Lectures, Articles and Interview Notes, 1960.

21. This is a general consensus feeling among many historians and writers as to the inherent "evil" of Taylorism—machine over man. Walter Shewhart, to his credit and genius, tries to marry quality control and scientific management. In the foreword to his 1931 master work referred to in Endnote 8, he writes, "Broadly speaking, the object of industry is to set up economic ways and means of satisfying human wants and in so doing to reduce everything possible to routines requiring a minimum amount of human effort. Through the use of the scientific method, extended to take account of modern statistical concepts, it has been found possible to set up limits within which the results of routine efforts must lie if they are to be economical. Deviations in the results of a routine process outside such limits indicate that the routine has broken down and will no longer be economical until the cause of trouble is removed."

22. Bonstingal, John Jay. *Schools of Quality*, New York: Free Press, 1992.

23. The Hawthorne Experiments, Elton Mayo, 1938.

24. Voehl, F.W. "The Deming Prize." *South Carolina Business Journal*, 1990 edition, pp. 33–38.

25. This was first pointed out by Robert Chadman Wood in an article about Homer Sarasohn, published in *Forbes* in 1990.

26. Figure 2.2 ©1991 F.W. Voehl. Figure 2.3 ©1992 Strategy Associates, Inc.

ARTICLE

THE DEMING PRIZE VS. THE BALDRIGE AWARD*

Joseph F. Duffy

The Deming Prize and the Baldrige Award. They're both named after Americans, both very prestigious to win, both standing for a cry for quality in business, both engaged by their share of critics. One is 40 years old; the other a mere four. One resides in an alluring, foreign land; the other on American soil. One is awarded to the paradigm of Japanese business, individuals and international companies; the other to the best of U.S. business. One has grown in what a psychologist might call a mostly safe, nurturing environment; the other amongst a sometimes sour, sometimes sweet, bipolar parental image of government officials, academia and business gurus who seem to critically tug every way possible. One represents a country hailed as the world leader in quality; the other is trying to catch up—trying very hard.

A battle between Japan's Deming Prize and the Malcolm Baldrige National Quality Award would be as good a making for a movie as *Rocky* ever was: You have the older, wiser Japanese, who emanates a wisdom that withstands time, against the younger, quickly maturing American who has an outstanding reputation for being a victorious underdog. Who would win? We took the two awards to center ring, made them don their gloves and have a go.

ROUND 1: HISTORY

Although residing almost half a world apart, the Deming Prize and the Malcolm Baldrige National Quality Award are bonded by influence. After

* This article is reproduced from *Quality Digest*, pp. 33–53, August 1991. In it, the author interviewed four individuals representing organizations with a reputation for being involved in the formation of the Baldrige Award. While no conclusions are drawn, the topics are central to total quality and worthy of debate.

the ravages unleashed during World War II took a ruinous toll on Japan, W. Edwards Deming came to aid this seemingly hopeless land. With his expertise in statistical quality control (SQC), Deming helped lift Japan out of the rubble and into the limelight by having Japanese businesses apply SQC techniques.

In 1951, the Union of Japanese Scientists and Engineers (JUSE) created an accolade to award companies that successfully apply companywide quality control (CWQC) based on statistical quality control. In honor of their American quality champion, JUSE named the award the Deming Prize.

Not until 31 years later did a similar prize take root in the United States, mainly due to the efforts of Frank C. Collins, who served as executive director of quality assurance for the Defense Logistics Agency and has formed Frank Collins Associates, Survival Twenty-One—a quality consulting firm; he also serves on the board of directors of the Malcolm Baldrige National Quality Award Consortium.

Collins, after many trips to Japan, based his U.S. quality award idea on the Deming Prize. "That's where I got the idea for the Malcolm Baldrige Award," he explains, "although I never in my wildest dreams expected it to be connected to Malcolm Baldrige."

Malcolm Baldrige, Secretary of Commerce in the Reagan administration, was killed in a rodeo accident in 1987. Reagan chose to honor Baldrige by naming the newly created award after him.

"The original concept was that it would be the National Quality Award," says Collins. "It would be strictly a private sector affair. The government would have no part in it other than the president being the awarder of the recognition."

ROUND 2: PROCESS

The Deming Prize has several categories: the Deming Prize for Individual Person, the Deming Application Prize and the Quality Control Award for Factory. Under the Deming Application Prize and the Deming Application Prize for Small Enterprise and the Deming Application Prize for Division. In 1984, another category was added: The Deming Application Prize to Oversea Companies, which is awarded to non-Japanese companies.

The Deming Application Prize has 10 examination items and is based on CWQC—the Prize's main objective.

A company or division begins the Deming Prize process by submitting an application form to the Deming Prize Committee, along with other pertinent information. Prospective applicants are advised to hold preliminary consultations with the secretariat of the Deming Prize Committee before completing and submitting the application.

After acceptance and notification, applicants must submit a description of quality control practices and a company business prospectus, *in Japanese.* If successful, the applicant will then be subject to a site visit. If the applicant passes, the Deming Prize is awarded.

Sound easy? Sometimes the applicant's information can fill up to 1,000 pages, and the examination process for U.S. companies is expensive.

The Baldrige Award applicant must first submit an Eligibility Determination Form, supporting documents and $50. Upon approval, the applicant must then submit an application package—running up to 50 pages for small business, 75 pages for a manufacturing or service company—and another fee. Among seven categories, 1,000 points are awarded. No particular score guarantees a site visit.

Each of the three categories—manufacturing, service and small company—are allowed up to two winners only.

ROUND 3: PURPOSE

The American obsession for winning is enormous. From Watergate to Iran-Contra, the American Revolution to Desert Storm, Americans have shown that they love to win no matter what the cost. So it's no wonder that as soon as quality awards and prizes have an impact, they fall under scrutiny. But most critics of these two world-class quality awards think these coveted prizes are mostly pristine in purpose.

Frank Voehl, *Quality Digest* columnist and corporate vice president and general manager of Qualtec Inc., a Florida Power & Light Group company, oversees the implementation of the total quality management programs within Qualtec's client companies. In 1987, Florida Power & Light (FPL) became the first and only U.S. company to win the Deming Prize. Through his work with hundreds of Japanese and U.S. companies, Voehl feels that there are seven reasons why companies quest for the Deming Prize or the Baldrige Award.

"The first general comment that a number of companies that I've talked to in Japan that have applied for the Deming Prize said was, 'We did not apply for the Deming Prize to win but to drive us toward better quality control,' says Voehl. "Second is applying for and receiving the examination had more meaning than did winning the Prize." Voehl's other five reasons are:

- The audit or the exam itself helped point out many areas of deficiencies and continuous improvement activities that they hadn't noticed.

- Since the Deming Prize dictates a clear goal and time limit, quality control advanced at an extremely rapid rate.

- The company going for the quality award was able to accomplish in one or two years what would normally have taken five or 10 years.

- There was a unification of a majority of the employees.

- They were able to communicate with a common language to the whole company. This is where the cultural change takes place.

Robert Peach, who was project manager of the Malcolm Baldrige National Quality Award Consortium for three years and now serves as a senior technical advisor to the administrator, feels the Baldrige Award "is not an award for the sake of the award—it is the 200,000 guidelines and applications that go out that matter, not the handful that actually apply."

And the companies that experiment with and implement the Baldrige criteria, as well as the Deming criteria, can only learn from their endeavor. However, for the companies taking it a step further and committing to win the prize, it isn't Little League, where the profits extracted from learning and having fun are supposed to outweigh the benefits of scoring more points than the other team. The Deming and the Baldrige are the Majors, where going for the award may mean 80-hour work weeks, quick hellos and goodbyes to spouses and missing your child's Little League games.

ROUND 4: GOING TO WAR

So your boss comes up to you and says, "Get ready—we're going for it." How you react may depend on the attitude of your senior-level management and the present quality state of your company. Ken Leach, a senior examiner for the Baldrige Award and founder of Leach Quality Inc., implemented the quality system at Globe Metallurgical—1988 winner of the Baldrige Award's small company category. He says winning the Baldrige was easy because its quality system was in place well before the birth of the Baldrige Award criteria.

"We got into it before Baldrige was even heard of, and we got into it at the impetus of our customers—Ford and General Motors in particular," explains Leach. "So we implemented a number of specific things to satisfy the customer, and you don't have a choice with them—you have to go through their audit system. We did that and did it very well. So that gave us the base to apply for the Baldrige and win it the very first year without trying to redo what we were already doing."

Leach says that because Globe was in such a readied state before the inception of the Baldrige Award, the company did not add any people or spend large sums of money on the implementation of a quality system. In fact, Globe was so advanced in its quality system that Leach claims he took the Baldrige Award application home after work on a Friday and returned it complete by the following Monday.

But even Leach agrees that Globe was exceptional and that not all companies can implement the Baldrige criteria as smoothly as Globe did.

Yokogawa-Hewlett-Packard (YHP) won the Deming Prize in 1982. Unlike Globe and its easy conquest of the Baldrige, YHP claims the quest for the Deming was no Sunday stroll. The company released the following statement in *Measure* magazine:

"Japanese companies compete fiercely to win a Deming Prize. Members of a management team typically work several hundred extra hours each month to organize the statistical charts, reports and exhibits for judging."[1] YHP also says that "audits had all the tension of a championship sports event."[2]

Voehl calls these extra hours and added stresses "pain levels and downside effects" and found that they were typical of most companies going for the Deming Prize. And because the Baldrige Award is a "second generation" of the Deming Prize, Voehl says the Baldrige Award is no exception to possible disruption. He explains that the quest for winning becoming greater than the quest for quality is a "natural thing that occurs within these organizations that you can't really prevent. Senior management focuses in on the journey and the overall effects that will happen as a result of going for the examination and the prize."

Voehl adds, "Getting ready for the examination and the site exams brings a tremendous amount of pressure upon the organizations, whether it's the Deming or the Baldrige, because of the implications that you should be the one department that results in the prize not being brought home."

William Golomski, who is the American Society for Quality Control's representative to JUSE, says deadline time for the award may be a time of pressure.

In the case of the Baldrige, there have been a few companies that hired consultants to help them get ready for a site visit after they've gone through an evaluation by examiners and senior examiners," recalls Golomski. "So I can understand that people who are still being asked to go through role playing for a site visit might get to the point where they'll say, 'Gosh, I don't know if I'm interested as I once was.' "

Collins looks at customers in a dual sense: your internal customers—employees or associates—and your external customers—the people who pay the freight to keep you in business.

"To me," Collins says forcefully, "when you *squeeze* your internal customer to win an award, you're really making a mockery of the whole thing."

But for the companies that take the Baldrige application guidelines and implement them without competing, Peach says the quality goal remains the biggest motivator.

"In my exposure both to applicants and other companies that are using the practice and guidelines independent of applying, I feel that they have the right perspective, that companies identify this as a pretty good practice of what quality practice should be," expounds Peach. "And they're using it that way. That's healthy; that's good."

Deming says it best: "I never said it would be easy; I only said it would work." And this piece of wisdom can pertain to the implementation and competing processes of both the Baldrige Award and the Deming Prize. But although sometimes not easy to pursue, these awards spark many companies to the awareness and benefits of a quality system. But as more companies win the Baldrige, more critics are discussing which accolade— the Baldrige or the Deming—holds more advantages over the other.

ROUND 5: ADVANTAGES VS. DISADVANTAGES

With a U.S. company capturing the Deming Prize, U.S. businesses are no longer without a choice of which world-class quality award to pursue. Motorola, before it went for the Baldrige Award, contemplated which award would improve Motorola's quality best, according to Stewart Clifford, president of Enterprise Media, a documentary film company that specializes in management topics. In a recent interview with Motorola's quality staff, Clifford asked if Motorola was interested in questing for the Deming Prize.

"I asked them the question about if they were looking at applying and going for the Deming," remembers Clifford. "And they said that they felt frankly that while the Deming Prize had some valuable points for them, the reason why they liked the Baldrige Award better was because of its much more intense focus on the customer."

But Voehl claims this is a misconception and that both approaches focus heavily on the customer. "Florida Power & Light really got a lot of negatives from our counselors that we weren't zeroing in on the external and internal customers enough," recalls Voehl. "We had to demonstrate how our quality improvement process was a means of planning and achieving customer satisfaction through TQC."

Section Seven of the Baldrige Award covers total customer satisfaction, and it's worth more points than any other section. In the Deming criteria, total customer satisfaction may seem lost among the need for applicants to document, document, document and use statistical approaches.

One reason Collins says he would compete for the Baldrige instead of the Deming is the Deming's unbending demand to have everything documented. "If you say something, you have to have a piece of paper that covers it," he jokes. "Having worked for the government for 33 years, I see that as a bureaucratic way of doing things. And the Japanese are extremely bureaucratic."

And in an open letter to employees from James L. Broadhead, FPL's chairman and CEO, printed in *Training* magazine, his employees confirm Collins' beliefs: "At the same time, however, the vast majority of the employees with whom I spoke expressed the belief that the mechanics of the QI [quality improvement] process have been overemphasized. They felt that we place too great an emphasis on indicators, charts, graphs, reports and meetings in which documents are presented and indicators reviewed."[3]

However, Collins says that what he likes about the Deming Prize criteria that's missing in the Baldrige Award criteria is the first two examination items of the Deming Prize: policy organization and its operation.

If you want people to understand what you mean by quality, you have to spell it out, you have to define it as policy, explains Collins. As far as objectives go, he remembers asking a Japanese firm what their objectives were. The president of this company said, "First to provide jobs to our company." "How many American firms would say that?" asks Collins. Organization and understanding its operation is extremely important. He says, "Those two criteria are the bedrock foundation of the Deming Prize that makes it somewhat stronger and of greater value than the Malcolm Baldrige National Quality Award."

Another point that may persuade a U.S. company to compete for one of the two awards is cost. All things considered, U.S. companies going for the Deming Application Prize to Oversea Companies seems more costly than U.S. companies competing for the Baldrige Award. Leach describes Globe's venture as very inexpensive: "It doesn't have to cost an arm and a leg for the Baldrige. You don't have to reinvent the wheel of what you're already doing." Peach worked with a small-category company that spent $6,000 on its Baldrige Award venture, and that included the application fee and retaining a technical writer for $1,000.

But these are small companies with 500 employees or fewer. FPL, on the other hand, with about 15,000 employees, spent $1.5 million on its quest for the Deming Prize, according to Neil DeCarlo of FPL's corporate communications. And there are some Baldrige applicants that have spent hundreds of thousands or even millions of dollars on their quality quest, according to *Fortune* magazine.[4]

But no matter how much the Baldrige applicant pays, whether it be $6,000 or millions, it still receives a feedback report as part of the application cost. In comparison, those companies not making it past the first level of the Deming Prize criteria may pay JUSE for counselors, who will come into the company and do a diagnostic evaluation.

Because FPL was a pioneer in the oversea competition, many of the costs that would have otherwise been associated with this award for an overseas company had been waived by JUSE, according to Voehl. But still, FPL dished out $850,000 of that million-and-a-half for counselor fees, says DeCarlo—an amount Voehl claims would be three or four times more if FPL had to hire a U.S. consulting firm.

One of FPL's reasons to go for the Deming award was because in 1986 when it decided to go for a quality award, the Baldrige Award did not yet exist. In fact, what many people, including some FPL critics, don't now is that the company heavily funded the activities leading to the Baldrige Award. FPL agreed not to try for the Baldrige Award for five years to deter any conflict of interest, says Voehl. Also, FPL had an excellent benchmarking company in Japan's Kansai Electric, which had already won the Deming Prize.

The Deming Prize puts no cap on the number of winners; the Baldrige allows a maximum of two winners for each of the three categories. Leach contests that by putting a limit on the winners, you make the Baldrige Award a more precious thing to win. Peach agrees. "I think there should be a limit," he says. "You just don't want scores of winners to dilute this."

Voehl disagrees. "We should take the caps off," he argues. "I think we'd do a lot more for the award, for the process if we didn't have a win-lose mentality toward it."

ROUND 6: CONTROVERSY

"The Baldrige is having such an impact," asserts Peach, "that now people will take a look at it and challenge. That will always happen—that's our American way." And at four years old, the Baldrige Award has already received a fair share of controversy. One of the most disturbing criticisms aimed at the Baldrige Award comes from Deming himself. Deming called the Baldrige Award "a terrible thing, a waste of industry" in a recent issue of *Automotive News*. The article states: "Among the reasons Deming denounces the award is its measurement of performance and the effects of training with numerical goals, which he cites as 'horrible things.'"

"'It's a lot of nonsense,' he said. 'The guidelines for 1991 (make that) very obvious.'"[5]

Golomski says that Deming is unhappy with two parts of the Baldrige guidelines. One is the concept of numerical goals, which Deming believes can cause aberrations within companies. "I don't take quite as strong a stand as Deming does," Golomski explains. "He makes another statement about goals and that far too often, goals are set in the absence of any way of knowing how you're going to achieve these goals."

Leach does not know what to think of "Deming's non-supportive or active disregard for the Baldrige Award." He finds it ironic that "a company could very much have a Deming-type philosophy or a Deming-oriented kind of company and could do quite well in the Baldrige application. I'm sure that Cadillac [1990 Baldrige Award winner] must have had a number of Deming philosophies in place."

Even if Deming is trying to be the burr under the saddle and spark U.S. companies into a quality quest, Leach doesn't think that Deming's "serving the pursuit of quality in general or himself very well by making public statements like that."

But Voehl agrees with some of Deming's points. "Cadillac got severely criticized by the board of trustees of the Baldrige because Cadillac took the Baldrige Award and General Motors tried to use it as a marketing tool," he says. "And that's not the intention. Those sort of things do not do the Baldrige Award any good because it seems like all you're interested in is public relations.

Cadillac has fallen under scrutiny from many critics for taking home the Baldrige Award.

After returning from consulting in Israel, Collins heard that Cadillac had won the Baldrige Award. "I couldn't believe my eyes," Collins exclaims. "Cadillac has gotten so much bad press over the last decade— transmission problems, difficulty with their diesel engines, their service record—a whole number of things that to me when they said Cadillac won it, I said, 'Impossible. They couldn't win it. Somebody's pulling a cruel joke.' "

Deming is not the only quality guru criticizing the Baldrige Award. Philip Crosby says in *Quality Digest* (February 1991) that customers should nominate the companies that compete for the Baldrige, not the companies themselves.

It is difficult to come by harsh criticism about the Deming Prize since few Americans are familiar with it. However, Collins questions FPL's quest for winning as superseding their quest for quality.

"There's no question in my mind that Florida Power & Light's John Hudiburg was intent on leading Florida Power & Light in a blaze of glory," insists Collins. "And money was absolutely no consideration as far as winning the Deming Prize. I don't know what the final tab on it was, but he bought the prize—there's no question about it."

Collins' comments do not go without backing. A number of articles on FPL's quest contain complaints from disgruntled employees who worked long hours to win the Deming Prize.

Deming Prize Application Checklist: Items and Their Particulars

---

1. Policy

- Policies pursued for management, quality and quality control
- Methods of establishing policies
- Justifiability and consistency of policies
- Utilization of statistical methods
- Transmission and diffusion of policies
- Review of policies and the results achieved
- Relationship between policies and long- and short-term planning

2. Organization and Its Management

- Explicitness of the scopes of authority and responsibility
- Appropriateness of delegations of authority
- Interdivisional cooperation
- Committees and their activities
- Utilization of staff
- Utilization of quality circle activities
- Quality control diagnosis

3. Education and Dissemination

- Education programs and results
- Quality-and-control consciousness, degrees of understanding of quality control
- Teaching of statistical concepts and methods and the extent of their dissemination
- Grasp of the effectiveness of quality control
- Education of related company (particularly those in the same group, subcontractors, consignees and distributors)
- Quality circle activities
- System of suggesting ways of improvements and its actual conditions

4. Collection, Dissemination and Use of Information on Quality

- Collection of external information
- Transmission of information between divisions
- Speed of information transmission (use of computers)
- Data processing, statistical analysis of information and utilization of the results

5. Analysis

- Selection of key problems and themes
- Propriety of the analytical approach
- Utilization of statistical methods
- Linkage with proper technology
- Quality analysis, process analysis
- Utilization of analytical results
- Assertiveness of improvement suggestions

6. Standardization

- Systematization of standards
- Method of establishing, revising and abolishing standards
- Outcome of the establishment, revision or abolition of standards
- Contents of the standards
- Utilization of the statistical methods
- Accumulation of technology
- Utilization of standards

7. Control

- Systems for the control of quality and such related matters as cost and quantity
- Control items and control points
- Utilization of such statistical control methods as control charts and other statistical concepts
- Contribution to performance of quality circle activity
- Actual conditions of control activities
- State of matters under control

8. Quality Assurance

- Procedure for the development of new products and services (analysis and upgrading of quality, checking of design, reliability and other properties)
- Safety and immunity from product liability
- Process design, process analysis and process control and improvement
- Process capability
- Instrumentation, gauging, testing and inspecting
- Equipment maintenance and control of subcontracting, purchasing and services
- Quality assurance system and its audit
- Utilization of statistical methods
- Evaluation and audit of quality
- Actual state of quality assurance

9. Results

- Measurement of results
- Substantive results in quality, services, delivery, time, cost, profits, safety, environment, etc.
- Intangible results
- Measuring for overcoming defects

10. Planning for the Future

- Grasp of the present state of affairs and the concreteness of the plan
- Measures for overcoming defects
- Plans for further advances
- Linkage with long-term plans

"If the goal is to win an award then the cost of winning the award is not worth the award itself," Voehl admits. "The focus needs to be on the outcomes for the organization." And Voehl feels that FPL's quality outcomes very much outweigh the cost put forth.

ROUND 7: CONSULTANTS

With the two awards, there's a big difference in the use of consultants or counselors, as they're called in Japan. In the case of the Deming Prize, a successful applicant uses counselors trained by JUSE throughout the examination, explains Golomski. "For the Baldrige, you're on your own or you use whomever you wish to help you—if you think it's worth it."

"Considering the tremendous number of brochures I get every day," says Collins, "it appears that everybody and his brother is an expert on the Malcolm Baldrige National Quality Award. And my experience tells me that there *ain't* that many experts on the Malcolm Baldrige National Quality Award."

So, are some consultants or counselors using the Baldrige Award to prey on aspiring companies? Voehl says he sees it happening all over and calls it "absolutely preposterous and absurd and unethical."

Voehl compares it to just like everybody jumping on the TQC bandwagon. "Everybody from a one-man or two-man mom-and-pop consulting company to a 1,000-employee consulting arm of the Big 8 seems to be an expert in TQM," he says. "It's like a dog with a rag: They're shaking it and shaking it, and they won't let it go because they see it can mean money to their bottom line. It's giving the consulting field a terrible black eye. It's giving the people who bring in these consultants the expectations clearly that they are going to win the award. These are false expectations, false hopes and false starts. They shouldn't even be looking at winning the award; they should be looking at implementing a quality system that can ensure customer satisfaction."

But there are good reasons to have consultants help you through the Baldrige quest. Leach points out that if a CEO of a company needs to change his or her approach on something, an employee will probably be intimidated to approach the CEO; instead, a consultant can do this. Also a consultant may carry in an objective view that brings different ideas to the company.

Deming Prize counselors, however, have a reputation to guard. That's why Golomski feels FPL had no chance to "buy the Prize."

"The counselor simply wouldn't agree with them that they [FPL] were ready," Golomski argues. "The counselors help an organization improve itself, but if they don't think the company is ready for the big leagues, they simply won't recommend it."

ROUND 8: MODIFICATIONS

The Baldrige Award criteria are constantly modified to meet changing expectations. This is how it grows stronger, becomes more mature. When awarded the Baldrige Award, recipients must share their knowledge of total quality, but Golomski wants to see better ways of technology transfer.

Collins thinks we will probably have a follow-up award similar to the Japan Quality Control Prize—which is awarded to Deming Prize winners if they have improved their quality standards five years after winning the Deming Prize and pass rigorous examination—but not until the Baldrige Award can be further improved.

Peach feels the Baldrige criteria are at a position where modifications will be in smaller increments. He says cycle time might become important enough to be emphasized more.

The possible modifications of the Deming Prize are hard to predict. However, modifications of the Baldrige Award may be based on the Deming Prize's influence.

ROUND 9: SAVING FACE

Junji Noguchi, executive director of JUSE, was contacted for an interview for this article. When he learned of the subject matter—comparing the two world-class quality awards—he declined to answer. He said, "I am sorry I have to reply that I cannot answer your interviews. That is because the contents were not preferable and that they are not what I was expecting."

Noguchi continued, "Awards or prizes in the country have been established under the most suitable standards and methods considering their own background of industries, societies and cultures. We do not understand the meaning of comparing awards in different countries that have different backgrounds."

Noguchi is displaying some of that ancient wisdom and showing a difference in our cultures that even Americans find difficult to explain. Is this why their award has been going strong for 40 years and why the Baldrige Award is a 4-year-old child growing much too fast thanks to our intrinsic desire to slice it up, examine it and try to put it back together more completely than before? Maybe. But as a result, our U.S. quality award will always remain provocative and exciting and keep the people talking. And this is good.

REFERENCES

1. *"YHP Teamwork Takes the Prize,"* Measure *(January-February 1983), 3000 Hanover St., Palo Alto, CA 94304, pg. 6.*
2. Measures, *pg. 6.*
3. *James L. Broadhead, "The Post-Deming Diet: Dismantling a Quality Bureaucracy,"* Training, *Lakewood Building, 50 S. Ninth St., Minneapolis, MN 55402, pg. 41.*
4. *Jeremy Main, "Is the Baldrige Overblown?"* Fortune *(July 1, 1991), Time & Life Building, Rockefeller Center, New York, NY 10020-1393, pg. 62.*
5. *Karen Passino, "Deming Calls Baldrige Prize 'Nonsense,' "* Automotive News *(April 1, 1991), 1400 E. Woodbridge, Detroit, MI, 48207.*

CHAPTER 3

THE PRESENT
R&D PARADIGM

Those social, management, and technical systems that exist today within R&D organizations are discussed in this chapter, including their effects on the environment. The discussion builds on the previous chapter and the development of the total quality movement and structure by identifying specific influences that affect R&D. The "environment" in which R&D must operate is examined in the first section. The specifics of the social, management, and technical systems (the existing paradigm) are considered in Chapter 4, and a narrative on each individual component is presented.

THE ENVIRONMENT SURROUNDING
THE SOCIAL, MANAGEMENT, AND TECHNICAL SYSTEMS

Before examining the present R&D system, described in general in Chapter 1, it is critical to address the environment that surrounds this system. This gives the social, management, and technical systems a multidimensional perspective by examining those influences that constantly affect the environment in which R&D operates.

Values, Vision, and Ideology

The first such influences on the R&D environment are the values and principles that guide the organization or business. Organizations that strictly value the financial aspects of a business communicate cost-driven tangibles to employees. Employees perceive these tangible as both confusing and unfamiliar measures. For many researchers, business practices such as cost accounting, marketing, and financial management remain mysterious. The researcher's unfamiliarity with business practices often leads to poor recognition of the bottom line. Bottom-line management practices measure only the tangible elements of the business and not items such as creativity and innovation.[1] Companies solely dedicated to financial performance may create a R&D department that is driven to meet quarterly financial objectives. Costs are forced lower at the risk of losing creativity and innovation. Cost-driven goals infuse stress into the R&D environment. This bottom-line-driven management style[2] becomes the prevailing environment. R&D objectives such as new product/process development, product innovation, new market penetration, etc. become secondary to corporate financial accounting objectives. Cost-conscious managers strive to alleviate excessive expenses at the risk of exchanging cost cutting for creativity. The "bottom-line approach" to determining research projects may produce "relevant science but not necessarily good science" because it risks losing creativity for the sake of a financial result.[3]

Organizations that stress teamwork, creativity, long-range planning, and strategies geared toward future growth and performance are well positioned for supporting total quality thinking. These organizations will continue to integrate effective managerial structures with an environment that encourages innovation and creativity.

Included in the first environmental influence is the concept of vision and ideology. **Vision** provides the "road map for change" and defines goals and objectives for the organization. Developing a corporate vision requires seven to twenty years.[4] Sustaining that vision involves strategies, complete management commitment, and achievable goals. Long-term corporate vision provides leadership and creates an environment in which creativity and innovation can flourish.[1]

Rapidly changing economic conditions result in instantaneous change, competitive marketplaces, and rapid product technology. Companies that lack vision cannot adequately scan the marketplace for technological opportunities. Organizations that generally rely on short-term goals often respond with knee-jerk reactions.[2] Short-term thinking by executives is reflected in a R&D department occupied with meeting objectives rather than creating new products and processes. Short-term strategies may force a reactive rather than proactive environment—one filled with improper or haphazard decision making, inconsistency in procedure and human resources, and incomplete management systems. Short-term analysis fosters a "CYA" mentality among and between researchers, which affects performance. Organizations, companies, or even R&D departments void of vision (or a strategy to reach that vision) become mired in day-to-day activities, losing sight of their long-term objectives and mission. One example of how vision greatly affects quality is the emphasis placed on this characteristic by the Malcolm Baldrige National Quality Award. Having a vision that supports total quality principles and a strategy to reach that vision is a required element for organizations striving to implement total quality.[5]

Strategic Emphasis

Often R&D is viewed from the boardroom as an appendage to the organization. It neither manufactures nor markets (sells) the product it creates. R&D may "cost" the company more than it "profits" the company if adequate performance measures do not exist. R&D often suffers from cost reductions when the economic climate is weak. Ask yourself the following questions concerning your R&D function:

- Does R&D participate in formulating organizational strategies?

- Is R&D a cost center in my organization?

- Is it treated as such?

- Has R&D truly quantified its performance?

- Do indicators now exist to measure the output performance from R&D?

Since financial and accounting personnel constantly examine cost-cutting strategies, it is quite natural for R&D to be examined using the same criteria. Given this premise, is it any wonder that R&D expenditures have been significantly reduced in so many organizations? One reason for this lack of strategic emphasis may be that R&D produces few "measurables" related to success. If financial measures such as profit and loss dictate success, then R&D performance must have a direct connection to these measures. Otherwise, R&D must develop clear performance standards[6] using criteria (measures) that uniquely define its function. For example, throughput (cycle time) is one such measure that indicates overall performance. Efficiencies developed for improving cycle time can be traced to improvements in costs and profits.

R&D must continue to play a vital and integral part throughout the entire product development cycle. R&D personnel must be seen not just as "developers" but as implementors and problem solvers. There must be a direct link to those measures that dictate organizational success. The strategic emphasis must ensure that R&D takes an active role in developing and implementing the master plan. For R&D to have a truly strategic influence, organizations must recognize their full potential and use this expertise to develop new technical or scientific advancements based on sound business practices. (For additional information, see Abstract 3.1 at the end of this chapter.)

A lack of strategic emphasis for R&D can also lead to a distancing of the entire department from organizational goals and objectives.[3] North American research facilities have a hierarchical approach to management and, therefore, a top-down philosophy when sharing or participating in the development of strategies.[7,8] Unlike their U.S. counterparts, Japanese research organizations participate in formulating strategies directly related to their function.[9] Japan's implementation of total quality occurred through "managed" strategies using a bottom-up approach.[8]

Japanese research facilities, unlike those in the United States, stress an atmosphere of personal contact and teamwork.[8,10] This interpersonal contact is one reason for the growth of new technical and scientific developments in Japan.[10] In the United States, research organizations have developed their own "operational agendas" and cultures which have removed them from day-to-day activities.[9] The "egghead" phenomenon associated with many R&D facilities is one such example and has been responsible for some negative corporate reactions. Reactive decision making has decimated many R&D departments through micro-management. These decisions, perceived as negative by researchers, have alienated the work force. The more a person or group of persons is seen as disjointed (dysfunctional) within the organization, the less dependent the organization sees itself on that department or function. Many researchers find themselves "outside" the corporate norm and for this reason dissociate themselves from the corporate or organizational infrastructure. This disassociation leads to a feeling of disenfranchisement, lack of control, and often a feeling of helplessness. Disenfranchised individuals cannot function properly within an organization; therefore, their actions and behaviors affect productivity. Freundlich and Schroeder[3] point out that the most difficult aspect of change for R&D is "getting the corporate message." This suggests that researchers are removed from the channels of communication and, therefore, are often disenfranchised from corporate goals and programs. Common sense tells us that researchers must be informed and secure within their environment before they can be free to innovate and experiment.

Strategies and strategic planning should examine the commonality between R&D and other business functions. Common business practices should measure indices of performance such as productivity, efficiency, and customer satisfaction. Strategies are needed to relate these measures to performance indices developed within the R&D department. A customer focus within the organization is one such measure of performance. Especially when geared to the internal customer, R&D plays a natural and critical role in developing new and unique products for consumers. The internal customers are those individuals, departments, and divisions that one encounters within the business. These customers are the key to a successful, healthy organization. Satisfying these individuals becomes primary for the effective and efficient operation of the organization. Without this cooperation and coordination, the business can never truly serve its external customers. The integration of R&D into the entire organization is critical for a successful organization. R&D must be viewed as both supplier and customer to the entire business. Products delivered by R&D should be measurable and capable of satisfying all customers.

Meeting diverse customer needs requires an internal strategy that depends upon a collective effort. A strategic emphasis on teamwork is needed to achieve customer satisfaction. Teamwork involves both cooperation among the employees of a department and collaboration between departments. Clear communication of goals and objectives to employees signifies commitment and supports team objectives. A process to reward and recognize employees who practice and institutionalize total quality principles should be implemented.

In summary, three key strategies for implementing total quality in R&D must exist for success. The first strategy for R&D is a clear and unambiguous vision. The second consists of performance (productivity) measures that directly relate to efficiency and effectiveness of operational systems. The final strategy includes successful human interaction through total teamwork. Without addressing these three key strategies, total quality will never succeed. (For additional information, see Abstract 3.2 at the end of this chapter.)

THE CYCLE OF SUCCESS

One strategy useful for R&D is the **cycle of success**[x] (Figure 3.1). This is a "natural cycle" for R&D, project management, or team development based on evaluating goals. This strategy allows for failures as a learning mechanism and calls these setbacks declines. Three stages characterize this cycle: (1) achievement, (2) status quo, and (3) decline. The achievement stage is where the organization, department, or person meets its established goals in a systematic manner. The second stage (status quo) represents a "no change" scenario, where projects or R&D ventures change little. The third stage constitutes decline in interest, technology, or commitment or failure.

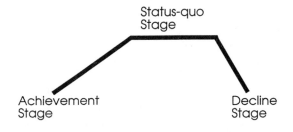

Figure 3.1 The Cycle of Success.

The **achievement stage** is characterized by:

1. Meeting or exceeding goals

2. A sense of continuous improvement

3. Opportunities for growth (expansion of goals)

4. An increase in employee potential

5. Empowerment and accomplishment

6. A preventative mentality

The slope of the line represents positive growth. The steeper the slope, the greater the gains as compared to goals and objectives.

The **status quo stage** is characterized by:

1. A protected environment

2. Limited control

3. Small risk taking

4. Minimal or selective growth

5. Static management

6. "Rollover strategy"

7. Status quo mentality ("if it ain't broke, don't fix it")

Change is minimized during this stage. This stage may be used to begin renewal or growth.

The **decline stage** is characterized by:

1. Reactive behavior

2. Severe retrenchment of resources

3. A proliferation of short-term goals and objectives

4. Volatile decision making

5. Frequent changes in management and personnel

6. Minimal long-term strategy

7. Declining growth (shrinkage)

8. Increasing costs

9. Reduced productivity

This stage can serve as either a precursor to achievement or a reassessment of priorities. The slope of the downward line is dependent upon an ability to recognize the decline and address new goals and objectives (strategy) to begin the achievement stage.

The success cycle runs counter to traditional business paradigms which suggest that achievement and growth are natural and symptomatic of success. This cycle accepts both growth and decline as natural and interconnected. Individuals, teams, and R&D departments need to accept a more realistic viewpoint by preparing for all contingencies. Strategies developed to move the organization from decline to achievement form the framework of lasting success. R&D departments and organizations need to assess themselves against these criteria and determine whether project and human goals can be achieved. A department in the decline stage can develop strategies to change and can begin to achieve success.

Individual success strategies for use in a R&D organization are important for achieving continuous improvement. In a *Harvard Business Review* article,[6] Kelley and Caplan studied those characteristics of "star performers" at AT&T's Bell Labs. Nine strategies were identified by the researchers:

1. Taking initiative—accepting responsibility and accountability willingly

2. Networking—access to technical expertise and knowledge

3. Self-management—empowered workers

4. Teamwork effectiveness

5. Leadership—building consensus to achieve goals

6. Followship—ability to follow others when needed

7. Perspective—holistic/global thinking

8. Show-and-tell—persuasively presenting one's ideas

9. Organizational savvy[6]

A sound strategic emphasis for both individuals and the organization ensures permanent and sustainable growth. **Strategy**, then, is formulating business plans, actions, and performance measurements around a central vision or set of guiding principles. The strategy must extend beyond ensuring shareholder value into such issues as ethics, responsibility, growth, employee development, and customer value. The core values of total quality must become permanently ingrained in the R&D environment.

CULTURE/EMOTIONAL ENVIRONMENT

The cultural environment that surrounds R&D has been described as "unstructured,"[3] where barriers may form to protect ideas, projects, and personnel. Often, R&D has functioned comfortably in a vacuum, where customers are little more than an afterthought.[3] What is often seen as normal is an "ideas over the wall" effect whereby products and processes arise from an unstructured cycle of development.[3] Scientists and research personnel tend to be "very cynical–control adverse" people[3] who may not adapt quickly to change. The culture that influences R&D is one formulated in academic research openly practiced at North American universities. Scientists and researchers have been influenced by those academicians who guided their graduate research efforts. Individualism, protectionism, adherence to the scientific method, and "academic freedom" are all descriptive of the research culture. Two distinct cultural elements exist within the R&D environment: (1) meticulous experimentation and (2) innovation.[11] Thus, many national research institutes as well as corporate R&D organizations tend to be modeled after nationally acclaimed academic institutions. This culture infiltrates and controls the destiny of many research organizations. Obviously, this culture is in direct opposition to the administrative structure often established at the same academic institutions.

The emotional as well as psychological environment influencing R&D is essentially the most critical aspect of those factors that directly impact R&D. Emotionally stable institutions (those organizations and businesses that truly value employees) establish both direct communication and an emotional link with their employees. This communication link maintains a bond of trust with employees and allows employees to express themselves without fear. Emotionally stable organizations put the human perspective before financial decision making and shareholder value. These organizations empower their employees through an emotional transmission pathway.[4] Emotions, such as sorrow, disappointment, grieving, and happiness, can be expressed through channels created by the organization. By permitting employees to express their emotions, the organization recognizes the entire or whole person. The expression of feelings and emotions, however, is recognized as a feminine style of managerial leadership[12] and as such is becoming a more accepted norm. This approach is in stark contrast to the traditional model, which rejects emotions and feelings as inappropriate. Most organizations continue to follow the "masculine model," which considers emotions a business liability.[12] The organization or department that ignores emotional transmission paths blocks the deepening of worker—including the R&D scientist—commitment.[4]

The emotional environment is directly linked to corporate decisions and guiding principles. Organizations that provide continuous learning (training) opportunities supply an emotional platform from which employees can expand their skills. Managers who encourage "the whole person" transform the environment into a positive and receptive workplace. The "transformational leader"[13] is a visionary who believes in and encourages lifelong learning for employees. This transformational leader empathizes with employees and encourages a realistic emotional environment.[13] Accepting the emotional environment energizes and motivates employees. Organizations that include this understanding of the whole person in their corporate values (principles) can implement total quality strategies.

An organization or business is considered an "entity" for tax purposes and as such develops a "personality." This personality may be either fully functional and emotionally stable or it may be dysfunctional and emotionally starved. The emotional environment pervades the entire organization, affecting decisions, policies, employees, product development, and future growth. The ability to adjust and compensate is the result of a positive emotional environment. Well-adjusted persons are better at handling difficult day-to-day business problems. Proactive behavior is the result of a healthy environment. Those organizations that have a well-adjusted personality will behave in a responsible manner using logical and rational decision making. Rational thinking will be translated throughout the organization to the R&D department/division. This consistency of behavior will result in a positive response from employees. Consistency of actions, strategy, and policy is an important concept of total quality and is one measure of the emotional health of the organization.

A dysfunctional environment creates physical and emotional problems for those individuals who interact with the business entity. A high-stress, negatively charged environment destroys motivation and inhibits creativity within R&D. The emotional environment greatly affects those products and services delivered.

Assessing the emotional health of the organization through surveys, interviews, and focus groups is essential. Those organizations that "audit" this environment can then adjust their strategies to compensate for negative reactions. Unfortunately, most organizations have no method for auditing the emotional health and psychological state of the business, as they do for auditing costs. (For additional information, see Abstract 3.3 at the end of this chapter.)

BUSINESS CLIMATE

The competitive and business climate dramatically affects productivity and effectiveness within the R&D organization. Good economic conditions generally bode well for R&D departments, with spending available for additional projects. Poor or uncertain economic conditions can cause havoc with R&D funding and personnel. These uncertain conditions have a dramatic and powerful psychological effect on projects, innovation, and creativity. Protectionism in the R&D function is a sign of poor health. Here, protectionism refers to defensive behavior, lack of cooperation between researchers, and an overall environment of retrenchment. For example, an unhealthy R&D department is like a retreating army whose disenfranchised soldiers (employees) constantly focus on negative or defeatist sentiments. Favorite projects are given high priority and the general environment becomes confrontational, as researchers and scientists retreat into "their own world."

The prevailing business climate affects employee motivation and creativity. Favorable business results can deliver a powerful motivator to the R&D function. In contrast, poor or uncertain results can provide a powerful demotivator to individuals and projects. Traditional business logic (costs and profit drive the entire business) is often foreign to and misunderstood by researchers. Researchers comprehend best what they understand and practice. Breakdowns in communication occur when goals are translated from financial business language into operational conversation. A "bad feedback loop" encourages reactive management. Open, two-way communication is required for effective operations and decision making. Reactive managers quickly respond to a negative result, forcing reactionary decision making.[14] Stimulus–response management permits few opportunities for total quality.

Competitive pressures, through increasing world trade, also continue to influence R&D. As product cycle and turnaround times decrease, the efficiency of the research effort must increase. AT&T Bell Labs increased its efficiency through benchmarking. Benchmarking provided a value-added approach to improving cycle time through six integrated steps:

1. Establish expected levels of success

2. Create opportunities for new ideas

3. Suggest approaches for implementing process improvements

4. Motivate change by knowledge of industry and competition

5. Develop role models for positive change

6. Include employee input in strategic planning process[4]

AT&T's Bell Labs proved that improving cycle time was possible through implementing total quality principles. (For additional information, see Abstract 3.4 at the end of this chapter.)

The ability of the business or organization to adapt to change becomes important for success. A business that adapts quickly and positively to change creates a paradigm for success. R&D departments that become adaptable build for future growth. Partnerships, cooperative ventures, and collaborative efforts are key results of adaptability. If the business acculturates itself to these principles and practices, then innovative and creative solutions should arise from the business challenges of the 21st century.

The internal environment/culture is as decisive in dictating underlying productivity and creative potential as is the external environment. How would your R&D organization answer the following questions?

1. Do departments/division cooperate or compete?

2. Is synergy between departments and individuals commonplace or rare?

3. What is the environment that surrounds failure?

4. Does failure breed fear or is it seen as a mechanism for growth?

5. Is cooperation among and between individuals destructive at times?

6. Can the internal environment be characterized as coordinated or haphazard?

The internal environment sets the tone for the entire organization. Tension, unhealthy competition, back-stabbing, infighting, and lack of direction are symptomatic of an internal environment that does not motivate or create innovation.

TYPES OF BUSINESS/BUSINESS SYSTEMS

The type of business influences the R&D function within many organizations. Businesses with a substantial R&D commitment will continue to support their efforts because of R&D's valuable contribution to the bottom line. Those organizations dedicated totally to research (for example, Sandia Laboratories) do not tend to have these difficulties. The "business" of these internationally recognized laboratories is research. Businesses heavily dependent on new products to remain competitive, such as the pharmaceutical industry, must maintain an extensive R&D effort. Those companies that prosper economically from new products generally support their research efforts with a serious commitment. Although a mood of corporate cost cutting exists today, these R&D departments will continue to provide their employees with a certain amount of security. Those businesses not totally dependent on a flood of new products risk a future of continued downsizing and loss of security. Growth industries, such as medical products/pharmaceutical, electronics, and software, are minimally assured of some sense of security. This security reassures personnel and helps to add safety to the overall environment. Security and emotional stability provide a positive environment that stimulates creativity and innovation.

Companies in less growth-potential industries risk losing ground to corporate cost cutters and restrictive financial policy. A strategic policy of "lean and mean" may be good for the short-term bottom line but it affects the environment and corporate culture. Thus, the industry (type of business) and economic conditions affect the entire R&D effort. (For additional information, see Abstract 3.5 at the end of this chapter.)

Business systems (i.e., operational practices and policies) affect the R&D function. Business systems form the policies, strategies, rules, and regulations within which R&D departments must operate. A prevention-oriented business system yields the best results. Business systems that are designed to detect problems at the end of the product line create inefficient and ineffective processes. Most modern business practices still treat the quality department as a "final inspector." Quality monitors the product and declares it fit for use. This mechanistic approach has created a system that facilitates errors, scrap, and rework. This mentality works its way into the R&D department by allowing the "bugs" in any product to be worked out at a later date. Quality is passed on to the plant or manufacturing facility. The customer is seen as a distant entity which only rarely affects day-to-day activities. Researchers see that the number of products introduced on schedule pays better dividends than products developed correctly. Business systems also dictate the level of efficiency at which products are introduced without major delays or serious quality problems. Systems more attuned to the bottom line or immediate payoff reward production rather than quality. Systems that follow the Shewhart process model and are monitored for inconsistency yield the best results.

An examination of the social, management, and technical systems that exist in many R&D organizations is presented in Chapter 4. This snapshot view examines a composite of R&D organizations and their concurrent systems.

ENDNOTES

1. Keller, Robert T. "Transformational Leadership and the Performance of Research and Development Project Groups." *Journal of Management*, 18(3), 1992.
2. Stumpe. P&L Frenzy, 1989.
3. Freundlich, Naomi and Schroeder, Michael. *Business Week/Quality*, pp. 149–152, 1991.
4. Voehl, Frank, personal comment as outlined in *Leadership and Management Quality*, Coral Springs, FL: Strategy Associates, 1994.
5. Stutski, K.J. "Conducting a Total Quality Communications Audit." *Public Relations Journal*, 48(4), pp. 29–32, 1992.
6. Kelley, Robert and Caplan, Janet. "How Bell Labs Creates Star Performers." *Harvard Business Review*, pp. 128–139, July–August 1993.
7. Maccoby, Michael. "Move from Hierarchy to Heterarchy." *Research & Technology Magazine*, pp. 46–47, September–October 1991.
8. Rogers, Rolf E. "Managing for Quality: Current Differences between Japanese and American Approaches." *National Productivity Review*, pp. 503–517, Autumn 1993.
9. "The Rise and Fall of Industrial Research." *Financial World*, pp. 64–68, June 25, 1991.
10. Wolff, M.F. "Working Japanese Laboratories." *Research-Technology Management*, pp. 9–11, 1989.
11. Smith, G. "Corning Laboratories: A Warm Feeling Inside." *Business Week*, p. 158, 1991.
12. Loden, M. *Feminine Leadership: Or How to Succeed in Business without Being One of The Boys*, New York: N.Y. Times Books, 1985.
13. Tichy N.M. and Devanna, M.A. "The Transformation Leader." *Training and Development Journal*, p. 298, 1986.
14. Yahagi, Seuchiro. "After Product Quality in Japan: Management Quality." *National Productivity Review*, pp. 501–515, 1992.

ABSTRACTS

ABSTRACT 3.1
IS STRATEGY STRATEGIC? IMPACT OF
TOTAL QUALITY MANAGEMENT ON STRATEGY

Schonberger, Richard J.
Academy of Management Executive, November 1992, pp. 80–87

While doing research in 1982, the author was struck with the fact that executives in superior Japanese companies seemed to do little of what is thought of as strategic planning. Instead, they spent more time overseeing organizational dedication to the basics of competitive advantage: high quality and short cycle time. He lists 19 principles of TQM, the first of which is "get to know the next and final customer." Many of these principles are aimed at (1) driving out costly overhead, (2) speeding up the design and production process, (3) improving flexibility of human and physical resources, and (4) eliminating uncertainties caused by rework and shaky suppliers—many of the knotty strategic decisions facing senior management. "Today," he says, "a minority opinion is that high-level managers should *not* engage in numerical goal-setting," perhaps because of Deming's emphasis on the elimination of numerical productivity and work standards goals. On the other hand, he observes, numerical targets for sales, profit, and so forth *are* necessary for budgeting and financial management. "A tenet of TQM is that 'you only improve what you measure,'" he acknowledges. "But aggregate numbers planned and measured high in the organization have little relevance to the work of most people in the organization." He sees self-imposed or team-imposed goals as more acceptable. There is no need, he says, to concoct a number as the improvement goal ("managerial tinkering"). Instead, he believes the focus should be on the *rate* of improvement. "Given their extensive inculcation of TQM practices," he says, "do fine companies like Motorola and Hewlett-Packard *need* high-level numerical goals? Perhaps not," he answers. He believes top managers' time should be spent in "frequent, active involvement in implementation of TQM-based policy, with successes and problems made visible on wall charts." Time spent visiting internal customers he sees as more valuable than time "in conference rooms over computer sheets and flip charts." Instead of a "by the numbers" approach to strategic planning, he says, "it's time to alter the mental image. The leader becomes strategically influential less by making decisions and more by seeing that good decisions are made." (*©Quality Abstracts*)

ABSTRACT 3.2
CRITICAL STEPS TO SUCCESS

Johnson, Homer H.
Total Quality Management, March–April 1992, pp. 9–11

Unless the management/culture component is taken seriously in implementing TQM, says the author, it is very likely that the process will flop. He discusses nine steps to create a TQM culture:

1. Develop a values statement that clearly specifies the values that will govern how the organization will conduct its affairs.

2. Conduct a values audit of each function or critical area.

3. Redesign policies and procedures to express quality values.

4. Plan and implement the culture change.

5. Measure and monitor key culture indicators.

6. Reward and recognize value-supporting behavior.

7. Have top management send clear values signals—repeatedly.

8. Communicate values constantly—everywhere.

9. Apply the continuous improvement process to the culture. (©*Quality Abstracts*)

ABSTRACT 3.3
CCI NEWS

Total Quality Management, March–April 1992, pp. 6–8

For continuous improvement to exist at all levels and across functions, says the author, there needs to be an environment that supports and encourages those activities. And in order to develop a culture which supports continuous improvement, the Council for Continuous Improvement has developed a business and organization review model:

1. Review the current business situation and strategy.

2. Examine the business results to see if expectations have been met.

3. Examine the organizational strategy of the company.

4. Observe the company's change strategy.

5. Probe the company's unique culture to see what in the culture is not supportive of continuous improvement.

6. Then, develop an improvement plan that examines and prioritizes all necessary business and organization changes, how these changes occur, who will be involved, and who will be responsible for assuring that they get made.

7. Finally, assess the impact of the changes on business results.

The article concludes with an overview of how a company culture emerges from the initial decisions made by a young company in the area of organizational structure, leadership style, boundaries, technology, decision-making processes, information systems, a rewards system, and a human resource system. (©*Quality Abstracts*)

ABSTRACT 3.4
R&D BENCHMARKING AT AT&T

Bean, Thomas J. and Gros, Jacques G.
Research-Technology Management, July–August 1992, pp. 32–37

Benchmarking has benefitted the R&D enterprise at AT&T Bell Laboratories in several ways, say the authors: (1) establishing expected levels of success, suggesting approaches for implementing process improvements, (4) motivating change through knowledge of performance levels of industry leaders and competitors, (5) offering role models for cultural change, and (6) serving as input for the strategic planning process. Benchmarking involves specific measures of R&D performance, R&D technology and process capabilities, and R&D management systems. Benchmarking teams include members from a small R&D benchmarking support function, as well as members solicited from process teams across the organization. Often, the authors report, benchmarking activities are resulting in the development of Best Current Practices which are then disseminated widely across AT&T's R&D enterprise. Some of the successes brought about by benchmarking have been shortening design cycle times and enhancing software development. Since AT&T has 21 business units, Bell Labs has set up a prototype information system to connect and catalog benchmarking contacts and allow for direct communication via an information-sharing electronic bulletin board, thus reducing duplication of efforts. The authors conclude by sharing three precepts for successful benchmarking: (1) make sure benchmarking teams have a clear idea of the organizational mission and customer needs they are serving; (2) provide teams with a vision of the change or improvement they are seeking to make, supported by their management; and (3) have teams build a complete picture of the practices studied. A sidebar to the article describes four objectives for benchmarking at Bell Labs.   (©*Quality Abstracts*)

ABSTRACT 3.5
MASTERING THE DYNAMICS OF INNOVATION

Utterback, James M.
Harvard Business School Press, Cambridge, Mass., 1994, 266 pp.

In this noteworthy ground-breaking book by Utterback, the author discusses how the uses of past technological breakthroughs have influenced corporate success. He shows how the industry type and economic conditions affect the entire R&D effort. He uses the invention of the typewriter as an example to show how innovation and new products are the cornerstones of competitive advantage. He also discusses the premise that top management must encourage innovation as a "company-wide" trait in order to ensure long-term survival. Although heavy on the academic emphasis, the work offers a depth of insight not often found in more practitioner-oriented texts. Some references are provided.

CHAPTER 4

PRESENT
R&D SYSTEMS

The viewpoints in this chapter represent a synopsis of observations and experiences over the last ten years. Most organizations practice some but not all of these behaviors. R&D organizations have the potential to perform above current expectations but are more often constrained by traditional managerial paradigms (see those influences affecting the environment). Although the tone may be considered at times negative, or at least unflattering, it represents an informed personal view.

THE SOCIAL SYSTEM

The largest system present in R&D is the social system (see Figure 4.1). The social system encompasses human issues such as interpersonal relationships, authority, and cultural and ethical standards. Interactions between and among employees of an R&D organization are determined by the existing social system. Social systems govern appropriate behaviors, creating mechanisms to monitor and control the environment. As discussed previously, environmental influences greatly impact the social system. The social system impacts R&D on a daily basis.

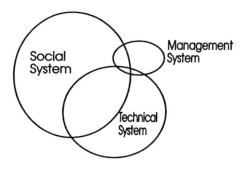

Figure 4.1 The Social System.

The social relationships between peers, subordinates, and supervisors are governed by an underlying code of ethical behaviors learned during graduate research years at a university. These behaviors are generally individualistic, unstructured, creative, often defensive, and generally protectionist. Behaviors such as these are rewarded by the university and become the social norms. Scientists and researchers bring these behaviors with them to work. Social standards developed for academic research become the norm for organizational or institutional research.

Research at most universities is strictly controlled through the graduate level and then structured by the government or private industry. These structures, rules, and regulations are often quite restrictive and limit the method by which research is conducted. The philosophy of research is generally contradictory; on the one hand, the need for individual creativity is highly encouraged, but the method, practices, and reporting of the research must follow strict prescribed norms. This contradictory philosophy adds to the confrontational nature of the R&D department. There is a strong drive for creativity in R&D, but in a structured environment that supports the individual. Many researchers are motivated "almost exclusively by technical challenges and opportunities to excel as world-class developers."[1] This drive affects the entire social structure of the organization, rewarding individual behaviors at the risk of discouraging team behavior. To the outsider, this may appear haphazard, but it is identical to the academic environment that promotes and encourages research. This dichotomy is difficult for the corporate executive to discern since he or she is accustomed to a traditional operational paradigm. Researchers create operational and administrative systems that model their academic counterparts. To examine the research paradigm practiced and encouraged at most research organizations is to examine the academic research paradigm. The "pseudo-university" structure represents one such way of naming the social structure so common in R&D. (For additional information, see Abstract 4.1 at the end of this chapter.)

The cultural environment that encompasses the R&D facility possesses a potentially different aspect for human resources. Given that the social paradigm for R&D differs significantly from that of business, a challenge arises for managing human resources. Human resource personnel must acknowledge and accept a very different culture for R&D. Their policies must reflect these differences while focusing all employees on corporate goals and objectives. Empathetic and concerned human resource personnel understand these differences and capitalize on their positive effects. Treating R&D personnel as typical plant or administrative personnel may further intensify the disenfranchisement experienced by many R&D employees. The disenfranchised employee is unable to produce efficiently and lacks the ability to change systems to improve effectiveness. Human resource policies, equalized for the entire organization, must respond to intra-class social standings yet recognize and celebrate differences. R&D social structures must be integrated into the framework of the entire organization.

Interpersonal skills for R&D personnel are generally refined within the academic environment. Issues such as teamwork are frequently seen as negative (because it reduces the effect of individual effort). Scientists and engineers develop most of their professional interpersonal skills in contact with other engineers and scientists. Few, if any, interpersonal skills are taught to scientists and engineers. Interpersonal relationships between and among R&D peers is often characterized as both collaborative and competitive given the prevailing environment common in R&D departments. Although competition is strong, there is also an identifiable camaraderie that binds personnel into a group. Group dynamics, peer pressure, and an accepted standard of excellence all cement the research group into a functioning unit. Protectionism, if it exists, extends beyond the research unit and serves to "shield" the department from outside influences. Training in interpersonal skills is needed for researchers as they develop a customer focus. Good interpersonal skills encourage teamwork and prevent conflict. Developing and honing these skills is a requirement for researchers committed to total quality principles.

THE MANAGEMENT SYSTEM

The most predominant management structure in R&D departments is found in most university research units; that is, a hierarchical structure, with freedom of expression and both structured and unwritten rules for scientific pursuits. It would be inappropriate to say that one system directly mirrors the other since environmental influences (discussed previously) differ at the university. There is a blending of management structures common to most business with the university research model. Business management structures that affect personnel, such as the employee review process, are identical to those established outside the research department. Creative and innovative processes, so essential to R&D, differ greatly from the reward–motivation process found in most businesses. Creativity and innovation incorporate individual energies and knowledge manipulation. These processes require personal initiative and technical interaction (networking).[2] Bell Labs "star performers" recognize these qualities as essential to achieving quality within the organization.[2] Management systems must infuse these strategies into the R&D organization. These qualities, often considered secondary in a typical business environment, may conflict with rewarded behaviors such as loyalty and commitment to business objectives. These systems more typically resemble the university research model. Unfortunately, this R&D management model lacks the intense competitive/ reactive business pressure that is usually found operating in a corporate environment.

The university model (management structure) is one based on individual initiative and creativity. It begins with strict attention to detail and uses the "Scientific Method" as a benchmark. The manager or supervisor's goal is to ensure the methodology and scientific accuracy. Duties resemble those of a mentor. These people guide the process, and their goal is to ensure accurate and reliable results. Accuracy and reliability are the ke words of this philosophy, just as profit and loss are the keywords for many American businesses. Ethical research produces accurate and reliable results. These ethical principles and practices constitute standards by which the research management process is judged. Standards are applied to the research method (process) and the quality of the results produced.

Fortunately for R&D, much more emphasis is placed on "process" than is often observed in American industry. Although management practices focus on results, the research model does allow for mistakes and errors as part of the learning process. The university research model stresses learning and exploration and openly encourages discovery. On the other hand, businesses generally do not have time for these qualities—yet they are essential for new product or process development. Here then is the major point of disagreement between business and research managerial practices. Business must recognize and fully understand the R&D process and reward qualities such as innovation and creativity. For example, industries that have devoted time to innovation and creativity, such as 3M, have found the process both successful and rewarding. The fact that employees at 3M have the time (10% of their work week hours) to be creative and innovative is one reason for their success rate in developing new products.

Most businesses continue to assure product performance by setting stringent standards and then delegating control of quality to the quality control department. The quality department performs the task of "assuring" that products meet specified requirements. Quality assurance/control is either nonexistent in R&D or generally assigned prior to final product acceptance. Since R&D has no product responsibility, traditionalists have seen little use for quality control. Therefore, a majority of the research, data collection, and analysis is completed without specific or monitored quality procedures. Like many businesses, R&D has few required or audited procedures. Quality is judged rather than designed into the product. Without specific quality procedures to guide the researcher, the individual is forced to use both good judgment and self-audits to achieve positive results. The individual is charged with a great deal of responsibility, but has little accountability. Accountability should remain with the individual, especially with those who "control" the design or development of such products.

International quality standards, such as the ISO 9000 series, incorporate quality assurance philosophies into the initial product or service design. These standards reinforce the concept of a functioning quality management system intent on assuring reliable customer-focused products and services. ISO 9000 permits customized products and services without compromising integral systems that assure quality. We can expect in the future that quality standards, such as those found in ISO quality procedures, will provide an operational framework for R&D. (See Chapter 8 for additional detail.)

The lack of specific quality procedures influences those measurements that define success within the R&D function. Concerns such as turnaround time, cycle time (from idea formulation to prototype), failure/success rate, expenditures, transfer time, and delays are some of the measures that R&D needs to define its success. Also, the procedures used to develop a new product process also need documentation. Documentation of the Navy's "PERT" process led to advances in project management.[3] In addition, "CPM," developed by DuPont researchers, was invented to assist in scheduling and project activity management.[3] Obviously, the management of projects (the actual work effort in R&D) should be of concern to managers. With time and commitment to total quality principles, "management quality" becomes more important than the quality of the results produced.[4] Considering the uniqueness of new product development, an established method for managing the project is needed. Although project management has received a great deal of attention, little work has been done to determine the "process" individuals use.[5] This relates directly to the competitive environment discussed previously. A system of indicators is needed within R&D to track progress, prevent errors and mistakes, and reduce the cycle time needed to complete a project. This idea will be discussed in detail in Chapter 5.

In examining the management structures that surround the R&D system, we cannot forget to mention those risks and rewards that employees encounter. Risks of failure always surround the R&D effort. Failure for R&D is defined as the inability to meet objectives in a timely manner. Failure is not the problem; rather, the problem is how the research department or business organization deals with the failure. Failure in R&D is natural and leads to improved products and processes as humans learn best from their mistakes. Many businesses will not accept failure from their R&D departments. A business failure is often defined (framed) as a defeat. These two opposing definitions are one reason for conflict and disagreement. Failure in R&D is a natural learning process that assists in defining future direction. Those managers and executives who confuse the intent and meaning of failure may misread the results causing reactive behavior. Applying a business management paradigm to R&D results in conflict and misunderstanding. Management systems must encourage the learning process and use the "failure" process along with the "catchball" process to prevent future problems. Often this involves the integration and deployment of indicators across all areas of the organization, both vertically and horizontally.[6]

Rewards also play an enormous role in motivating individuals and improving their overall productivity. What is rewarded in R&D—successful results or an improved method? As in business, rewards in R&D tend to be for only those accomplishments that are tangible. Unfortunately, much of the progress made in R&D is accomplished on intangible items, such as discovery or exploration that may have only limited commercial value. Rewards that only complement tangible business objectives may often be looked upon as punishment by the research community. Momentary thinking devastates R&D long-range planning since development time is not easily measured. This is one reason for suggesting that new and innovative measures be developed to adequately recognize and reward the R&D function.

Finally, the R&D department management must create and integrate an internal environment that encourages creativity and innovation.[7] If the management structure of the business or organization parallels a traditional paradigm, then an acceptable alternative must be found to counteract the "business paradigm." In order to counteract this tendency, many research organizations "shield" or protect their employees from traditional business measures and practices. This shielding or protection can lead to a misunderstanding of true business objectives, initiate or maintain fear, and generally foster a sense of mistrust among and between employees. (For additional information, see Abstract 4.2 at the end of this chapter and Abstract 3.5 at the end of Chapter 3.)

In order to create a management system that promotes innovation, the following six steps are needed:

1. Reduce fear

2. Establish a strong sense of values and ethical principles

3. Establish achievable goals

4. Accept failure as a learning device

5. Remove threats and unwarranted risks

6. Reward commensurate with both individual and team problem-solving and creativity

Innovation and creativity are the results of an open, secure, and interactive environment where knowledge is readily available.[8] Creativity comes from the individual when needs are met and the mind is free to explore the universe of all possibilities.

The management system must measure the environmental influences, cultural aspects, and interpersonal relations among employees. Measurement requires standards (benchmarks), guidelines for consistency, design of appropriate instruments, audit procedures, and constant feedback.[5]

Many measures for R&D require coordinating pieces of information from multiple data sets that are widely dispersed throughout the company. This is a recurrent feature in all companies, and the situation is a strong argument for computer implementation of database systems that facilitate accessing multiple data sets.[9] (For additional information, see Abstract 4.3 at the end of this chapter.)

In addition to measurement, management must design and implement a system that promotes:

1. Collective leadership and rewards[10]

2. Cooperation between employees

3. A "win–win" team perspective[7]

4. Consistent communication within and outside the department

5. A process for developing new products, such as quality function deployment, that is customer oriented[11]

THE TECHNICAL SYSTEM

The primary technical driver for R&D is the Scientific Method, along with the many tools that support its application The Scientific Method is a "systematic form of reflective thinking and inquiry."[10] This approach has guided scientists and researchers and has become a method of auditing the quality of research. The Scientific Method serves as a performance standard. Research serves the purpose of widening the boundaries of knowledge through the application of the Scientific Method. There are four major elements to the scientific approach:

1. Problem–Obstacle–Idea

2. Hypothesis

3. Reasoning–Deduction

4. Observation–Test–Experiment[10]

This paradigm of scientific exploration and discovery advises the researcher and becomes the primary guiding principle for the department. This research paradigm (research model) differs greatly from the paradigm traditionally used for day-to-day business. Businesses use a form of deductive reasoning that is less stringent than the Scientific Method and more dependent upon "conventional wisdom." The scientist, however, formulates problems and resulting solutions within this scientific framework. Researchers define success in terms of the ability to achieve a result with the Scientific Method. From a technical system perspective, the Scientific Method guides the operational activities of the R&D department.

The Scientific Method is a systematic process to accomplish the research premise. From a total quality perspective, this systematic method provides a strategy for success. Each element represents a benchmark for measuring progress. Although the Scientific Method ensures a degree of consistency, individual elements are open to interpretation and therefore may vary from researcher to researcher. When applied with total quality principles, the Scientific Method becomes a guidepost for success.

Quality Technical Tools

One such total quality technical system, **quality function deployment** (QFD), is useful for defining customer needs, wants, and desires. These customer requirements can then be correlated to internal R&D business (operational) requirements. QFD is discussed in Chapter 7.

Other technical systems available to the researcher include simulation and modeling. **Simulation** provides the researcher the ability to test various theories with hypothetical situations controlled through selective probabilities. The researcher rates or determines the probability that a certain event will occur based on previous knowledge or observed behavior. In a cost-cutting environment, simulation provides an alternative to lengthy experimentation. **Modeling** is also a probabilistic alternative to costly experimentation using the Scientific Method. Modeling assumes the behavior of certain events, based on observation and theory or known relationships. Both simulation and modeling have expedited product breakthroughs and reduced development times. Both methods contribute positively to the researcher's ability to solve problems and test theories. The risk, however, is that these techniques will replace the scientific process of exploration and discovery. Researchers must have guidelines to help them in deciding when to use these technologies and when to conduct serious research. A product or process with an established history and consistent results (statistically in-control) makes an ideal candidate for simulation or advanced modeling. With modifications, a process (product) is theoretically revised and therefore improved.

Technologies such as advanced microprocessors, computers, expert systems, and artificial intelligence all assist research. These technologies are tools for the researcher and improve the efficiency and effectiveness of scientific exploration. Technology improves the quality of results. Tools, however, cannot become the "means to an end." Innovation and creativity are the results of human ingenuity, not technological advances. Also, guidance and training tools for the R&D and staff client community will be needed to solve their business problems.[12]

As described previously, quality assurance and quality control provide a key technical system for the researcher. Ensuring accurate and reliable results increases the scientific and market potential of the research. Researchers who scoff at quality procedures only diminish the believability of their results. Scientists support quality principles and improvement when they eliminate hassles.[12] There is a need to develop procedures that monitor the entire research process, not just the results. Like quality procedures, standard operating procedures (SOPs) create benchmarks for the entire research process. SOPs define the boundaries in which to operate scientific research without the restraints that prevent creativity and innovation. These procedures prevent unnecessary failure by establishing a master plan for success. In addition, researchers can use SOPs to monitor progress, report on results, and review activities.

By instituting a total quality philosophy, the overall environment changes from reactive (inspection oriented) to proactive (prevention oriented). The culture must change from one that considers quality as judge and jury to that of a mentor and facilitator. (For additional information, see Abstract 4.4 at the end of this chapter.)

SUMMARY

Examining the systems that form the structure of the R&D organization is critical for allocating resources for a total quality effort. Different perspectives, upon assessing these systems, indicate inconsistency in perception. Assessment also highlights systems (subsystems) that require improvement. The exercise at the end of this chapter is a detailed assessment tool that is useful for indicating potential problems in the organization.

ENDNOTES

1. Maccoby, Michael. "Move from Hierarchy to Heterarchy." *Research and Technology Magazine,* pp. 46–47, September–October 1991.
2. Dilworth, J.R. *Production and Operations Management,* New York: Random House, 1986.
3. Schine, E. "Sandia National Laboratories: Weapons to Plowshares." *Business Week,* p. 156, 1991.
4. Davis, D.C. "QA in the R&D Environment." *Defense Electronics,* 26(2), pp. 30–31, 1994.
5. McKenna, Joseph F. "Coach Lets His Team Play the Game." *Industry Week,* 24(9), pp. 12, 16, 1992.
6. Baldrige examiner Garvin, in his 1991 work, describes vertical integration as the process within Hoshin Planning called "catchball." This deployment is the cascading of senior management's vision down through the organization so that each succeeding level is still aligned with and derived from higher goals as activities become more operational and detailed. In addition to vertical deployment, it is also essential to link various targets of total quality measurement, such as process improvement and customer satisfaction. This is needed to prevent suboptimization and avoid dysfunctional outcomes. Catchball was a popular strategy and technique of JUSE and became an integral part of the FPL Deming Prize qualification during 1988 and 1989. Stories are legend within FPL as to the power and effects of the catchball process, especially when played with seasoned Japanese counselors, who are among the world's very best at this total quality practice.
7. Keller, Robert T. "Transformational Leadership and the Performance of Research and Development Groups." *Journal of Management,* 18(3), 1992.
8. Fitzgerald, M. "Quality: Take It to the Limit." *Computer World,* 25(6), pp. 71–73, 1991.
9. Melan, E.H. "Quality Improvement in an Engineering Lab." *Quality Progress,* pp. 18–25, June 1987.
10. Kerlinger, F.R. *Foundations of Behavior Research* (3rd edition). Fort Worth, TX: Holt, Reinhart and Winston, 1986, p. 11.
11. Freundlich, N. and Schroeder, M. *Business Week/Quality,* pp. 149–152, 1991.
12. Most organizations have not yet begun to grapple with the problem of systematic training in knowledge, skills, and behavior to ensure that

their computer system is effectively used. One useful approach to this difficult training problem is to use a model. Each manager—whether a specialist or executive—has a specific set of objectives to achieve, which are typically summarized in the key results analysis and job improvement plan. At regular intervals, the job-holder and his or her boss sit down together and carry out a review of performance. From this discussion, a gap between results expected and results actually achieved may be identified. Although not the only possible explanation, the failure to reach agreed performance standards *may* stem from lack of knowledge or skills. Three examples of good training are team training, in-house project-based training, and perceptive use of outside courses.

ABSTRACTS

ABSTRACT 4.1
THE TOPIC OF QUALITY IN BUSINESS SCHOOL EDUCATION AND RESEARCH

Kaplan, Robert S.
Selections, Autumn 1991, pp. 13–21

The author starts out by describing his search for literature on the teaching of quality in business schools. Having come up empty, he went to Jack Evans, former dean at North Carolina University, who in 1991 performed an extensive survey on the subject which resulted in responses from 89 schools. His conclusion was that there was virtually no coverage on how total quality management (TQM) changes the way organizations are managed. Therefore, Kaplan decided to do his own case study of 20 universities considered to be heavy hitters. Of the 19 that responded, the author was most impressed with the University of Chicago's offerings. Other schools included Columbia, Duke, NYU, Penn, Northwestern, Virginia, and Yale.

The results of Kaplan's survey showed that leading business practice in quality management is well ahead of current academic research and teaching. Business schools' teaching programs are adjusting to contemporary developments with lags that are long (10 years or more) and variable, and there is no evidence that an adjustment has been made in faculty research programs. For example, 15 of the schools had 3 or fewer sessions on quality in their introductory operations management courses. Even more damaging is that what is taught in the quality segment is not material that has emerged from academic research. Kaplan notes that of the more than 1500 possible papers on productivity and global competition, far fewer than 1% were produced by business school research on total quality.

The study of TQM in business schools will require individuals with multidisciplinary skills. Changes must be made in journals, doctoral programs, and the kinds of research and educational innovation that are rewarded by promotion committees. Business schools must be prepared to face competition from company-sponsored MBA and executive programs and European business schools. Compare Kaplan's analysis with the comments of William Glavin, who left Rank Xerox in London to become president of Babson College in Boston. Unlike Kaplan, Glavin feels that in many areas, academia is thinking further ahead than corporations which he feels "manage today's problems today." This is an important work for understanding the motivation of the research paradigm practiced in both the business and academic environments.

ABSTRACT 4.2
BUILDING A TOTAL QUALITY CULTURE

Batten, Joe
Crisp Publications, Menlo Park, Calif., 1992, 88 pp.

"People want to be led, or driven," insists the author. Providing the kind of tough-minded leadership that will produce a total quality culture is the focus of this motivating book (which includes a foreword by Zig Ziglar). Rather than presenting a formula for TQM, the book aims at developing the attitudes which support successful leaders. Chapter titles are:

1. The Path to the Future

2. The New Leaders

3. Making Quality Possibilities Come True

4. Peak Performance at All Levels

5. Winners Can Be Grown

6. Tomorrow's Culture

Some of the themes include tough-minded leadership (the title of one of the author's former books), servant leadership, being a winner, motivating one's subordinates, excellence, and dreams. The author draws on upbeat quotations from a variety of individuals to bolster his points. The book concludes with a 14-page glossary of terms which serve to spell out Batten's philosophy of leadership. For example, he defines "builder" as "The CEO who stands tall is, above all, a builder. Committed to vision, stretch, empowerment, synergy, responsiveness, flexibility—toughness of mind—a builder ensures that all dimensions of each P in the pyramid are intensely focused on creation, growth, and building." (©Quality Abstracts)

ABSTRACT 4.3
MEMORY VERSUS RANDOMIZATION IN ON-LINE ALGORITHMS

Raghaven, P. and Snir, M.
IBM Journal of Research and Development, November 1994, Vol. 38 No. 6, pp. 683–707

Many measures involved in the R&D process require coordinating pieces of information from multiple data sets that are widely dispersed. The authors discuss the use of on-line algorithms which help to service sequences of requests, one at a time, without knowing future requirement requests. They compare their performance with the performance of algorithms that generate the sequences as well as service them. They discuss the many settings in which these formulas perform almost as well as optimal off-line algorithms, by using statistics about previous requests in the sequences. They point out that since remembering these sequences of information may be expensive, the use of randomization to eliminate memory is explored.

The method and process of devising and studying performance measures for the randomized on-line formulas is discussed, along with developing and analyzing memoryless randomized on-line algorithms for the "cacheing problem" and its generalizations. Although very technical in parts, this is a worthwhile article for the practitioner as well as the scientist. Theorems and proofs are provided, along with extensive references.

ABSTRACT 4.4
MANAGING QUALITY: THE PRIMER FOR MIDDLE MANAGERS

Schuler, Randall S. and Harris, Drew L.
Addison-Wesley, Reading Mass., 1992, 202 pp.

Most overviews of total quality management are written to convince executives who have the power and resources to effect change in their companies. This book, however, is written for the middle manager, who may be in one of three positions: (a) the company has a well-planned quality improvement process, (b) the company has merely given a mandate to "improve quality" but little direction, or (c) the manager has no company support but still desires to improve quality in his or her department. This thoughtfully written book gives a helpful overview of: quality issues, where middle managers fit into the larger picture, a glance at quality improvement tools, the human resource aspect of quality management, and quality interfaces with suppliers as well as customers. In order to tie all the parts together, the authors include two case studies of quality improvement: at Ensoniq Corp., an electronic musical instrument manufacturer, and at the HR department of Swiss Bank Corp. Two useful appendices include an annotated reading list on quality and a glossary of terms used in TQM. Chapter contents include:

1. **Why Look at Quality and the Middle Manager?** The authors identify with middle manager issues and offer a simple plan for quality improvement.

2. **What Is Quality?** They discuss the contributions of Juran and Deming, and then they define quality as: "delivering loyalty-producing products and services along all dimensions of quality with a single effort." They discuss quality from a process and systems viewpoint.

3. **Tools for Improving Quality.** Using a narrative describing a quality improvement project, the authors introduce elements of a typical quality improvement process, as well as tools such as control charts, flowcharts, cause-and-effect diagrams, and other diagnostic tools.

4. **Quality Enhancement, the Manager, and the HR Function.** They discuss the transformation of the HR function to the line manager and vice president for quality and describe alternative HR management philosophies.

5. **Choices in Human Resource Management.** The authors link HR practices with competitive strategy, and they describe HR decisions which must be made in planning, staffing, appraising, compensating, training, and labor–management negotiating.

6. **Quality from External Relationships.** They describe varying relationships between customers and suppliers and the differences between internal and external relationships. (©*Quality Abstracts*)

EXERCISE

EXERCISE 4.1
ASSESSING A COMMUNICATION SYSTEM

RESPONSES

5 = Strongly Agree	2 = Disagree
4 = Agree	1 = Strongly Disagree
3 = Neither Agree nor Disagree	U = Unknown

1. **Are communication systems identified within your company or organization?**
   Yes ❑   No ❑   Not Sure ❑

   a. Communication is a "true" process   5 4 3 2 1 U

   b. A method or mechanism exists for   5 4 3 2 1 U
      communication within the organization

   c. Transmission is clear and precise   5 4 3 2 1 U

   d. Transmission is erratic   5 4 3 2 1 U

   e. Reception is clear and precise   5 4 3 2 1 U

2. **What are the means and percentages of communication within your organization?**

   a. Verbal (spoken instructions)   _____%

   b. Visual (e.g., posters, newsletters)   _____%

   c. Electronic   _____%

   d. Written (e.g., memos)   _____%

3. **How would you characterize** *formal* **communications within your company or organization?**

   a. Structure of communication systems:
      Highly ❑   *Some* ❑   *Loose* ❑   *No structure* ❑

   b. Are communications goal oriented?
      Yes ❑   *Sometimes* ❑   *No* ❑   *Not sure* ❑

c. Are communications patterned or haphazard?

Patterned ❑   Haphazard ❑

d. Characterize the amount of control:

Tight ❑   Moderate ❑   Loose ❑   No control ❑

e. Communication is transmitted effectively	5	4	3	2	1	U
f. Communication is transmitted efficiently	5	4	3	2	1	U
g. Communication is frequently filtered	5	4	3	2	1	U

h. Describe the environment in which formal communication exists

Supportive ❑   Neutral ❑   Threatening ❑

i. Formal communications motivate and energize employees	5	4	3	2	1	U
j. Information is frequently filtered	5	4	3	2	1	U
k. Feedback on the communication system is encouraged	5	4	3	2	1	U

l. A formal communication presentation style exists

Yes ❑   Sometimes ❑   No ❑   Not sure ❑

m. Are formal communications consistent?

Yes ❑   Sometimes ❑   No ❑   Not sure ❑

4. **How would you characterize *informal* communications within your company or organization?**

a. The amount of control:

Tight ❑   Moderate ❑   Loose ❑   No control ❑

b. Do structures frequently change?

Yes ❑   No ❑   Not sure ❑

c. Informal communications are affected by:

I. Cultural norms	5	4	3	2	1	U
II. Social values	5	4	3	2	1	U
III. Gossip	5	4	3	2	1	U
IV. Rumor	5	4	3	2	1	U

d. Information is disseminated:

I. Effectively	5	4	3	2	1	U
II. Efficiently	5	4	3	2	1	U

    e. Are informal systems sustainable?

       Yes ❑   *Sometimes* ❑   *No* ❑   *Not sure* ❑

    f. Informal communications usually denote:

I. A positive influence	5	4	3	2	1	U
II. A negative influence	5	4	3	2	1	U

5. Is communication a two-way process?

    Yes ❑   *No* ❑   *Not sure* ❑

6. Are formal communication channels established?

    Yes ❑   *No* ❑   *Not sure* ❑

7. Communication channels (pathways) are:

a. Confused	5	4	3	2	1	U
b. Complicated	5	4	3	2	1	U
c. Clear	5	4	3	2	1	U
d. Concise	5	4	3	2	1	U
e. Understandable (unambiguous)	5	4	3	2	1	U

8. Communications flow:

a. Evenly	5	4	3	2	1	U
b. Effectively	5	4	3	2	1	U
c. Efficiently	5	4	3	2	1	U

9. When communicating, employees and managers:

a. Add additional channels	5	4	3	2	1	U
b. Circumvent the established system	5	4	3	2	1	U
c. Confuse information with conversation	5	4	3	2	1	U
d. Intertwine information with personal bias or comment	5	4	3	2	1	U
e. Always get the actions desired	5	4	3	2	1	U
f. Always "get the message" across	5	4	3	2	1	U
g. Frequently receive "noise"	5	4	3	2	1	U
h. Change the message	5	4	3	2	1	U
i. "Shoot the messenger"	5	4	3	2	1	U

j.	Stress consistency	5	4	3	2	1	U
k.	Stress factual information	5	4	3	2	1	U
l.	Stress opinions	5	4	3	2	1	U

10. When communicating, the message is:

a.	Clear and well received	5	4	3	2	1	U
b.	Understood by those who receive the message	5	4	3	2	1	U
c.	Filled with "noise"	5	4	3	2	1	U

11. Do barriers exist to improving communication in your organization?

Yes ❑   No ❑   Not sure ❑

12. Are communications measured in your business or organization?

Yes ❑   No ❑   Not sure ❑

13. Employees and managers listen:

a.	To commands or directives	5	4	3	2	1	U
b.	To guidelines	5	4	3	2	1	U
c.	To the actual message or the tone	5	4	3	2	1	U
d.	To opinions without facts	5	4	3	2	1	U
e.	To facts substantiated with data	5	4	3	2	1	U

CHAPTER 5

BEGINNING THE SYSTEMATIC IMPROVEMENT PROCESS

Implementing continuous improvement within any R&D organization or department is a five-stage (or phase) process. This process involves numerous outcomes at each stage. Outcomes represent performance criteria for each stage of the improvement process.

This book is based on three central principles. The first relates to a sound theory of total quality which integrates the principles of people, tools (functions or technology), and management. These three components represent the fundamentals of a sustainable total quality effort within any R&D organization. All three components must be addressed at each of three major building blocks found in a successful effort. These three building blocks—foundation, structure, and sustaining forces—drive the improvement effort and form the House of Quality. This "house" must be built upon a firm foundation of management support, involvement, and commitment (risk). This is further supplemented by a structure or framework that facilitates the effort and gives it direction and drive. Finally, support and sustainment complete the structure by strengthening the effort while individualizing the focus.

Stages 1 and 2 of the five-stage process for implementing continuous improvement are covered in this chapter, and Stages 3 to 5 will be covered in Chapter 6.

STAGE 1: ASSESSMENT PHASE

In the assessment stage, the entire organization is examined and reviewed. R&D management, in cooperation with employees, examines operations and organizational and communication systems from a global perspective. Prior to review, performance measures which describe system output must be established. Typical measures consist of financial (costs, overruns, allocations), productivity (efficiency, cycle and development time, "loss time"), and quality (on-time performance, amount of rework, customer satisfaction) indicators. The infrastructure of the R&D organization (management, social, and technical systems) is examined and compared to benchmark performance. Those mechanisms that drive systems (organizational structure, hierarchy, size, culture, competitive standing, work force potential, customer dependence, etc.) are reviewed and assessed for overall improvement potential.

Assessment requires objective and subjective information. Assessment begins on an organization-wide basis through the use of the R&D Organization Infrastructure Self-Assessment Checklist (see Exercise 5.1 at the end of this chapter). Through the use of a subjective rating scale (such as a survey), those systems requiring improvement are identified. Since management is driven top-down, systems are best viewed from a more global perspective. This prevents suboptimization (focusing on small subsystems) and begins the improvement process.

Outcomes of Stage 1

The outcomes of this stage are twofold. Outcome 1 involves a realization by management that continuous improvement both adds value and yields significant benefits. The R&D department can positively review its operations, organization, and communications from a strategic perspective. Realization of the need for change is the first measure of success.

Outcome 2 deals with the establishment of criteria to evaluate system performance. These criteria represent measures of improvement potential and are formulated from the assessment tools completed by management. The assessment tools provide management with a consensus opinion of improvement opportunities.

Outcome 1: Realization

Critical for corporate and company change is realization of the need for change, in particular for the implementation of a continuous improvement mindset throughout the R&D organization. Change management techniques are introduced to management to facilitate the cultural evolution required for success. Resistance to change is addressed through constant reinforcement and discussion focusing on internal and external benefits.

Outcome 2: Measurement

Outcome 2 involves establishing performance measures to evaluate performance and completing the assessment instruments. Measurements include both internal performance indicators and external customer-related evaluations. The organization searches to measure performance and distinguish systems from discrete events. Measures of performance enable the system to be tracked, documented, and improved. Goals and objectives for the improvement process are initialized at this stage. Success criteria in the form of critical success factors, which detail the road map for change, are initiated in Stage 1. These criteria should be multifaceted (quality, productivity, cost–benefit, cycle time improvement, etc.), interconnected, and related to one another.

The concept of critical success factors (CSFs) was first popularized by Jack Rockart.[1] CSFs for any business are the limited number of areas in which satisfactory results will ensure successful competitive advantage; in other words, these are the areas where things must go right if the effectiveness of the organization is to flourish.

The following excerpt is from *Building the Corporate Measurement System* by Frank Voehl (Strategy Associates, 1992):

> Critical success factors for R&D can be categorized as either "monitoring," "building" or "benchmarking" types. The more competitive pressure for current performance that the chief R&D executive feels, the more his or her CSFs tend toward monitoring current results. The more that the organization is insulated from economic pressures or decentralized, the more CSFs become oriented toward building for the future through major change programs aimed at adapting the organization to a perceived new environment. The more the organization has identified the need for comparison and adaptation of other organizations' best practices, the more CSFs become oriented toward benchmarking the operations of others,[2] as exemplified in the Key Indicators approach.

In general, at least five criteria can be used on the corporate level to determine which factors are critical to the effectiveness of an organization:[3]

1. Overall impact on performance measures, such as profitability, cash flow, return on investment and competitive positioning[4]

2. Overall relationship to the strategic direction and issues, such as differentiation, turnaround and segmentation[5]

3. Relationship to more than one business activity[6]

4. Relationship to stages in product or organizational life cycle, such as introduction, growth and decline[7]

5. Overall impact involving large amounts of capital and resources in relation to activities of the organization

Once the corporate level CSFs are established, each department is encouraged to identify indicators that can be used to measure its contribution. In this way, a corporate-wide system of indices can be linked and tied into the organization's performance measurement system.

It is not uncommon to see management begin to develop operational procedures for handling discrete events and systems difficulties. This outcome may also result in the definition of performance measures of less quantifiable R&D organizational systems such as human behavior and self-esteem. Success depends upon employee involvement and positive feelings and attitudes. Employee and management self-esteem is critical for participation and creative contributions (see discussion on social system in Chapter 4).

External measurement includes customer, competitor, and supplier assessments. These measures are ultimately linked to internal performance (process) measures. External measures facilitate the process of managing customers (both external and internal) and monitoring suppliers for performance. (For additional information, see Abstract 5.1 at the end of this chapter.)

STAGE 2: MANAGEMENT CONCURRENCE PHASE

The management concurrence phase is the most critical phase in the systematic improvement process. Management accepts the challenge of continuous improvement by practicing a more proactive management style. Commitment and support begin to develop as the organization experiences both human and business-related benefits.

This phase involves the largest number of outcomes and is critical if the organization is to implement and sustain its continuous improvement effort. During this phase, management begins to change practices, implement core values, and reward (recognize) employee behavior. It is essential that individual efforts concentrate on developing methods to begin the total quality process. At this stage, R&D management demonstrates that initial commitment and support. This commitment must be in the form of both words and action.

Stage 2 requires a multifaceted set of outcomes, each one building upon the other. Seven major outcomes comprise this stage. An evaluation of each outcome at this stage requires performance measures. At the completion of this stage, the evaluation process begins. Feedback on system performance is critical for judging and documenting success.

Outcomes of Stage 2

Outcomes involved in this stage consist of:

1. Accepting the challenge of the total quality philosophy

2. Realization of the long-term perspective

3. Development of both commitment and support

4. Willingness to change both organizationally and personally

5. Willingness to measure the business beyond traditional business measures

6. Establishing management structures that recognize added value

7. Improved communications and feedback throughout the organization

Rewards and recognition are tools that management can use to introduce the concepts throughout the department. As in all lasting improvements, R&D will experience changes slowly at first. Progress serves to reduce resistance, which remains the most potent negative force. For sustained success, Stage 2 must become the centerpiece of the total quality effort.

Outcome 1: Accept the Challenge

The R&D organization accepts the challenge of total quality and begins a systematic approach. Initial resources are allocated for the effort, and management begins by organizing its structure, authority, and "power grids" into alignment with total quality goals. Improvement goals tied directly to organizational and business objectives are formulated. Goals should be multifaceted, with levels of improvement interconnected, related to one another, and designed to meet the needs of the R&D function.

Outcome 2: Realization of the Long-Term Perspective

After accepting the challenge of total quality, management must begin to realize the long-term effort needed to accomplish this goal. A definitive time frame for successful implementation is initiated. Total quality evolves within the organization or business. It is measured in increments rather than tremendous accomplishment—improvements rather than miracles. Months and years become realistic time frames for implementation.

Criteria for success are developed and disseminated to the entire management staff. Management establishes **core values** (those distinct values that define the R&D department or organization, its approach to customers, and its commitment to employees, in concert with business or corporate [organizational] goals). Core values signify those characteristics and goals that become measurable benefits to the organization.

Outcome 3: Develop Support and Commitment

The appointment of an organizational-wide implementation team represents the first essential element of Outcome 3. The purpose of this implementation team is to provide a management framework for those involved in the systematic improvement process. The responsibilities of an implementation team include:

1. Develop a mission statement that captures the level of commitment and involvement of all management in the systematic improvement process

2. Lead the improvement process

3. Guide and direct improvement teams

4. Allocate resources

5. Evaluate progress of teams

6. Publish success stories and develop and implement improvement guidelines

7. Resolve conflicts with corporate/organizational goals

8. Direct future efforts

9. Develop training schedule

10. Act as an interface with teams to top management

The implementation team does not, however, have responsibility for the quality improvement effort. The implementation team is management's tool for communicating throughout the organization. It is an outward sign of management's commitment and support. It also has operational guidelines, functions (tasks), and responsibilities to both employees and upper management within R&D. The first order of business is to develop internal operational guidelines. Major departmental areas within the R&D organization should be represented on the committee. Designated individuals should hold management technical positions within the organization. The committee's authority is essentially that of coordination, delegation, and evaluation. It serves as a communication link between upper management and the improvement teams. The measure of success for this stage is the formation of an operational implementation team.

Outcome 4: Organizational and Personal Change

Outcome 4 operationalizes core values into a departmental/organizational mission statement which details the entire organization-wide quality improvement effort. The statement should be issued from the implementation team and be signed by all committee members. It should include a detailed explanation of the purpose and intent of the mission so as to elicit support. Employees should also be informed about planning, actions, and level of effort expected. Trust is needed in order for employees to accept change and see the positive elements of total quality. Employees have learned to "read between the lines" and react accordingly. Management has a difficult task in introducing this mission statement in an environment that is open to communication and free of fear. Any hint of demand or any "power play" will be recognized by employees, who will ensure the ultimate demise of the improvement effort. One such element in removing fear/anxiety (establishing trust) is to introduce the preliminary mission statement and solicit changes from employees. Include with the mission statement an estimated timeline, activities to be accomplished, and responsibilities. Let employees participate in the formulation process with guidance from management.

Outcome 5: Measure the Business Beyond Traditional Financial Measures

Management begins to quantify attributes beyond traditional measures which often gauge only the balance sheet of the organization. Measures related to key concepts of total quality include:

1. Customer satisfaction, specified requirements, and needs
2. Supplier input requirements and process performance
3. Internal performance (operations, organization, communication)
4. Productivity (efficiency, maximized employee effort)
5. Effectiveness potential (how well activities/tasks are accomplished)
6. Human measures of performance

    - Knowledge, skills
    - Experience
    - Judgment/decision making
    - Willingness/capacity to learn
    - Attitude
    - Cooperation/creativity/innovation
    - Initiative
    - Problem-solving, problem-prevention potential
    - Self-esteem, self-motivation
    - Teamwork potential
    - Leadership ability
    - Self-management potential

7. Timeliness
8. Accuracy

See Abstract 5.2 at the end of this chapter for additional information.

Emphasis on human and technical skills development becomes the cornerstone of the total quality effort. Measurement provides an assessment of progress as well as highlighting areas for continued improvement. Total quality philosophy requires that management use the concept of measurement and evaluation to track system performance, establish benchmarks, and improve employee productivity.

Outcome 6: Establish Management Structures that Recognize Added Value

Sustained success requires implementation of an effective recognition and reward system to identify positive behavior. Individuals will most often recognize the weakness in a total quality program when communications are positive but rewards continue to benefit traditional individualistic behavior. Positive actions such as problem prevention, teamwork, leadership, and conflict resolution need to be consistently and effectively recognized.

A recognition system consists of five major elements:

1. Establish criteria for rewards and recognition:

   - Specify those actions and behaviors that merit reward
   - Define the scope and magnitude of those actions
   - Establish a mechanism for identifying positive behaviors
   - Define a specific awards process
     - o Guidelines
     - o Rules
     - o Evaluation criteria
     - o Selection
     - o Reviewer selection/qualifications
   - Monitor progress
   - Establish effective feedback
   - Make "fairness" a central issue

2. Identify and confirm behavior and actions

3. Communicate and showcase recognition award winners

4. Model positive (effective) behavior

5. Constant review and update

   Additional structures that add value include:

1. Proactive employee evaluation that highlights positive behavior and actions

2. Consistent feedback to and from management

3. Employee/manager role models

4. Expectations clearly stated, frequently reviewed, and consistently updated

5. Respect for diversity, talent, and the community

Finally, a formalized training effort for the entire business is initiated at this stage. Training provides the work force and management with the tools and theory to continue the total quality process. At this stage, management begins training in the basics and proactively examines its structures through assessment, searching for improvement.

Outcome 7: Improved Communication and Feedback Throughout the Organization

Finally, initial responsibilities and tasks are assigned and communicated throughout the organization. Upper management accepts the responsibility for its actions and begins to set in motion the task of improvement. Upper management's tasks include:

1. Define, publish, and communicate central core values

2. Identify realistic goals and objectives for the improvement process, and accept its evolutionary perspective

3. Set and initialize time frames for success

4. Fully support the implementation team and commit to the effort

5. Supply appropriate resources including support for middle management and the work force

6. Establish mechanism for evaluation

Communication remains the key element for establishing trust among all employees. Keep employees informed and consult with them on issues that directly pertain to them. Effective communication requires that employees be informed as well as consulted on the issue of quality (systems) improvement. Design and use an effective communication system that is truly two way. Assess intra- and intercommunications for effectiveness and accuracy. Accurate and precise information facilitates the improvement process and is another cornerstone of this effort. Evaluate R&D communication systems by completing the Communication System Assessment Survey (Exercise 1.1) provided at the end of Chapter 1. (For additional information, see Abstract 5.3 at the end of this chapter.)

Outcome 7 also involves the initialization of an ongoing evaluation/appraisal stage to monitor progress, detect difficulties, and inform the work force. This appraisal process provides a mechanism for improvement for all business, customer, and human systems. Consistent and comprehensive evaluation begins a feedback loop and a framework to improve all operations and personnel.

ENDNOTES

1. Rockart, Jack. "Chief Executives Define Their Own Data Needs." *Harvard Business Review*, March–April 1979.

2. In most cases observed to date, however, there is a mixture of the three types. Every chief executive appears to have, at some level, monitoring, benchmarking, and building (or adapting) responsibilities. Thus, a great deal of the information needed will not continue to be needed year after year. Rather, it is relatively short-term "project status" information that is needed only during the lifetime of the project. Periodic review of CSFs will, therefore, bring to light the need to discontinue some reports and initiate others.

3. George Albert Smith was a pioneer in providing "hard, penetrating questions concerning organizational experience, human relations and integrity which must be asked and answered truthfully" if CSFs are to have a real-world impact.

4. Bill Ward, past president of Amerace Corp., is known in the industry for having developed a CSF-based corporate measures and culture change program called BEST. This is also a planning process that integrates total quality management and advanced value analysis to achieve and maintain competitive advantage. Endnotes 5, 6, and 7 contain an outline of questions developed by Mr. Ward to identify weaknesses in management commitment.

5. The following questions should be asked: (1) Does the management distinguish between symptoms and causes? The failure to understand this obvious distinction results in band-aids and not the elimination of the root cause(s). (2) Does top management frequently ask itself, "In our industry, what are the fundamental tasks we perform?" "What must we do as well as, or preferably better than, someone else in order to compete and to excel?" (3) Do executives watch day-to-day developments in their own industry so closely that they lose track of some big, sweeping, long-range developments in the world, or their part of, which may affect their business vitality? Do they take time to think about these major trends?

6. In dealing with more than one business activity, the following question must be asked: Do the executives have integrity? It must be answered in terms of the following: (1) Integrity in relationships with other people: Are we honest with them? Do we tell them the truth? (2) Integrity with ourselves: Do we face up to the tough situations? Do we just close our eyes and pretend that the problem does not even exist? (3) Integrity in presenting all of the facts—real facts: Do we present only that which will support some pet notion of our own?

7. The following questions revolve around product timing: (1) Does management frequently ask, "What is wrong with our product or our competitor's product which, if corrected, would put us out of the pa-

rade?"(2) Are there people in the organization with commercial sense who can translate research and new ideas into marketable products? (3) Does the management of the company have a good sense of timing? (4) Is the organization afraid to make exceptions? Does it recognize them for what they are and return to a general policy?

ABSTRACTS

ABSTRACT 5.1
THE IMPACT OF JUST-IN-TIME INVENTORY SYSTEMS
ON SMALL BUSINESSES

Sadhwani, A.T. and Sarhan, M.
Journal of Accountancy, January 1987, pp. 118–132

This article by Sadhwani and Sarhan, although written in 1987, is as timely today as the day it was written. The key notion is that just-in-time (JIT) inventory management systems, used to reduce inventories and improve quality and productivity, are being adopted more frequently by large manufacturing corporations, thus presenting new challenges for small businesses as well. JIT, a "pull" system (assembly line triggers withdrawal of parts from preceding work centers), has two aspects that are heavily emphasized by manufacturers: just-in-time purchasing and just-in-time delivery and transportation. JIT purchasing, which relies heavily on a dependable supplier network, calls for manufacturers to deal with fewer suppliers, small lot sizes, and statistical quality control (SQC) techniques.

In addition to using fewer suppliers and signing larger contracts (with suppliers), JIT manufacturers are working with smaller lot sizes, thereby reducing unnecessary inventories and freeing storage areas to reduce cost and improve quality. SQC is a powerful problem-solving tool that pinpoints variations and their causes and eliminates after-the-fact inspection—an expensive, wasteful procedure that rarely detects the causes of poor quality.

More recently, JIT manufacturers have encouraged their suppliers to form "focused factory" arrangements which enable the supplier to focus on a limited number of products and become a specialized maker to a major manufacturer. This usually leads to suppliers relocating closer to their respective manufacturer, one of the tenets of JIT delivery and transportation. In addition to the elimination of centralized loading docks and staging areas, another benefit is the use of information sharing and microcomputers, which exposes small businesses to computerized information systems. The implications of JIT for small businesses are profound, such as better customer relationships and stable product demand. Not all the benefits come easy, though. For example, suppliers must institute statistical process control and understand freight economics, but the benefits of long-term contracts, smooth production, improved quality, and reduced scrap and rework greatly enhance the success of small businesses. Good graphs are provided, but no references.

ABSTRACT 5.2
THE BALANCED SCORECARD—MEASURES THAT DRIVE PERFORMANCE

Kaplan, Robert S. and Norton, David P.
Harvard Business Review, January–February 1992, pp. 71–79

"What you measure is what you get," begin these authors. "Traditional financial accounting measures like return on investment and earnings per share can give misleading signals for continuous improvement and innovation—activities today's competitive environment demands." The remedy, they say, is a "balanced scorecard," a group of measures that summarize progress toward the objectives most important to the organization. Anything else is like trying to fly a plane by watching just the altimeter and ignoring measures like air speed, remaining fuel, and so on. The authors conducted a year-long research project with 12 companies to explore ways of finding the combination of operational and financial measures that would constitute a "balanced scorecard." They concluded that there are four important measurement perspectives:

- Financial perspective (How do we look to shareholders?)

- Customer perspective (How do customers see us?)

- Internal business perspective (What must we excel at?)

- Innovation and learning perspective (Can we continue to create value?)

Each of these perspectives implies a set of goals that in turn imply measures of performance in reaching those goals. To illustrate possible goals and measures, the authors describe how a disguised electronics firm derived its own balanced scorecard of goals and measures from these four perspectives, and the authors supplement these examples with measures adopted by other businesses. They conclude with some suggestions on how to ensure that balanced scorecard measures will result in improved financial results. (©*Quality Abstracts*)

ABSTRACT 5.3
TRY THINKING BACKWARDS

Nadarajah, Raj
Total Quality Management, July–August 1992, pp. 164–166

Why has the goal of quality not been realized? According to the author, a failure to communicate effectively is one of the major reasons. Little is said about communication in TQM literature, and prescriptive advice is scarce. Most organizations lack a communications expert, so the author gives advice on meeting communication needs. He recommends adapting the message to different cultures within the organization, anticipating what the listener wants to hear, and keeping the vision statement simple. The author then outlines the communication needs in the four phases of TQM-inspired corporate culture evolution:

1. **Introspection:** Everyone is thinking about doing things right the first time on an individual basis. The role of communications is to support education and training.

2. **Timeliness:** Everyone is doing things on a timely basis. The communications message should motivate teams to implement quality improvement.

3. **Zero defects:** People are striving to do things right the first time, both as individuals and as teams. The message is geared towards individuals identifying waste and eliminating it.

4. **Innovation:** People are finding new ways to meet time requirements and eliminate waste and defects. The message is aimed at improving the way the business is run.   (©*Quality Abstracts*)

EXERCISE

EXERCISE 5.1
R&D INFRASTRUCTURE CHECKLIST

DIRECTIONS
Evaluate the entire R&D organization from your personal perspective. Circle the response that most closely represents your opinion. Do not sign or indicate your name on this form. Your honest evaluation is critical.

RESPONSES

5 = Strongly Agree	2 = Disagree
4 = Agree	1 = Strongly Disagree
3 = Neither Agree nor Disagree	

STRATEGY

1. **There is a complete strategic plan for R&D.**   5 4 3 2 1

   The strategic plan includes:

   a. Organizational mission   5 4 3 2 1

   b. Purpose and reason for being   5 4 3 2 1

   c. Goals/objectives for the present and future   5 4 3 2 1

   d. Methods for achieving those goals   5 4 3 2 1

   e. Priorities   5 4 3 2 1

   f. Established time frames   5 4 3 2 1

   The strategic plan lists the top three organizational   5 4 3 2 1
   goals.

   Management fully supports these strategies.   5 4 3 2 1

   Management commitment is identifiable.   5 4 3 2 1

2. **The strategic plan for R&D is:**

   Clearly understood and communicated to all   5 4 3 2 1

   Recognized by all managers as a framework for   5 4 3 2 1
   operating the organization

Implemented at all (any) levels	5	4	3	2	1
Able to be accomplished	5	4	3	2	1
A guide for managing activities and tasks	5	4	3	2	1
A plan for managing future activities	5	4	3	2	1
Systematic in execution	5	4	3	2	1
A series of discrete events	5	4	3	2	1

3. **The planning process for your department (organization):**

Is haphazard or incomplete	5	4	3	2	1
Can be completed by using a distinctive method	5	4	3	2	1
Is established without viable methods to accomplish these goals	5	4	3	2	1
Management participates in the planning and formulation stage	5	4	3	2	1
Management "buys-in" to the strategic plan	5	4	3	2	1
Employees "buy-in" to the strategic plan	5	4	3	2	1

CORE VALUES

1. **Core values (those goals and objectives that the company considers critical) are well established.**   5 4 3 2 1

   Core values are stated as numerical (profits, ROI, revenue, etc.) goals.   5 4 3 2 1

   Core values are community based (employment, environmental, etc.).   5 4 3 2 1

   Core values refer to human potential (self-respect, dignity, self-esteem, etc.).   5 4 3 2 1

2. **Executive management participated in creating the "core value" statement for R&D.**   *Yes* ❏   *No* ❏

Corporate buy-in is a reality.	5	4	3	2	1
Executives and managers frequently discuss these values with employees.	5	4	3	2	1
Managers are evaluated against these values.	5	4	3	2	1

3. **What percentage of the values are:**

   Business related   _____%

Community based _____%

Human resource potential _____%

4. Core values represent goals or purpose (reason for existence). 5 4 3 2 1

5. Core values are communicated to all employees. 5 4 3 2 1

6. Core values are clearly stated, in unambiguous terms 5 4 3 2 1

7. Your company or organization periodically evaluates these values. 5 4 3 2 1

8. Employees contribute to the establishment and continuance of values. 5 4 3 2 1

9. Employees openly discuss these values. 5 4 3 2 1

10. There is a company core value (policy) statement.
    Yes ❏   No ❏

11. The company or organizational policy statement contains (or states) these core values. 5 4 3 2 1

PLANNING

1. How would you accurately describe the management structure of your business or organization?

    Hierarchical ❏   Participative ❏   Authoritative ❏   Mixed ❏

2. The present management structure facilitates:

    Accomplishing tasks 5 4 3 2 1

    Ordering subordinates 5 4 3 2 1

    Planning 5 4 3 2 1

    Coordinating 5 4 3 2 1

    Staffing 5 4 3 2 1

    Controlling 5 4 3 2 1

    Operating in a (place percentage next to activity):

    Cooperative environment _____%

Reactive environment   _____ %

Crisis environment   _____ %

Planning environment   _____ %

3. **Conflicts frequently exist between managers and employees**

   Yes ❑   *No* ❑   *Don't know* ❑

   If yes, what percentage of the time is the conflict:

   Productive   _____ %

   Counterproductive   _____ %

   Demotivational   _____ %

   Demoralizing   _____ %

	5	4	3	2	1
Managers'/employees' duties are clearly defined.	5	4	3	2	1

   What percentage of the time would jobs be:

   Poorly defined   _____ %

   Poorly communicated   _____ %

   Improperly organized   _____ %

   Improperly managed   _____ %

   Poorly coordinated   _____ %

   Inappropriate, given the employee   _____ %

	5	4	3	2	1
4. **Teamwork exists within your department or organization.**	5	4	3	2	1
Teamwork is encouraged.	5	4	3	2	1
Teamwork is discouraged.	5	4	3	2	1
Teamwork is possible, given present constraints.	5	4	3	2	1
5. **Continuous improvement is a management goal.**	5	4	3	2	1
6. **The levels of management are restrictive.**	5	4	3	2	1

   There are too many or too few?

   Too many ❑   *Too few* ❑   *Acceptable* ❑

	5	4	3	2	1
7. **Employees are productive.**	5	4	3	2	1
8. **Employees are overburdened.**	5	4	3	2	1

What are the reasons for employees being overburdened?

Too much to do ❏   *Time spent on unnecessary activities* ❏

Not enough time ❏   *Managing people too frequently* ❏

Managers are overburdened.   5   4   3   2   1

What are the reasons for managers being overburdened?

Too much to do ❏   *Time spent on unnecessary activities* ❏

Not enough time ❏   *Managing people too frequently* ❏

9. **Communications are adequate within your**   5   4   3   2   1
   department or organization.

   There are "grapevines" within the organization.   5   4   3   2   1

   They carry incorrect information.   5   4   3   2   1

   There are "rumor mills" in your organization.   5   4   3   2   1

   They are destructive.   5   4   3   2   1

   Employees generally communicate well with their   5   4   3   2   1
   managers.

   Managers generally communicate well with their   5   4   3   2   1
   employees.

   There is frequent communication between top   5   4   3   2   1
   management and employees.

10. **Personnel policies are consistent.**   5   4   3   2   1

    Personnel policies are consistent with corporate   5   4   3   2   1
    organization strategy.

    Employees are evaluated:

    Yearly ❏   *Monthly* ❏   *When needed* ❏   *On a scheduled basis* ❏

    Systems (processes) are evaluated:

    Yearly ❏   *Monthly* ❏   *When needed* ❏   *Never* ❏

    Job descriptions exist for all employees.   5   4   3   2   1

    These are updated regularly.   5   4   3   2   1

    Employees participate in preparing these job   5   4   3   2   1
    descriptions.

    Job descriptions are:

    General ❏   *Specific* ❏

    Employees participate in the review process.   5   4   3   2   1

| Employees are given written reviews. | 5 | 4 | 3 | 2 | 1 |

What type of recourse is available to employees?

Many types ❑   *Some types* ❑   *One* ❑   *None* ❑

Employees are permitted to modify or change their reviews.	5	4	3	2	1
Feedback with employees is regularly scheduled.	5	4	3	2	1
Teamwork (team behavior) is evaluated.	5	4	3	2	1
Teamwork (team behavior) is rewarded.	5	4	3	2	1
Teams are recognized in your organization.	5	4	3	2	1
Individuals are rewarded for their behavior.	5	4	3	2	1

Teams are:

A regular occurrence ❑   *Used only for special events or reasons* ❑

Employees are rewarded for:

Cooperation	5	4	3	2	1
Competition	5	4	3	2	1
Team building	5	4	3	2	1
Managing other employees	5	4	3	2	1
"Best Employee of the Month" activities	5	4	3	2	1
Problem solving	5	4	3	2	1
Decision making	5	4	3	2	1
Systems thinking	5	4	3	2	1
Crisis management	5	4	3	2	1
Reactive behavior	5	4	3	2	1
Active involvement	5	4	3	2	1

11. Resources are dedicated to employee enrichment. 5 4 3 2 1

Resources in the organization are dedicated for:

Employee/manager empowerment skills	5	4	3	2	1
Employee attitudes and professional behavior	5	4	3	2	1
Skills enhancement	5	4	3	2	1
Employee morale	5	4	3	2	1
Organizational effectiveness	5	4	3	2	1

Customer satisfaction   5   4   3   2   1

Internal/external communications improvement   5   4   3   2   1

12. What type of training is currently available to employees?

Management training   *Yes* ❑   *No* ❑   *Don't know* ❑

Job responsibility/task assignment   *Yes* ❑   *No* ❑   *Don't know* ❑

OJT (on-the-job training)   *Yes* ❑   *No* ❑   *Don't know* ❑

Job-related skills   *Yes* ❑   *No* ❑   *Don't know* ❑

Specific, please list: _____

_____

_____

13. The training offered by the organization or   5   4   3   2   1
department is effective.

The result of the training is consistent and predictable.   5   4   3   2   1

Training yields positive result.   5   4   3   2   1

14. If you answered #13 with a 3, 2, or 1, please list the reasons for negative results: _____

_____

_____

PERFORMANCE EVALUATION

1. Your R&D department (organization) measures   5   4   3   2   1
performance.

If you answered 5, 4, or 3, list those key performance measures:

1. _____

2. _____

3.. _____

4. _____

5. _____

2. These performance measures relate to customer   5   4   3   2   1
satisfaction.

Customers' needs are continually met.   5   4   3   2   1

Quality is a key measure.   5   4   3   2   1

3. **These performance measures are accurate and reliable.** 5 4 3 2 1

   Mistakes do occur with these measures. 5 4 3 2 1

   How frequent are these mistakes (errors)?
   Frequent ❑   *Occasional* ❑   *Seldom* ❑   *Never* ❑

   Reasons for these mistakes are known. 5 4 3 2 1

   The errors are traceable to a particular cause or reason. 5 4 3 2 1

   You know who (what) is responsible. 5 4 3 2 1

   Errors (mistakes) are mainly due to employees. 5 4 3 2 1

   Errors (mistakes) mainly occur in the business's/organization's:

Accounting systems/balance sheet	5	4	3	2	1
Accounts receivable	5	4	3	2	1
Accounts payable	5	4	3	2	1
Invoices/bills	5	4	3	2	1
Payroll	5	4	3	2	1
Financial reports	5	4	3	2	1
Inventory	5	4	3	2	1
Costs	5	4	3	2	1
Profit-and-loss (P/L) statement	5	4	3	2	1
Quality	5	4	3	2	1
Variances/standards	5	4	3	2	1
R&D	5	4	3	2	1

4. **External performance information is presently available to the R&D department/organization.** 5 4 3 2 1

   If this information is available:

   It is relatable to internal performance. 5 4 3 2 1

   External measures are stable and predictable. 5 4 3 2 1

5. **There is an internal performance monitoring system.** 5 4 3 2 1

   Measurement system reveals accurate systems information. 5 4 3 2 1

It is reliable (it warns management of potential problems or signals future opportunities).   5 4 3 2 1

List these internal measures:

1. _____

2. _____

3. _____

4. _____

5. _____

Internal measures relate to:

Employees (attitude, behavior, etc.)	5 4 3 2 1
Opportunities	5 4 3 2 1
Prevention	5 4 3 2 1
Efficiency	5 4 3 2 1
Productivity	5 4 3 2 1
Quality	5 4 3 2 1
Customer satisfaction	5 4 3 2 1
Profitability	5 4 3 2 1
Bottlenecks	5 4 3 2 1
Costs	5 4 3 2 1

Overall, are the internal measures positive or negative?

Positive ❑   Negative ❑

Employees are aware of the department's internal performance measures.   5 4 3 2 1

Employees are aware of external measures of performance.   5 4 3 2 1

Internal measures receive priority.   5 4 3 2 1

The priority of internal measures changes:

Frequently ❑   Occasionally ❑   Seldom ❑   Never ❑

6. **The R&D organization or business evaluates the measures of performance with:**

An established audit (review) system	5 4 3 2 1
External measures	5 4 3 2 1
Internal measures	5 4 3 2 1

What is the frequency of the evaluation process?

Monthly ❑   Quarterly ❑   Yearly ❑   As needed ❑

Who conducts the review?

Management ❑   Employees ❑   Mixed ❑   Outsider ❑

After completing a review, what is done with the results?

Prepare a report	5	4	3	2	1
Summarize results	5	4	3	2	1
Act on results	5	4	3	2	1
File	5	4	3	2	1
Communicate within the organization	5	4	3	2	1
Search for improvement opportunities	5	4	3	2	1
Fix or repair	5	4	3	2	1
Actions based on these measures are then initiated.	5	4	3	2	1
There are written procedures established to initiate action.	5	4	3	2	1

If not, should a procedure be established?

Yes ❑   No ❑   Don't know ❑

Based upon results, R&D goals and objectives are modified.	5	4	3	2	1
Actions (i.e., an action plan) are established.	5	4	3	2	1

Management reacts to or studies the results?

Reacts ❑   Studies ❑

The organization gives a priority to the action items established.	5	4	3	2	1
These action plans frequently change.	5	4	3	2	1
Resources are identified to carry out tasks, assign responsibilities.	5	4	3	2	1
A performance monitoring (evaluation) system presently exists.	5	4	3	2	1
Resources are identified.	5	4	3	2	1
Requirements are identified.	5	4	3	2	1
Management adheres to these requirements.	5	4	3	2	1
Staffing is flexible to meet changing requirements within the organization.	5	4	3	2	1

The staff (management and employees) understands   5 4 3 2 1
job tasks and responsibilities.

COMPETITION AND TECHNOLOGY

1. **Your organization or company regularly does a**   5 4 3 2 1
   competitive analysis.

   Does the competitive analysis measure:

   Customer satisfaction   5 4 3 2 1

   Market share   5 4 3 2 1

   Pricing (competitive market strategy)   5 4 3 2 1

   Delivery of service/product   5 4 3 2 1

   Process analysis   5 4 3 2 1

   Technology assessment   5 4 3 2 1

   Organizational analysis   5 4 3 2 1

   Cost analysis   5 4 3 2 1

   Design/development analysis   5 4 3 2 1

   Number (and type) of customer complaints   5 4 3 2 1

   Other (indicate): _____

   _____

   _____

2. **Your organization or company assesses itself against**
   its competition:

   Frequently ❏   *Rarely* ❏   *Never* ❏   *Unknown* ❏

   Your company or organization has a competitive   5 4 3 2 1
   advantage over its competition (e.g., niche product
   or service, unique marketing strategy, etc.).

   If so, list these and rate yourself against these criteria:

   List of Competitive Advantages   *Rating*

   _____   _____

   _____   _____

   _____   _____

   _____   _____

Your company has considered competitive disadvantages.	5	4	3	2	1
Your company has completed a competitive product or service comparison.	5	4	3	2	1
Your company has listed your competition's comparative advantages (e.g., special features).	5	4	3	2	1
Your company or organization has listed your competition's comparative disadvantages (i.e., their weak points).	5	4	3	2	1
You have compared your strong points against your competition's weak points (and vice versa).	5	4	3	2	1
Your customers know of your competitive advantages and comparative strong points.	5	4	3	2	1

Should they?   *Yes* ❑   *No* ❑

3. **How fast can your competition adapt to new economic conditions, that is, changes in the business environment?**
   Faster than your business ❑   *Same* ❑   *Slower* ❑

Your adjustment time (time needed to change) can improve.	5	4	3	2	1

4. **Technology is a concern for your business.**　　5　4　3　2　1

What types of technologies are important for your business or organization (please list): _____

_____

_____

Your organization maintains a competitive *advantage* or *disadvantage* with each listed technology.
   Advantage ❑   *Disadvantage* ❑

Time is a critical component of your technology (ability to change products, services, pricing, etc.).	5	4	3	2	1

If you answered with a 5, 4, or 3, what amount of time is required to successfully reorganize the R&D organization in order to change the cycle time?
   List time: _____

People resist change.	5	4	3	2	1
Management resists change.	5	4	3	2	1

The amount of time needed to change is restrictive.   5   4   3   2   1

This can be made more efficient and effective.   5   4   3   2   1

5. **Rate the importance of technology within your organization:**
    1st ❑   *2nd* ❑   *3rd* ❑   *4th* ❑   *Other* ❑

6. **A continuous revision of your strategic plan, market   5   4   3   2   1
    assessment, pricing, technology, customer evaluation,
    and internal systems is part of your R&D
    organization**

    If you answered 5, 4, or 3, which of these *components*
    are reviewed and what is the *frequency* of the review?

Component	*Frequency*
_____	_____
_____	_____
_____	_____
_____	_____

PRODUCT/SERVICE DEVELOPMENT AND DELIVERY

1. **What is the cycle time (time from initiation to
    completion) to develop a new service or new product?**
    1–2 mos. ❑   *6 mos.* ❑   *1 yr.* ❑   *2 yrs.* ❑

    This is competitive with similar organizations.   5   4   3   2   1

    It is appropriate, given present systems.   5   4   3   2   1

    It can be significantly shortened.   5   4   3   2   1

    It meets your present needs.   5   4   3   2   1

    If you answered 1 or 2, what are the reasons for the delay?

    _____

    _____

    _____

2. **External customers are completely identified (those   5   4   3   2   1
    who use your products or services).**

    All internal customers are identified.   5   4   3   2   1

    All potential suppliers/vendors are identified.   5   4   3   2   1

    Users are linked to the development process.   5   4   3   2   1

Customers (users) are linked with your delivery process.   5   4   3   2   1

Development is seen as a *process*, or a set of *activities* (set of tasks)?

   Process ❑   *Activities* ❑

To develop a new product or service, how many divisions or departments are required (involved)?

   Number _____

3. **Users receive a quality product on time.**   5   4   3   2   1

4. **Customers evaluate your delivery performance.**   5   4   3   2   1

5. **Is R&D's delivery system a set of related activities or tasks?**

   Related activities ❑   *Tasks* ❑

R&D's delivery system is inconsistent.   5   4   3   2   1

It is haphazard.   5   4   3   2   1

6. **R&D systems are "in-control" (stable) and predictable.**   5   4   3   2   1

7. **Customers of R&D delivery have clearly communicated their needs.**   5   4   3   2   1

These needs relate to the delivery process.

These needs are clearly defined as requirements established to meet customer desires.   5   4   3   2   1

Customers complain.   5   4   3   2   1

The R&D organization analyzes customer complaints or collects information concerning dissatisfaction.   5   4   3   2   1

R&D measures customer satisfaction with delivery systems.   5   4   3   2   1

Customer complaints are acted upon.   5   4   3   2   1

8. **List those problems encountered in developing a new product or service:**

_____

_____

_____

R&D is addressing these needs.   5   4   3   2   1

9. **Product or requirements are developed:**

By a team of experts	5	4	3	2	1
Through communication with the customer	5	4	3	2	1
By management decision	5	4	3	2	1
By the engineering/quality control/design department	5	4	3	2	1
Through the R&D department	5	4	3	2	1
By the legal department	5	4	3	2	1
Through government regulation	5	4	3	2	1
Other	5	4	3	2	1

CUSTOMER SATISFACTION AND SERVICE

1. **There is an existing customer satisfaction measurement program within R&D.**   5   4   3   2   1

It measures *satisfaction* or *dissatisfaction?*
Satisfaction ❑   Dissatisfaction ❑

It quantifies the satisfaction measures.	5	4	3	2	1

It measures:

The amount of customer feedback	5	4	3	2	1
The usefulness of customer feedback	5	4	3	2	1
Internal business performance as compared to customer (user) assessment	5	4	3	2	1
Customer perceptions	5	4	3	2	1
Customer expectations	5	4	3	2	1
System or process efficiency (effectiveness)	5	4	3	2	1
Competitor performance	5	4	3	2	1
Accuracy and reliability of customer data	5	4	3	2	1
Satisfaction on a continuous scale (or continuum)	5	4	3	2	1
Customer complaints	5	4	3	2	1
If you answered 5 or 4, is the feedback informative?	5	4	3	2	1
Losses (costs) related to poor performance	5	4	3	2	1
Future success and profitability	5	4	3	2	1

2. **Customer satisfaction is measured between departments.**   5 4 3 2 1

3. **R&D is responsible for delivering a "quality product."**   5 4 3 2 1

   Quality is defined in a R&D setting.   5 4 3 2 1

   A total quality approach is applied.   5 4 3 2 1

   Quality and performance are frequently monitored.   5 4 3 2 1

   R&D is responsible for its own quality.   5 4 3 2 1

   R&D is responsible for correcting problems.   5 4 3 2 1

   A corrective action plan exists.   5 4 3 2 1

   Causes/sources of quality problems are identified.   5 4 3 2 1

   Reactive solutions are implemented.   5 4 3 2 1

   Proactive solutions, meant to alleviate the problem, are instituted.   5 4 3 2 1

   Root cause problem analysis is common.   5 4 3 2 1

4. **Your department concentrates on "human quality."**   5 4 3 2 1

   Human resources are valued.   5 4 3 2 1

   You can achieve your potential in this department.   5 4 3 2 1

CHAPTER 6

PLANNING AND DIAGNOSING

This chapter deals with Stages 3 through 5 in the transformation process.

STAGE 3: PLANNING PHASE

Stage 3 comprises the organization's effort to establish and coordinate the philosophy of total quality within the strategic plan. The plan takes on both a short- and long-term focus. Short-term planning is guided by the need to demonstrate results quickly and efficiently and is results oriented, benefiting the organization based on goals established in Stages 1 and 2. Long-term planning focuses primarily on sustainment, growth, and development by impacting the management cycle of the organization.

This stage facilitates the generation of success stories, which are critical for future success, demonstrating total quality principles, and laying the groundwork for the organization's future efforts. By preparing and disseminating information on the *how, what, where,* and *when,* management and employees can begin to decipher the intent and direction of the total quality effort. Without sharing the framework of "the plan," quality improvement takes on the characteristics of a program, which implies a short-term perspective. Employees need to be convinced of the criticality of total quality for survival and growth.

Management should also inform all employees that the plan is evolutionary; it will change and evolve over time. Planning is not static but rather is stepwise (i.e., a dynamic process that provides the organization with flexibility). The goal remains the same—total quality, exceeding customer needs and wants, community involvement, environmental concern, and an organization that values its employees by empowering them to improve those systems in which they operate.

Competing in the future will require leaders and sets of managers who are adept at two kinds of management: organization maintenance management and organization development management. One set of managers helps keep the organization together under the strains of continual change and challenge. The other set keeps the organization fit to exist by leading it into challenge and change. The terms leadership and excellence are therefore permanently intertwined.[1]

Also, every system of work has its outputs. **Outputs** are products or services. The goal of the management cycle is to go beyond optimizing the quality of products and services; focusing on the product or service itself is inadequate. Outputs are the result of a set of processes, and quality must be built into the process. The process of hiring and training employees may determine the quality of service in a restaurant. Concentrating on the service itself is too late in the flow of processes. Management quality must be built into the system, beginning with the creation of a vision and strategies and extended to the hiring process.[2]

Similarly, quality of a product is often determined during the design process. Is it designed in a way that reduces the probability of variances in the manufacturing process? Do the specified materials reduce variability in the manufacturing process? Has it been designed in a way that will meet the customer needs of tomorrow? Again, quality is largely a function of the process of work as well as the management cycle, which consists of vision, strategies, planning, organizing, implementing, and controlling

Outcomes of Stage 3

Two outcomes comprise this phase and serve as a measurement for progress. Outcome 1 addresses short-term planning necessary to accomplish specific tasks (improvements), generating successes, utilizing tools and methods, and implementing the improvement process. Outcome 2 concentrates on a long-term perspective, sustained change, appropriate goals, and internal/external customer focus.

Outcome 1: Short-Term Perspective

A short-term plan should provide the strategy (framework) for implementation of total quality methods. The plan should address the following:

1. Results orientation that quickly benefits the R&D organization by selecting critical systems that cause:

   - Bottlenecks
   - Inefficient performance
   - Losses (Taguchi)
   - Increased costs
   - Poorer than expected customer satisfaction
   - Cycle time improvement
   - Effective project management
   - Time to task completion

   Results require measurable performance directly linked to process characteristics. The key idea is to demonstrate success with these methods and management styles.

2. Employee and organizational empowerment to meet short-term issues, including:

   - Creating "values" that promote a dynamic, viable, positive self-image for the individual and the organization
   - Creating an environment that challenges the individual, is responsive to proactive changes, benefits from and manages change, and results in the ability to shift paradigms
   - Building an organization that is proactive to teamwork, cooperation, collaboration, marketplace "scanning," information management, alliance building, and compromise management
   - Managing decision making in a responsive (rather than static) mode, where decisions are cooperative ventures; a process rather than a regimen
   - Communication in an effective, positive, open, rewarding, and supportive environment
   - Individual initiative and assertiveness, including *personal power* (control over inner and outer forces shaping the individual) and *organizational power* (the organization accepts responsibility for controlling its destiny rather than relying on fate)
   - Individuals eagerly accept responsibility and accountability, success and failure are celebrated, and blame is minimized as a punishment tool

Employee empowerment signals the organization's willingness to support and commit to total quality improvement. This commitment demonstrates the strategy management that will be used to reward behavior. It also addresses the issue of suboptimization (focusing on a part rather than the whole). The plan describes the framework (which employees will use) to improve the organization's strategy in order to accomplish improvement and those actions and tasks that form the professional criteria for acceptable performance. It also embraces the management control role of the chief executive, which can at least partially be served by means of routine, often computer-based, reporting.[3] (For additional information, see Abstract 6.1 at the end of this chapter.)

3. Use the Systematic Improvement Process as a guide for improving a system or process. Management needs to stress the adaptability of the process (remembering that it is a dynamic rather than static process). The organization can use the process flowchart to improve its operations. The flowchart can be modified and adjusted to meet the unique objectives of every improvement project.

SYSTEMATIC IMPROVEMENT PROCESS

Step 1: Select the System

I. Develop selection criteria

    A. Select system that is:

        1. Documentable (can be flowcharted)

        2. Repetitive

        3. Traceable

        4. Measurable

        5. Accountable

II. Determine performance measures

    A. Select performance measures that are:

        1. Systematic measures (measure performance of the system):

            a. People

            b. Procedures (methods)

            c. Machines (machine parameters, settings)

            d. Materials (inputs to the system)

            e. Environment (satisfaction, attitude)

2. Results measures (measure output of the system):

    a. Customer related

    b. Monitor progress

    c. Effectiveness

    d. Efficiency

3. Begin planning process:

    a. Define the scope of the system

    b. Choose appropriate performance measures which define the intended result

    c. Brainstorm outcomes related to requirements

    d. Assign success potential (possibility of achieving success)

    e. Review alternative approaches

    f. Obtain management approval/support

    g. Allocate resources

Step 2: Flowchart the System

I. Identify major system elements:

    A. Outputs (customer, receiver)

    B. Process steps

II. Arrange process steps sequentially

III. Include all decision steps

IV. Detail alternatives and flow back to process steps

V. Check for accuracy and repeatability (precision)

    A. Check the flowchart for accuracy: Does it truly represent actual system flow?

    B. Are "bottlenecks" identified?

    C. Are alternate paths (flows) available?

    D. Does the system regularly create new paths?

    E. Are documented procedures available? Does the system follow the documented procedure(s)?

VI. Update and refine as needed

Step 3: Establish Cause and Effect

I. Brainstorm all possible causes

II. Identify effects

III. Classify major causes into categories as:

    A. People

    B. Materials

    C. Procedures (methods)

    D. Measurements

    E. Environment

IV. Arrange in fishbone (cause-and-effect) format

V. Perform Pareto analysis, identifying critical few causes

VI. Update/refine as needed

Step 4: Identify Key Characteristics

I. Inputs and outputs

II. Assess measurement capability (accurate and repeatable)

    A. Determine and validate measurement systems

    B. Establish monitor (audit) process

    C. Develop improvement criteria

    D. Verify statistically

III. Directly related to the improvement process

    A. Evaluate improvement

IV. Establish operational definitions

    A. An operational definition is a definition which clearly communicates the meaning or function of a word (term) in such a way as to produce a desired result without further elaboration

    B. Establish operational definitions of all key characteristics

    C. Verify applicability

    D. Review periodically

Step 5: Collect Systems Data

I. Decide on critical information to collect

    A. Use basic tools to identify key characteristics (inputs, outputs, critical system elements) to collect data

II. Develop data collection "instrument":

    A. Check or tally sheet

    B. Form

    C. Survey

    D. Computer-generated information

III. Sample process (system) according to:

    A. Natural cycle time, i.e., normal (time-related) system rhythm

    B. Expected fluctuations in system performance

    C. Changes expected in the system

    D. Decision-making criteria (a natural point in time when a decision would be made)

IV. Review for effectiveness:

    A. Thoroughness of data (can confirmation of a decision be verified by the data?)

    B. Is the information appropriate, reliable?

Step 6: Is the System (Process) Stable?

I. Test system data for special causes

    A. Use run charts and run tests

        1. Length of run test

        2. Number of run tests

        3. Trend test

II. Use control charts for variables and attribute data

    A. If there are no subgroup data points outside the control limits and the presence of runs or trends is not confirmed, then judge the system (process) to be *stable*

III. If the system is not stable (out-of-control):

    A. Identify the special causes

    B. Identify and specify those subgroup data points that indicate a special cause

    1. Special causes are the result of *discrete events*

        a. These discrete events cause the variation of the system to be inconsistent

        b. It is critical to identify both the event and its cause, so as to initiate corrective action

IV. Implement corrective action

    A. After identifying any special causes, a plan should be instituted to prevent the discrete event from occurring in the future

        1. A signal is needed that indicates the potential for the discrete event to occur

        2. Prevention is the key word at this stage

V. Establish monitor mechanism

    A. Prevention without vigilance is not continuous improvement; therefore, there must be some method established to evaluate progress

        1. A control chart is a natural monitor of an unstable system

Step 7: Prioritize Common Causes

I. Identify potential system elements

    A. If the system is stable, then the power of the management tools can be used to identify potential improvements (brainstorming, Pareto analysis, etc.)

II. Develop action plan for implementation of improvement cycle

    A. Establish Plan-Do-Study-Act cycle

    B. Identify tasks, activities, responsibilities

    C. Develop time frame for improvement

III. Attach measurable output to improvement

IV. Pick systems elements first, achieve success, and publish success stories

Step 8: Implement and Monitor Improvement

I. Document and standardize implementation plan

II. Begin system evaluation (audit)

    A. Establish evaluation mechanism

    B. Identify measurable parameters

    C. Involve those who are part of the system in performing the review periodically

    D. Create a feedback loop to those who are part of the system

        1. Develop a feedforward system for management

III. Begin system evaluation (audit)

    A. Monitor both outputs and system elements

        1. Outputs serve as the primary mechanism for review

IV. Develop customer surveys and evaluations

V. Include the supplier (input) as an evaluation point

Step 9: Is the System Meeting Requirements?

  I. If meeting stated requirements, specifications, or regulations, then go to Step 10

    A. Be sure to verify with process capability analysis

 II. If the process is *not* meeting its requirements, then:

    A. Evaluate the causes

        1. Use both the management tools and experimental design to identify potential problems

        2. Design of experiments is an extremely powerful tool for identifying potential causes and interrelated effects

    B. After experimenting with the process, implement suggestions and monitor improvement

        1. Further experimentation may be required

    C. Establish a monitor system as in Step 8

Step 10: Experiment with the System

  I. Use brainstorming and Pareto analysis to identify potential problematic areas

    A. Examine cause-and-effect diagrams for system elements interrelationships

    B. Choose elements (by Pareto analysis)

    C. Consider all possible effects and relationships

    D. Develop experimental plan

    E. Conduct experimentation and implement

Step 11: Audit (Review) Systems Output

  I. Establish monitor mechanism

    A. Define measurable outputs that reflect system performance

    B. Establish the time frame for review process

    C. Identify activities, tasks, and responsibilities

  II. Institute review process

    A. Determine cycle for monitoring systems that are improved

  III. Review each system periodically

Step 12: Is the System Improving?

  I. If not, continue with experimentation stage (Step 10)

  II. Institutionalization phase

    A. Management actively involved in the system of improvement

    B. Employee/customer survey actively supports concept and reveals that systematic improvement is visible and accomplishing success

    C. Improvement is organization-wide

  III. Continuous improvement

Outcome 2: Long-Term Perspective

Outcome 2 conceptualizes the vision of the organization concerning total quality. It should be incorporated into the strategic plan (or a portion of that plan). It should relate directly to the goal and mission of the organization and assist customers and employees in comprehending the intent, direction, and implementation of total quality. The plan should reflect the corporate culture and stress the dynamic element of change (evolution) needed for future growth and development. Rather than speaking about the present mission (vision) of the organization, it should relate to what the organization will become in the future. The plan should address the following.

1. Sustained cultural change. The plan should detail how and why the organization will change to adapt to future requirements and marketplace environments. It should stress that constant adaptation and modification are required for future growth. In conjunction with this need is the incorporation of this philosophy into the corporate identity. That is, total quality will enhance the present culture rather than destroy its unique and special character. Management orientation will both support and commit to this for the future.

2. Goals and objectives. The plan should continually refer to total quality as a sustainable and positive goal (i.e., an essential requirement for the organization). The plan should detail resources, training, evaluation, goals, consistency, level of effort realistic for the organization, and dedication. The plan should reinforce the benefits (to both the organization and employees) of total quality.

3. Customer as well as competition focus. Both internal and external customers require long-term efforts to ensure consistency and long-term improvement. Identifying key internal customers becomes an activity of improvement teams and the implementation team. Internal customers provide the link to overall organizational performance. Reinforcing this link removes barriers, improves communication flow, and involves employees in servicing (meeting the needs of) all customers.

A customer focus becomes the critical goal for the organization. Included in this goal are sustainable customer relationships, improved communications and feedback, a customer satisfaction measurement program, internal/external systems review, and evaluation.

"Next to knowing what your customers want, the most important thing is to know what your competitors are doing." This remark by John Rhode, Vice President of Marketing and Planning with Combustion-Engineering's Industrial Group, summarizes the case for competitive intelligence. Michael Porter of the Harvard Business School, one of the key players in his field, states that competitive strategy involves positioning a business to maximize the value of the capabilities that distinguish it from its competitors. It follows that a central aspect of strategy formation is perceptive competitor analysis. Porter argues that one of the key functions of the corporate measurement system is to provide information profiles on each key competitor.[4]

4. Total quality focus. Support and commitment for this methodology through rewards (benefits), communication, and practice.

STAGE 4: IMPLEMENTATION PHASE

This stage begins the formal training of employees, the development of teams, and the structuring of the improvement process. Implementation is an ongoing process. The implementation team has chosen team members and empowers the team with a project using the improvement process. This stage encompasses total quality projects. Prior to full implementation and with two to five trial projects completed, the implementation team develops and institutes a framework for success. The implementation team issues guidelines for implementation, optimal team size, project size and depth, goals and objectives, a formalized team improvement process/plan, feedback and monitoring mechanisms, and a reward structure for team behavior. (For additional information, see Abstract 6.2 at the end of this chapter.)

Outcomes of Stage 4

Guidelines for sustained success are developed at this stage. Outcomes are fivefold, dealing with actions and tasks. Structure, developed at this stage, guides and powers the continuous improvement effort. Training begins at this stage, as well as team development. Managers accept new responsibilities and behaviors. Communications improve throughout the business and with the customer. Finally, a monitoring mechanism is initiated.

Outcome 1: Guidelines for Sustained Success

Outcome 1 involves the creation, within the implementation team, of a set of guidelines to develop, support, enhance, and monitor implementation progress. These guidelines should encompass the activities, tasks, and responsibilities required of team members, managers, trainers, etc. In the first few months, the implementation team should observe team behavior and establish a set of guidelines for:

1. Creating teams with strong core values, team goals, and alignment

2. Team leadership, including team membership and function

3. Team–management interface

4. Implementing a foundation and framework for a successful team

5. Allocating sparse resources, time, and workload

6. Best utilization of time in teaming process

7. Monitoring team progress

8. Compliance with organizational goals and objectives

9. Communicating within and outside of the team

10. Identifying viable projects for teams

11. Identifying human and organizational benefits

12. Implementing a team recognition process

13. Team decision making and consensus

14. Participative management

15. Expression of individual creativity and initiative

16. Preventative conflict management

This is an evolutionary process and will eventually eliminate many of the initial implementation team responsibilities/activities. By providing structure and feedback for a total quality effort, most problems can be eliminated or prevented. The implementation team can issue preliminary guidelines on all major facets of the improvement process.

Outcome 2: Manager/Employee Responsibilities and Behaviors

The improvement process produces a set of behaviors and responsibilities unique to managers and employees. Responsibilities evolve, proactive behavior replaces reaction, and managers and employees accept new definitions of their roles, tasks, and actions. Managers may need to assume all or most of the following responsibilities:

1. Provide constancy of purpose

2. Establish trust

3. Lead employees rather than purely direct their actions

4. Improve efficiency and effectiveness for the entire department

5. Interact with and complement other departments rather than erecting barriers

6. Achieve organizational goals and objectives

7. Improve systems through and with subordinates

8. Empower workers to perform to their maximum potential

9. Establish communication and feedback with employees and superiors

Employees (workers) also share in responsibilities and are given the potential to exceed personal and company goals. Workers assume the following responsibilities:

1. Participate in improvement of the system

2. Offer creative, constructive solutions to problems as well prevent them

3. Assist managers in achieving company goals

4. Participate in maintaining an effective feedback system

5. Assist management and other employees in effective training

Change affects the responsibilities of all of the organization's employees and encourages cooperation, coordination, and mutual benefit.

Outcome 3: The Team Process

Outcome 3 signals the beginning of the team process. Training should begin with individuals interested in and motivated to support the team and the team's objectives. Teams should be facilitated by knowledgeable persons trained in the team improvement process. Teams will develop, with guidance and direction from management, a framework that defines the operational, organizational, and communication systems. Guidelines should include the following.

1. Identification of core values, mission, and purpose. Identify and "live" core values. Each team must have a stated purpose and mission, which describes its reason for existence. A shared purpose must unite and strengthen the R&D team. Members need to feel united in a joint effort that benefits each individual and the organization. Without this unity of purpose, individuals will become disenfranchised, and the team will struggle for its existence.

2. Choice of team leader and leadership behavior. The key participant during the formative stages of a team is the facilitator. The facilitator must understand the entire team process, be self-confident, communicate effectively, set achievable goals and objectives, encourage and motivate team behavior, create trust, maintain a sense of consistency, and be willing to yield for the good of the team.

Leadership behavior may be required of all team participants. Leaders set clear goals, establish strong values, and empower individuals to support their mission. Leaders prevent problems and give the team the chance to succeed and fail. Leaders use failure to improve the system rather than blame the participants.

3. Expectations for the team. Expectations for teams involve both a description of the method to achieve a set of objectives and a clear vision of the goals to be achieved. Expectations form the framework around which teams are structured and, therefore, must be measurable. Expectations of R&D teams should reflect the outcomes desired as a result of the team conforming to agreed-upon standards of performance. Realistic time frames, improvement potential, and employee effort are performance standards that must be agreed upon prior to embarking on a team improvement process. (For additional information, see Abstract 6.3 at the end of this chapter.)

4. Team behavior.   Creativity and innovation are direct results of an environment that promotes these attributes. Teams need to reach consensus on the behaviors that are acceptable and then recognize those actions that are positive contributors. Teams need to recognize the holistic nature of the individual by accepting both the emotional and cognitive person. Establishing a realistic range of expected behaviors and recognizing positive attributes provides the team a framework for examining its emotional health. Like any system, frequent audits (reviews) of the psychological and behavioral nature of the team reveal areas for improvement. The team needs to create a model of desired behaviors and then address the social and managerial systems that support and promote these results.

Preventing negative, destructive, or self-serving behavior should become a priority in the initial stages of development. Preventive systems, instituted to avoid conflicts and negative behavior, follow total quality principles for ensuring the "cycle of success."

5. Operational procedures.   Creating operational systems to effectively manage the team and accomplish objectives is a critical requirement to ensure a successful effort. Each R&D team must address the following structural elements: (1) methods to present ideas, needs, and requirements; (2) responsibility assignment; (3) task assignment and follow up; (4) discipline; (5) lateral and external communications; (6) rewards and recognition; (7) reporting structure; (8) "power sharing"; (9) creation of goals and objectives; (10) team behavior problems such as "groupthink"; (11) measuring progress; and (12) resource allocation.

6. Decision making and consensus.   Decision making within a team is a cooperative (joint), collaborative effort. It is a partnership between members to achieve common goals that strengthen and energize the team. Decisions are reached through consensus (i.e., mutual agreement between individuals operating in a nonthreatening environment).

Consensus is achieved through free and open expression in an environment where trust exists between the members. Each team member must respect the opinion of each individual, yet consider decisions in terms of the common good. Each team member should be accountable and responsible for his or her actions and the team's decisions.

7. Measuring team progress. In order for teams to improve, they must be measured. Measuring team progress requires that a "scoresheet" be used. The scoresheet measures team structure, communications (internal and external), ability to resolve conflicts, individual satisfaction, success of recognition process, effective team/management interface, level and magnitude of management support, adequacy of team behaviors, and the amount and quality of team effectiveness. Additional performance measures include regularity of team meetings, task and team accomplishments, frequency of interaction, clarity of purpose and meaning, number and frequency of delays and bottlenecks, maintenance of consistency, amount of "true" progress, amount and level of creativity, and a measurement of the "team comfort factor" (i.e., satisfaction level of team members with each other).

Each team should create a unique set of performance measures that describe its progress. In *The Human Side of Enterprise*, Douglas McGregor[5] describes ten such characteristics of an effective team:

1. Atmosphere (environment) of team is informal, comfortable, and relaxed.

2. Discussion exists freely, with active participation from all teams.

3. Objectives (goals) of the team are well understood and accepted by everyone.

4. Members listen to each other.

5. There is disagreement; it is constructive, not abusive.

6. Decisions are reached by consensus.

7. Team members are free to express their feelings. Hidden agendas are avoided.

8. Tasks, responsibilities, and assignments are made clear and accepted by all.

9. Team leader does not dominate the team, but facilitates progress.

10. The team is self-conscious about its own operations.

8. Team/management interface. A proactive management style that coaches rather than controls the team is recommended. Control of the team occurs from internal and external sources. Power is shared freely within the team, with guidance and direction provided externally by management to the team. Teams must structure their power-sharing ability and not leave it to chance. Teams should welcome "outsiders" who assist them in their efforts. It is the responsibility of the R&D team to communicate with management concerning its activities. The team should establish frequent reviews with management to focus on tasks, accomplishments, and resources rather than arguments, petty problems, and politics.

9. Rewards and recognition. Individual and collective recognition is required for healthy, productive teams. Individual efforts that benefit the team need to be celebrated. Structure rewards to recognize team members, management, and individuals. Recognizing team behavior builds self-esteem, pride of workmanship, and a sense of accomplishment. Develop a reward process, with management's support, and then evaluate its effectiveness. Keep rewards simple and straightforward and the process consistent and fair. Reward the team as a group, and let the team reward individual efforts.

10. Esprit de corps (motivation and team spirit). Team members form the foundation of any collaborative effort and as such require nurturing. Motivating people requires that (1) a person's critical needs be met, (2) self-worth be encouraged, (3) barriers that impede improvement be removed, (4) relationships be built upon trust, (5) stress-producers be reduced, (6) training and education be provided, and (7) people be empowered.

Team spirit (esprit de corps) refers to the enjoyment, energy, and camaraderie developed within the team. As a human enterprise, a team must ensure that individuals benefit from the interchange. Team spirit addresses those benefits that individuals use to support and commit to the enterprise. Without this component, individual "buy-in" is weak and fragmented and the team is ineffective.

Although a framework should allow some flexibility to account for team initiatives, haphazard planning can send negative signals throughout the organization. The key idea at this stage is to provide some type of structure up front, allowing for modifications (approved by the implementation team) and adjustments as needed. Little structure communicates lack of intent or justification. During the early stages, too little control is more negative than too much control.

Outcome 4: Communication

Outcome 4 focuses on communication. This is an ongoing process that informs the organization as to the progress of the improvement effort, changing goals and objectives, and other modifications/additions associated with the effort. At this stage, publicizing success stories, sharing favorable experiences, networking, and system-wide review represent positive feedback. One major component, lacking in many R&D total quality efforts, is positive reinforcing communication. This is a behavioral characteristic, especially when emulating leadership. Rewarding managers, individuals, and teams for positive behavior is critical for success, improved quality, and future productivity. Most rewards take the form of recognition, directed specifically at employees or teams. Rewarding positive behavior not only demonstrates commitment, but also adds credence and support to the effort. It requires a totally different attitude and behavior from management. Training, which begins formally at this stage, may be needed for managers to facilitate this behavior. Subtle forms of communication, such as body language, actions, support, and visible commitment, all communicate management's intent and priorities. Frequently, the best of efforts are killed at this stage due to lack of proper and effective communication.

Outcome 5: Monitoring Mechanism

Outcome 5 involves the creation of a monitoring mechanism for the total quality effort. This is a key ingredient for success and the most frequent omission. The implementation team needs to issue effective guidelines concerning achievable project goals, how to establish and monitor, team membership, resource allocation, reporting structures, and preparation of reports. The monitor system should include:

1. Monitor projects and activities to determine fit and applicability to corporate goals and objectives agreed to in Stage 3

2. Reporting of progress or delays by teams, management, etc.

3. Continue following objectives and guidelines

4. Benefit, application potential

5. Costs, resource requirements, employee/management requirements

6. Project completion to date

7. Training needed and required

8. Identification of key feedback indicators required to achieve success

By establishing a monitoring mechanism, management and teams complete the feedback loop. Progress is easily tracked and evaluated for potential benefit. Core values, company goals, and personal objectives remain synchronized.

STAGE 5: EVALUATION AND IMPROVEMENT PHASE

Evaluation and improvement complement those outcomes described in Stage 4. This phase involves monitoring progress while instituting improvements throughout the organization. Monitoring mechanisms and measurements need to consider both internal and external needs. During this stage, company (corporate/organizational) systems are prioritized and monitored. External efforts focus on meeting and exceeding customer requirements (satisfaction). Tasks include developing and implementing a customer satisfaction measurement program, supplier review and evaluation, and competitive review and evaluation. Internal measures include establishment of system-wide performance measures, system/employee/ management feedback, and internal process measurements and reviews.

Total quality must reflect a system-wide commitment to the goal of serving the strategic needs of the organization's customer bases, through internal and external measurement systems, information and authority sharing, and committed leadership. In "Making Total Quality Work," Olian and Rynes[6] list the following pertinent data: (1) organizational synergies critical to achieving a pervasive culture; (2) the essentials of total quality; (3) organizational processes that support total quality; (4) establishing quality goals, including a look at Six Sigma and benchmarking; (5) training for total quality; (6) recognition and rewards; (7) measuring customer reactions and satisfaction; (8) developing four areas of measurement: operation, financial, breakthrough, and employee contributions; and (9) getting stakeholder support. (For additional information, see Abstract 1.5 at the end of Chapter 1.)

Outcomes of Stage 5

Stage 5 encompasses internal and external measurements that relate to both R&D performance and customer satisfaction. Included is an evaluation of inputs (suppliers) and their effect on the company's operations and customers. Outcome 2 formalizes the systematic improvement process as an available method for total quality.

ENDNOTES

1. Source: Frank Voehl. *Leadership and Management Quality*, Coral Springs, FL: Strategy Associates, 1993/1994.
2. Miller Associates advocate that the "whole systems" process of planning the total quality organization is a breakthrough because it is a different way of thinking about change. See Design For Total Quality, pp. 15–16.
3. Management control can be defined as the integration of the process of (a) long-range planning of the activities of the organization, (b) short-term planning (usually one year), and (c) monitoring activities to ensure the accomplishment of the desired results. The management control

process thus follows the development of major strategic directions that are set in the strategic planning process. This definition roughly follows the framework described by Robert N. Anthony in *Planning and Control: A Framework for Analysis* (Boston: Division of Research, Harvard Business School, 1965).

4. Porter suggests that the objective of a competitor analysis is to develop a profile of the nature and success of the likely strategy changes each competitor might make, each competitor's probable response to the range of feasible strategic moves other firms could initiate, and each competitor's probable reaction to the array of industry changes and broader environmental shifts that might occur. Sophisticated competitor analysis is needed to answer such questions as, "Who should we pick a fight with in the industry, and with what sequence of moves?" "What is the meaning of that competitor's strategic move and how seriously should we take it?" "What areas should we avoid because the competitor's response will be emotional or desperate?" (Porter, Michael. *Competitive Strategy*, New York: John Wiley & Sons, 1988, p. 38.)

5. McGregor, Douglas. *The Human Side of Enterprise*, New York: McGraw-Hill, 1960.

6. In "Making Total Quality Work: Aligning Organizational Processes, Performance Measures, and Stakeholders" (*Human Resources Management*, 30(3), pp. 303–333, Fall 1991), Judy Olian and Sara Rynes identify integration of the corporate measurement system as one of the critical elements in successful total quality implementation and achieving competitive advantage.

ABSTRACTS

ABSTRACT 6.1
THE EMPOWERMENT OF SERVICE WORKERS:
WHAT, WHY, HOW, AND WHEN

Bowen, David E. and Lawler, Edward E. III
Sloan Management Review, Spring 1992, pp. 31–39

"Before service organizations rush into empowerment programs, they need to determine whether and how empowerment fits their situation," say the authors. They first compare the production-line approach to service with the empowerment approach and show how both have been successful. The authors then discuss the benefits of empowerment:

- There is quicker on-line response to customer needs during service delivery.

- There is quicker on-line response to dissatisfied customers during service recovery.

- Employees feel better about their jobs and themselves.

- Employees will interact with customers with more warmth and enthusiasm.

- Empowered employees can be a great source of service ideas.

- There is word-of-mouth advertising and customer retention.

The possible disadvantages of empowerment include:

- A greater dollar investment in selection and training

- Higher labor costs

- Slower or inconsistent service delivery

- Violations of "fair play"

- Giveaways and bad decisions

The authors describe three approaches which represent increasing degrees of employee empowerment. In the "suggestion involvement" approach, employees contribute ideas but maintain the same daily work activities. In the "job involvement" approach, employees have considerable freedom in deciding how to do the work. Often, this includes extensive use of teams.

In the "high involvement" approach, employees are involved in the total organization's performance. The authors offer a rating scale for determining whether the production-line approach or empowerment is best suited to a particular service organization. The ratings are based on basic business strategy, on the tie to the customer, on technology, on the business environment, and on types of managers and employees. (©*Quality Abstracts*)

ABSTRACT 6.2
HOW TO AVOID FAILURE WHEN IMPLEMENTING A QUALITY EFFORT

Numerof, Rita E. and Abrams, Michael N.
Tapping the Network Journal, Winter 1992–93, pp. 10–14

Quality is dead at ABC Corporation, say the authors, despite the official line that "Quality was now going back to the line. Quality was no longer a separate function but once again part of 'everyone's' job." The authors analyze the reasons for failure of the seven-year quality initiative at this nameless *Fortune 500* company, and they discuss seven reasons for TQM's demise there:

1. Quality was established as a parallel process to the existing organization rather than as an integral part of it.

2. Quality activities, such as training and building employee involvement, were seen as the measure of success, rather than as means to a specifically defined end.

3. The company failed to define a narrow range of strategic business issues to address systematically, leaving teams to charge off on their own.

4. They failed to see quality improvement as a continuous process with a myriad of internal and external customer interfaces managed as a strategic process.

5. They failed to define a specific role for the company's management team beyond creating vision and awareness.

6. They failed to see improved relations with the employee as the foundation for improved relations with the customer.

7. They failed to understand the complex process of organizational change and manage it carefully.

But TQM is not the "mystical, time-consuming, resource-intensive process that it's made out to be," the authors insist. "In fact, the steps involved are fairly straightforward." They conclude with a brief listing of 8 steps involved in a quality effort and 13 key questions to address for successful quality implementation. (©*Quality Abstracts*)

ABSTRACT 6.3
TEAM DEVELOPMENT: THIS IS HOW IT'S DONE

Gold, Jeffrey (editor)
Executive Development, 1992, Vol. 5 No. 3, pp. 1–32

This entire issue of *Executive Development* is devoted to the process of developing teams—both training members of a management team and training members of work teams. The individual articles include:

- "Building Our Team—From the End of a Rope"—which explores training a management team through outdoor training

- "Measures Which Help You Work Together as a Team"—which discusses three different feedback instruments: the Types of Work Index, the Team Management Index, and the Linking Skills Index

- "Improved Teamworking Using a Computer System"—which reviews the computer-based Belbin *Interplace III Expert System* that is used to help determine and understand an individual's team role

- "From Public to Private: The Team Approach at Scottish Hydro Electric plc"—which outlines a development program for 130 senior managers

- "Management Team Building: An Experience at BT"—which explains a management team development workshop at British Telecom

- "Organizational Change Through Team Development at BICC"—which describes a senior management team development exercise at a company implementing work teams throughout its organization

- "Team-Built Teams"—which reviews three-day team-building workshops at Colworth House Laboratories as part of a total quality initiative

- "Developing the Team at Northamptonshire Police"—which describes a management team development effort

- "Know Thy Team—and Play Your Trump Card!"—which outlines the *TeamBuilder* analysis of five team roles used at a London-based design company
- "Improvement Teams at Champion Spark Plug"—which describes workshops to train total quality management improvement teams at a manufacturing plant (©*Quality Abstracts*)

CHAPTER 7

QFD: A TOOL FOR MANAGING CUSTOMER SATISFACTION*

INTRODUCTION

Quality function deployment (QFD) assists business and service industry personnel in managing customer satisfaction. Managing customer satisfaction through understanding customer expectations and perceptions is a key aspect of total quality management and an essential requirement for lasting success. Although QFD is generally associated with the engineering design and development of products (or goods), this tool serves a useful and unique purpose in mapping customer satisfaction. How QFD can be utilized, in a simple form, to manage and profit from continuously

* From "1992 Proceedings of the Section on Quality and Productivity," Alexandria, VA: American Statistical Association, pp. 180–186.

improving customer satisfaction is the focus of this chapter. Overall, the following considerations should be addressed:

- Outline the place of QFD in product development
- Define QFD R&D and describe its uses
- How to expanded the House of Quality (major tool)
- Which tools and techniques to use
- Potential benefits/costs
- How and what implementation/applications are available
- Cost
- Timeliness
- The role of quality "conformance to requirements"

Why Products Fail (Crosby)

Misunderstood wants and needs	45%	Competitive action	17%
Product problems	29%	Poor timing	14%
Poor marketing	25%	Technical problems	12%
High cost	19%		

- A major issue for developers is whether to change the technology or the customer's perceptions. Traditional quality methods usually only focus on the communication gap between design and delivery.

$$\begin{array}{ccccc} \text{Customer} & \rightarrow & \text{Understood} & \rightarrow \\ \text{needs} & & \text{by organization} \\ \\ \text{Designed} & \rightarrow & \text{Delivered} & \rightarrow & \text{Perceived} \\ \text{by organization} & & \text{by organization} \end{array}$$

- QFD provides a better definition of product that requires less design.

QFD was developed by the Japanese to assure consistent quality of their automobiles and components, beginning with the initial engineering design. QFD brings together engineering, design, marketing, sales, and manufacturing people to design and build a product that meets customer requirements. QFD combines resources and facilitates corporate energies so that products can be manufactured quickly, with a high degree of acceptability, at appreciably lower costs. By making customer needs and requirements the prime requirement, satisfaction is more easily attained and a more lasting effect is achieved.

THE CONCEPT OF SATISFACTION

Satisfaction is an emotional response that dictates the behavior and actions of a customer's purchasing abilities. Those products and services that provide satisfaction are likely to be purchased in the future. Given its attitudinal component, satisfaction is readily defined as the difference between what a customer expects and what he or she perceives to occur. Therefore, managing these expectations and perceptions becomes critical for all businesses to maintain customer satisfaction and provide a unique and lasting quality experience.

QFD, applied in a simple but powerful form, provides business and service industries with a method to manage customer expectations and perceptions. This information provides a tool for designing services to meet ongoing (changing) customer needs as well as a useful evaluation tool for improving the quality of the service (or product). Those industries and businesses that practice this technique maintain a significant competitive advantage, provide consistent quality, improve customer satisfaction, and cut lead times significantly.

The methods for constructing a QFD grid to accomplish both design and evaluation functions are detailed in this chapter. QFD is especially useful in R&D organizations given its ability to match customer requirements with internal operations and functions. The R&D organization provides both service and product, satisfying its customers along a broader spectrum of needs, wants, and desires.

Before using the QFD format, researchers must address the unique needs, wants, and desires of their customers. Measuring these requirements for complete customer satisfaction demands that researchers fully understand design and development criteria, predicted product performance, and functionality. Given that customer satisfaction is the measurable gap between expected and perceived performance, it is critical to define customer requirements in terms of expectations and perceptions.

Expectations, traditionally the most critical component, measure what the customer expects combined with experiences and attitudes developed previous to the encounter. **Perceptions**, which occur after the product or service encounter, measure service delivery and post-consumption satisfaction. Ironically, R&D organizations offer many service-oriented characteristics and must also develop and manage customer satisfaction and service quality.

Satisfaction, as described, cannot be fully measured. Evaluating satisfaction requires a measurement of customer expectations, perceptions, attitudes, bias, past experiences, and likes and dislikes. Satisfaction is a *momentary*, emotional response which involves cognitive processes greatly affected by environmental factors. Those individuals and organizations that continue to measure satisfaction as a response rather than the result of numerous responses and causal factors do not grasp its full impact and may lose their ability to accurately and precisely gauge the customer.

Customers measure satisfaction with products or services on a changing scale called the **satisfaction continuum**. This continuum adequately describes the fluid nature of satisfaction and suggests its short-term perspective. Satisfaction is greatly affected by environmental factors, previous outcomes and experiences, bias, warnings, and pre- and post-consumption feelings and attitudes. In order to manage satisfaction and attitude (the long-term component of satisfaction), the manager must identify and measure the sources (causes) of both satisfaction and dissatisfaction. Satisfaction must be examined within the context of the decision made (i.e., those cognitive processes used to facilitate the feeling of satisfaction). In addition, factors surrounding immediate response include:

1. The interactional cooperation between provider and receiver

2. Multiplicity of emotional factor

3. The amount and type of customer involvement

4. Past experiences and influences

5. Perceived business/service competence

Management of expectations becomes a critical concern for R&D organizations. R&D organizations must manage the services or causes of satisfaction/dissatisfaction instead of reacting to a single response. Manage the situations and circumstances that can quickly affect the customer's perception. The momentary nature of satisfaction requires intensive measurement, education, and follow-through. Managing customer satisfaction as a result rather than an interlocking set of emotional, environmental, and decision processes is dangerous. Customer feedback becomes a necessity in an environment that is rapidly changing. Manage customer satisfaction by examining what supports the customer's positive view of the organization.

QFD used in the context of customer satisfaction examines both the customer's needs and desires based upon those characteristics that are deliverable by the organization. QFD will be examined as a tool for managing overall customer satisfaction as well as providing a measurement of continuous improvement. QFD, which is a design and development tool generally not associated with customer satisfaction, remains a viable and useful technique for evaluating R&D performance versus customer needs. QFD is a tool for developing and refining measures of internal and external performance that relate directly to elements of customer satisfaction.

QFD: USING CUSTOMER SATISFACTION
AS A BUILDING BLOCK

QFD is a fully integrated technique, which consistently correlates measures of performance with predetermined customer needs. It fully utilizes the team approach, relying heavily on brainstorming, Pareto analysis, cause-and-effect principles, and consensus. These concepts determine both internal and external measures of customer satisfaction. The QFD team discusses and analyzes products or services, detailing customer requirements, needs, expectations, and perceptions. Internal measures refer to process-oriented, systematic (operational) elements in contrast to external measures that are derived from customers through surveys, focus groups, and intensive competitive/comparative analyses. Customer feedback provides the control link to company performance. (For additional information, see Abstract 7.1 at the end of this chapter.)

Traditionally, QFD involves an evolutionary process of defining four key phases: design, planning, process, and product, with increasingly sophisticated methodological complexity. Each phase represents a further refinement of key characteristics (variables) that are critical to the customer. The QFD team refines these determinants through piggybacking, synthesis, and expansion.

A simplistic application of the QFD principle serves the purpose of illustrating its use. Systematically transferring customer requirements into tangible measures, which can be related to specific performance within the R&D department, can assist in improving customer satisfaction. By listening to the customer in order to understand and interpret the customer's needs and wants, the principles of QFD can benefit both the customer and the R&D organization.

For this application, three key components detail the QFD process. The first element is an intensive focus on the entire dimension of customer satisfaction. This phase involves data collection and synthesis, competitive awareness, customer feedback, and frequent internal/external dialogue. The second phase exists concurrently with the first phase and involves the use of multifunctional teams (including customers). The third phase (ongoing) encompasses detailed advance planning to include follow up, frequent evaluation, customer participation, and review.

CONSTRUCTING A QFD

Constructing a QFD into a grid format requires detailed information on two elements:

1. Customer needs, wants, and desires

2. Business deliverables that match customer requirements and expectations

After assembling the initial information, the QFD process begins by listing customer requirements. Requirements originate from the customer's expectations and perceptions of product and service performance. These requirements form the basis of what will satisfy the customer. Customer requirements should be formulated by asking three simple questions:

1. What do customers really want?

2. Why do they need it?

3. How do they know when they have received it?

Requirements define needs, wants, and desires instead of simply solutions. A defined and measurable benefit must be associated with each customer requirement. Customer requirements include basic needs and wants (not generally verbalized) and those additional requirements (often verbalized) that truly satisfy. In addition, requirements that surprise or excite (delight) the customer generally yield a competitive edge. Although focus groups of customers and surveys can provide this information, it is critical that researchers place themselves "in the shoes" of their customers to verbalize these requirements.

Concurrently, the QFD team lists those business deliverables that will be measured to gauge customer satisfaction, productivity, performance, and efficiency. Business deliverables represent internal measures of R&D performance. By assigning a priority to these, the QFD team evaluates for effectiveness, accuracy, and substance.

Customer requirements, needs, and expectations form the vertical axis of the QFD, with business deliverables listed horizontally (see Figure 7.1).

Each customer attribute must correspond to one or more business deliverables along the QFD grid. This phase represents the most dynamic and complex step in the QFD process.

The major difficulty in using the QFD technique results from the highly evolutionary, interactive process of choosing customer requirements and business deliverables. Choosing customer requirements involves both the customer (end user) and the researcher, management, or other suppliers. The process of choosing, evaluating, and finalizing choices is a distinctive learning process. It is not atypical to find that organizations offer solutions to customers prior to determining their true needs. This results in a distorted and biased view of customer needs. By "fitting" solutions to unwanted needs, the customer is distanced from the QFD process and left unsatisfied. The cognitive and emotional aspects of customer satisfac-

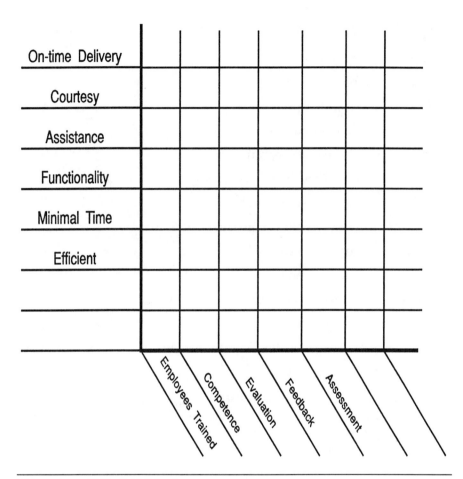

Figure 7.1 QFD Grid Matrix.

tion require a thorough review of potential customer needs prior to the QFD process. For these reasons and others, the Taguchi experiments are often combined with traditional QFD, especially in the design of experiments phase. (For additional information, see Abstract 7.2 at the end of this chapter.)

Customer requirements focus primarily on four main categories: employees, product and service performance, and support. Typical customer requirements related to customer satisfaction include:

- Minimizing existing rework
- Reducing existing scrap
- Loyalty

- Improved flow of products
- Improved communication
- Stable processes
- Successful production processes
- Improved routing of customer requests
- Identifying new market opportunities
- Access to new equipment and technology
- Eliminating nonvalue-added activities
- Maximizing resources (human, technological)
- Using technology for a competitive edge
- Timely access to new and existing technology
- Improved materials/components required for production
- Exceeding customer expectations
- Identifying and implementing key productivity/quality enhancements
- Utilizing the best technologies

In essence, the customer of the R&D organization wants to use the expertise and technology of R&D to enhance their customer's satisfaction. These requirements help to quantify those expectations and perceptions related to customer satisfaction.

Business (service) deliverables (internal R&D performance measures) relate directly to the requirements specified by the customer and are controlled by the organization. A typical listing of business deliverables follows:

Employees
- Teamwork
- Attitude
- Product/service knowledge
- Expertise
- Communication
- Creativity/innovativeness
- Experience
- Trust

Product performance
- Rework/scrap

- Reliability
- Thoroughness
- Applicability
- Cost benefit
- Process capability
- Compliance
- Consistency

Service performance
- Delivery performance
- Accuracy
- Timeliness
- Follow-through
- Satisfaction

Support
- Cooperation
- Coordination
- Planning and execution
- Productivity
- "Bottlenecks"
- Dissemination/distribution of information
- Feedback

After listing these business deliverables, the QFD team needs to examine the importance and strength of the relationship between them and customer requirements. A strong positive relationship (correlation) between a deliverable and a customer requirement is critical for control and monitoring for inconsistencies. A strong negative relationship, indicated by an asterisk (not shown in Figure 7.2), needs to be monitored closely for changes that could lead to adverse performance. (For additional information, see Abstract 7.3 at the end of this chapter.)

Detailing customer requirements and business deliverables assists the QFD process by providing measurable information to track overall performance. Those key characteristics with strong relationships form the nucleus of a complete customer satisfaction program.

In traditional applications, the QFD team produces a graphic representation of its endeavors. The QFD process yields what is commonly called the House of Quality. The House of Quality evaluates customer needs, business deliverables, competitive pressures, and product/process targets listed, with the importance of each characteristic indicated. A traditional House of Quality graphic representation of the QFD process is displayed in Figure 7.3. Given the implications for quality, the House of Quality for the R&D segment is illustrated in Figure 7.4.

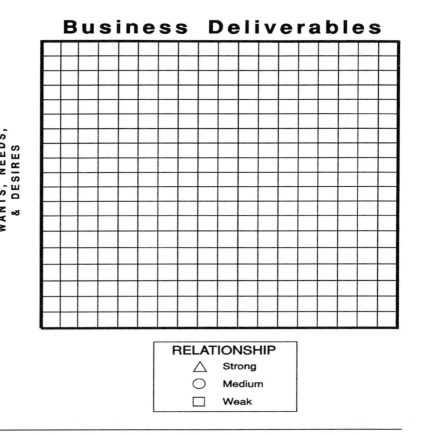

Figure 7.2 Relationship of Business Deliverables to Customer Requirements, Wants, Needs and Desires.

The benefits of using such a tool include:

1. Improved lead time (concept to market)

2. Flexibility

3. Accurate, reliable measures of provider and receiver performance

4. Competitive analysis

5. Critical evaluation of business operations

6. A method for measuring customer satisfaction and product/service performance

For additional information, see Abstract 7.4 at the end of this chapter.

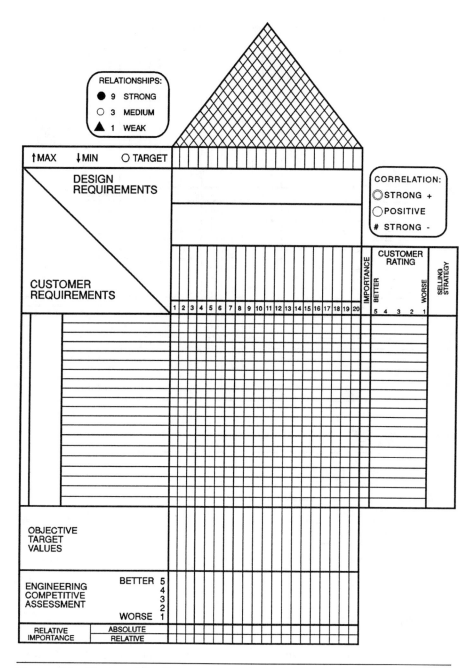

Figure 7.3 House of Quality.

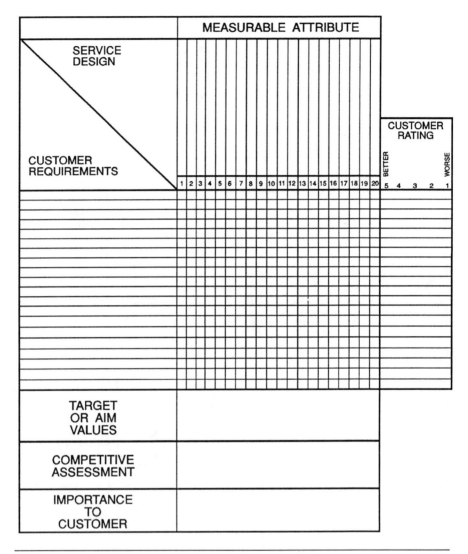

Figure 7.4 Service Deliverables Matrix.

CONCLUSION

The QFD process involves synthesis, data gathering, and communication. The key concept exposed by QFD is the development of a communication network between supplier and customer. QFD promises success if customer and performance both interact and interrelate. Measures of performance, developed by the QFD team and the customer, provide a road map (benchmark) for success. (For additional information, see Abstract 7.5 at the end of this chapter.)

ENDNOTES

Fortuna, R.M. "Beyond Quality: Taking SPC Upstream." *Quality Progress*, pp. 23–28, 1988.

McElroy. J. "QFD: Building the House of Quality." *Automotive Industries*, pp. 30–32, 1989.

Oliver, R.L. "What Is Customer Satisfaction?" *The Wharton Magazine*, 5(2), pp. 36-41, 1981.

Parasuraman, A., Zeithaml, V.A., and Berry, L.L. "A Conceptual Model of Service Quality and Its Implications for Future Research. " *Journal of Marketing*, 49(4), pp. 41–50, 1985.

Webster, C. "Influences upon Customer Expectations of Services. " *Journal of Services Marketing*, 5(1), pp. 5–17, 1991.

ABSTRACTS

ABSTRACT 7.1
AFTER PRODUCT QUALITY IN JAPAN: MANAGEMENT QUALITY

Yahagi, Seiichiro
National Productivity Review, Autumn 1992, pp. 501–515

This is one of the most important new articles to come out of Japan in 1992, and the implications are enormous. The author proposes the use of expert systems featuring a 12-factor model organized into 41 "elements" for measuring subfactors. Japanese management has moved beyond product quality, says the author, to an emphasis on total integrated management (TIM)—management concerned about each facet of the company and interrelating them into a concerted, comprehensive corporate management policy of innovation. The author has developed an expert system which measures the 12 factors that determine management quality, divided into 41 subfactors:

- Corporate history: past, present, and future

- Corporate climate: core climate and culture

- Strategic alliances: objectives and coherence

- Channels: suppliers and buyers

- Management cycle: vision, strategy, planning, organizing, implementing, and controlling

- Environment: economic, societal, and global

- Management targets: inputs, markets, technologies, and products

- Business structure: business fields, business mix, and market standing

- Management resources: money, materials, information, and people

- Management design: system, organization, authority, and responsibility

- Management functions: decision making, interrelationships, and quality

- Management performance: growth, scale, stability, profit, and market share

He sees six factors as critical to the success of a company: management cycle, business structure, management resources, management design, corporate culture, and management performance. These six factors are interrelated in a circulatory system of management quality factors which have a cause-and-effect relationship as follows. The management cycle acts as the driver and influences the four factors of structure, resources, design, and culture which, in turn, affect management performance. If the quality level of the management cycle is low, then the six factors generate a negative or bad feedback loop, which finds management passively waiting until poor results of management performance force reactionary feedback into the management flow.* If the quality level of the management cycle is "high," then these six factors generate an excellent feedforward loop in which management perceives the strategies and plans needed for success of each management factor and then proactively formulates and implements them.

The author's consulting organization conducts an annual survey of the management practices of Japanese firms, and in this article he presents the results of the most recent survey, which represented input from about 200 firms. Graphs and charts show comparisons between the worst-scoring and best-scoring companies, and the author uses creative graphics to illustrate his analytical technique and to summarize questionnaire responses. From this comparison he deduces a number of principles: (1) management quality factors must be well balanced, (2) management cycle is the key to the management quality loop, and (3) the dynamics of TIM must be considered. He then goes on to describe the management cycle, which consists of the following key components: vision, strategy, planning, organizing, implementing, and controlling. The author recommends using an annual questionnaire to first analyze management factors within a company and then develop a multiphase action plan to restructure an organization for TIM. This article by Yahagi is must reading for anyone who wants to remain on the leading edge of new application-oriented technology.

ABSTRACT 7.2
TAGUCHI METHODS: A HANDS-ON APPROACH

Peace, Glen Stuart
Addison-Wesley, Reading, Mass., 1993, 522 pp.

"The intention of this book," explains the author, "is to provide a basic guide for solving and gaining insight into the everyday quality problems and processes for which the reader is responsible...The focused audience is the supervisor, the engineer, the technician, or any other person who is on the front line and must handle quality problems...This is meant to be a

---

* According to Yahagi, the circulatory aspects of the management quality system are a key to understanding the relationship of this system to others, such as the Malcolm Baldrige National Quality Award. See Chapter 8 for additional detail.

basic step-by-step guide of simple techniques related in down-to-earth language." The author does succeed in providing a clear path, but the nontechnical user may be put off by the algebraic equations, orthogonal arrays, and linear graphs. However, the reader who sticks with the book will be rewarded. The author acknowledges but avoids the controversies which surround Taguchi's work. The first chapter provides a conceptual overview of Taguchi's contributions to quality. The remainder of the book's 23 chapters are divided into 4 sections which progress logically through the steps involved in designing, conducting, and analyzing experiments designed to isolate problems and optimize the manufacturing process:

1. **Planning the experiment.** Chapters focus on: forming the experimentation team, determining objectives and using basic quality tools, addressing measurement considerations, selecting the independent variables, and adopting an experimental strategy.

2. **Designing the experiment.** This section covers orthogonal arrays to meaningful and cost-effective experimental designs, degrees of freedom, linear graphs, incorporating "noise factors" into the experiment, and experimental error and bias.

3. **Conducting the experiment.** In this part, the author describes test plan development, preparing the experiments, and conducting the experiment.

4. **Analyzing the experiment.** In this section, he explains the various types of analyses needed to understand the experimental data: level average analysis, classified attribute analysis, signal-to-noise ratio calculations, nominal-the-best data analysis, and dynamic signal-to-noise computations. The book concludes with special cases: modifying experimental design to handle special case factors, multiple quality characteristic analysis, and dealing with missing and infeasible data.

The book contains three large appendices: orthogonal arrays, linear graphs, and interactions between two column tables. (©*Quality Abstracts*)

ABSTRACT 7.3
CONTINUOUS IMPROVEMENTS TO MEET
CUSTOMER EXPECTATIONS

Greenwood, Frank
Journal of Systems Management, February 1992, pp. 13–15

Raising office productivity, says the author, depends on matching the Voice of the Customer to the Voice of the Process, so process outputs will meet customer expectations. Ascertaining the Voice of the Customer, he says, involves three areas: (a) identifying customer needs and expectations, (b) translating those needs into specific customer targets, and (c) establishing a measurement system that captures the level of customer satisfaction. He discusses several tools to capture the Voice of the Customer: surveys/questionnaires, benchmarking, focus groups and interviews, market research, and watching and listening. To monitor the Voice of the Process, data must be identified which track important characteristics that impact customer satisfaction. "A measurement method provides a window through which the process can be observed," says the author. Once the critical characteristics have been selected, appropriate targets must be established that relate the Voice of the Process to the Voice of the Customer. He notes that the human or social aspects of the process must be considered as well. The article gives a theoretical basis for office productivity improvement, but few specific examples. (©*Quality Abstracts*)

ABSTRACT 7.4
WHAT HATH TAGUCHI WROUGHT?

Sprow, Eugene E.
Manufacturing Engineering, April 1992, pp. 57–60

An army of opportunists, touting Taguchi methods as the only "true" tool for problem solving, are misleading many, contends the author—particularly small companies that are stumbling into design of experiments (DOE) for the first time. The author reviews Taguchi's contribution to problem-solving methodology: simplifying, classical DOE techniques to study interactions between a matrix of fewer variables in a process, rather than testing the interactions of all of the factors with each other. This "fractional factorial" approach to DOE has saved time by turning a 25% reject problem into a 5 to 10% problem, and it has been instrumental in bringing quick results to many companies. However, an increasing number of DOE experts are complaining that using Taguchi matrices to the exclusion of other DOE approaches can be counterproductive. The author cites criticisms by Forrest Breyfogle, Hans J. Bajaria, Philip Ross, and Chuck Bradley—recent authors on statistical problem solving. "Taguchi experiments are rough cuts," says Bajaria. "They do not work at the refinement stage. Fractional factorial was designed for use in the research stage to find suspicions. Screening devices must always be followed by another experiment to confirm." To find the last few minor refinements, a full factorial experiment, or classical approach, is necessary. Bajaria suggests using multiple regression, which, in some situations, is almost equivalent to a full factorial. While Taguchi contributed the concept of nominal focus to the definition of quality, says Bajaria, his loss-function explanation complicates a simple concept. "What is often under attack," Bajaria concludes, "is not Taguchi's ideas, but their glamorization by entrepreneurs." (©*Quality Abstracts*)

ABSTRACT 7.5
UNDERSTANDING AND APPLYING QFD IN HEAVY INDUSTRY

Maduri, Omnamasivaya
Journal for Quality and Participation, January–February 1992, pp. 64–69

Quality function deployment (QFD), explains the author, is the process of (a) determining required product functions from the customer's point of view, (b) determining if there are additional features which can, as options, fill the needs of additional customers, and (c) identifying features to be developed and promoted to meet customer needs of which the customer is not yet aware. The QFD process is managed by a cross-functional team to anticipate impediments to quality at various stages in making a product right from the beginning. The author illustrates the QFD system in a research and development project of a 30- to 40-ton rear dumper. Figures in the article show examples of the first three of four key documents in the system:

- The product planning matrix, which translates customer requirements into specified final product control characteristics

- The product deployment matrix, which translates the outputs of the planning matrix into critical components or areas

- Component deployment charts, which identify the design and process parameters, as well as control or checkpoints for each of those parameters

- Operating instructions based on the critical product and process parameters, which identify operations to be performed by plan personnel (©*Quality Abstracts*)

CHAPTER 8

ISO 9000 IN R&D: A VIEW TO THE FUTURE

by Frank Voehl and Greg McLaughlin

PROLOGUE: THE COMING OF THE GLOBAL MARKETPLACE

Throughout history, most research and development organizations have served solely their corporations and local geographic regions. Their externally sponsored funds usually have also come from local or national public funds. All that is changing. First, we have seen the development of global research markets. Routinely, scientists travel thousands of miles to conduct an extended experiment. Also, satellite links are commonly used to join research labs across half the world. Second, we have seen the decreasing role of public funds as governments, both East and West, push R&D organizations to seek other sources of money.[1] Market-oriented training and education of R&D personnel are on the way to becoming market driven. Companies such as Motorola, Xerox, IBM, Proctor & Gamble, General Electric, and others are educating their executives and workers informally, using their own universities and corporate labs.[2] This has created the concept of the "living lab."

Once competition enters the research market, the providers must find ways to distinguish their service from that of their competitors. They look for competitive advantage. Some will seek that edge through providing specialist products or facilities, others through the flexibility of their products and offerings, and yet others through price reduction while adding value. Most, however, will have no option but to compete on the R&D variables of total quality.

While all providers doubtless like to think of themselves as providing a quality service, any provider who complacently assumes that quality will look after itself will rapidly be overtaken by those who listen to the market. Only those providers who consciously strive to meet and exceed the demands of their markets will survive. What does strive mean for R&D professionals? What it does *not* mean is expecting to be rewarded for hard work. The market rewards results, not effort. Clearly, striving for quality means working in some way which more effectively delivers results. Tom Peters would call this customer delight.

OVERVIEW

ISO 9000 Defined

What is ISO 9000? Let's start by defining ISO as a term. According to Sprow, it is short for *isos,* the Greek term for equal, homogeneous, or uniform, which is a deliberate transformation of the acronym for the International Organization for Standardization. This was done deliberately because IOS sounds too much like chaos, and the word order inevitably changes in different languages. One observer has quipped that ISO 9000 stands for International Strategic Opportunity for the 1990s, which it certainly might be. (It sounds a bit like the transliteration of the Union of Japanese Scientists and Engineers into the acronym known as JUSE.)[3]

Quality by Consensus

ISO 9000 began with the launch of Technical Committee 176 in 1979 to deal with generic quality principles to satisfy the need for an international minimum standard for how manufacturing companies establish quality control methods. This included not only control of product quality, but maintaining uniformity and predictability as well. Consumers wanted assurance that in the new world market—whether buying telephones, bread, wheat, or widgets—they would be getting reliable quality for their money today, tomorrow, or next year.

To accomplish this, 20 actively participating countries and half as many additional observer countries met and created, by consensus, a series of quality-system management standards called ISO 9000, which were finally issued in 1987. The standards were based in large part on the 1979 British quality standard BS 5750, as well as the Canadian standard CSA Z299, the American ASQC Z1.15 standard, MIL Q 9858A, and to a limited degree the JUSE-based Deming prize guidelines.[3]

ISO 9000 was a huge success from day one. It was the first ISO standard to go beyond nuts and bolts and attempt to address management practices. It quickly became the most widely known, widely adopted ISO standard and has sold more copies than any standard ISO has ever published. Although it is voluntary thus far, over 97 countries have adopted it as a national standard. According to a recent survey, 82% of European blue-chip companies are familiar with its content and 64% have initiated action to become registered to ISO. Although the numbers on this side of the Atlantic may not be as high, it is of interest here.[3]

The Interrelationships between Quality Assurance and ISO 9000

ISO 9000 is an international standard that requires certified businesses to create and integrate a working quality system. These standards examine the methods and practices a business uses to produce and deliver the products it sells. To understand the impact that ISO 9000 can have on R&D, it is first necessary to focus on the interrelationship that exists between quality assurance (QA) and ISO 9000. The approach that manufacturing organizations have taken to achieve the quality edge has traditionally been QA, and over the past ten years QA in the United States has evolved into total quality. Total quality involves a systematic approach to identifying market needs and honing work methods to meet those needs. Organizations can develop and run their own QA and total quality management (TQM) programs, but many prefer to adopt a recognized standard and to seek external approval for their system. In the United Kingdom, BS 5750 is the standard for QA and total quality systems. Internationally, BS 5750 is known as ISO 9000. The two standards are identical in all but name.

Many R&D organizations in Europe have begun to explore how they can adopt this standard; a few have attained the coveted BSI kitemark (certification symbol).[4] The main reason why so few organizations have achieved certification is the fact that BS 5750/ISO 9000 was initially designed for manufacturing industries and not the scientific community. Its language and approach are alien to most R&D operations. However, its underlying principles, which concentrate on meeting customer needs, are fully applicable in the new R&D marketplace of the global village. Somehow, then, we need to find a way to apply ISO 9000 to this field.

The ISO 9000 standards can be adapted for the benefit of scientists, technicians, and researchers without compromising the professional standards that have developed over many years. However, many ISO 9000 and TQM consultants whose backgrounds are in industry are inadvertently persuading professionals to apply the standard in a manner that is detrimental to good practice.[4]

A different approach is clearly needed. The ISO 9000 standards are a single system originally designed to cover all manufacturing, later extended to the service industries, and now being experimentally used in all types of professions. ISO 9000 certification could become a requirement for any research organization that wants to do business in the international marketplace, even though at this time that notion seems to be a bit of a stretch. ISO 9000 remains a very general set of principles about good management. As such, applying the principles to the specifics of the R&D process is often difficult. It is easy to monitor the outcome but very difficult to monitor the process. Of the 20 standards (modules) contained in ISO 9000, 12 modules have direct application, not including the module covering the use of statistics, which is covered elsewhere in this text.

Getting a Feel for ISO 9000 Integration

The following are the ISO 9000 modules that are of particular importance to R&D activities, especially from the administrative viewpoint:

Module 1: Management responsibility

Module 2: Quality system

Module 3: Contract review

Module 4: Design control

Module 6: Purchasing

Module 7: Purchaser-supplied product

Module 9: Process control

Module 13: Control of nonconforming product

Module 14: Corrective action

Module 16: Quality records

Module 17: Internal quality audits

Module 18: Training

Fundamentals of the Quality Assurance Management System

The words "quality assurance" in the context of total quality have a certain mystique about them, giving the impression of a complex set of skills which few will ever acquire. The early developers of QA no doubt kept themselves in the consulting business through continuing to foster that image. However, the reality is that QA is a fancy term for any well-run management system. This means that QA is not esoteric, complex, or beyond the reach of nonspecialists. If it were, what would be the point of it? Any QA system that is going to work has to be simple, fitting comfortably alongside—or even inside—everyday working practices.[4] It has to be economical, in that it saves more than it costs. And it has to be longlasting, not just a here today, gone tomorrow type of program.

In essence, total quality involves an approach to organizing work which ensures that:

- The mission and objectives of the organization are clear and known to all

- The systems through which work will be done are well thought out, foolproofed as well as possible, and communicated to everyone

- It is always clear who is responsible for what

- What the organization regards as "quality" is well defined and documented

- Measurement systems are in place to check that everything is working according to plan

- When things go wrong—and they will—there are proven ways of making them right

ISO 9000 is designed to provide a flexible structure that ensures the identification and enforcement of QA principles. For R&D organizations, a set of typical ISO 9000 QA principles is as follows:

- Precise goals/objectives related to specified requirements

- Clearly identified responsibilities and interaction of departments/functions

- Traceability of all activities/documents to source requirements

- Preventive and corrective actions
- Process control—flow down of requirements
- Consistent evaluation and feedback
- Plan-do-check-act cycle

R&D organizations that clearly state their quality principles and then create an operational structure to ensure them will have little or no difficulty implementing ISO 9000.

ISO 9000 QA Approach

The ISO 9000 QA approach to management is a documented system approach, but it adds three essential extras:[5]

- A method for monitoring how well the system is being adhered to
- A method for correcting mistakes
- A method for changing the system if it has become obsolete

This error-correcting aspect of ISO 9000 is very important for the lab. Mistakes and failures will occur, and the ISO 9000 based quality system recognizes that possibility and prepares for it.

Three types of failure are recognized:

- Human error
- Failure of input materials
- Obsolescence of the existing method

The ISO 9000 quality system carefully distinguishes between these causes. In the first case, the error or omission is corrected; in the latter two, the material or method is amended. ISO 9000 is, therefore, both a self-correcting and a learning system. It changes to reflect changing needs. It is known as a QA rather than a traditional quality control type system.[6]

GETTING STARTED WITH ISO 9000

The Documentation Process

This section provides an overview of the heart of the documentation process for setting up a QA-based ISO 9000 system. It looks at the basic building blocks that need to be created (see Figure 8.1):

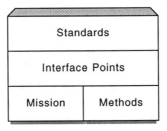

Figure 8.1 Documentation Building Blocks.

- Mission
- Methods
- Interface points
- Standards

Mission of R&D

ISO 9000 starts with a clear sense of what the R&D organization is to achieve: its mission. Dr. Deming calls this constancy of purpose. It is a timeless, qualitative statement, such as:

- To be the best developer of products and services in our field
- To maintain the highest possible level of creativity and innovation
- To have a reputation for excellence among customers and internal clients in our organization

In a well-established research center, it may seem unnecessary to document the mission. "We all know what we do here." "It's obvious what this place is for." Often, however, different people have different ideas of what the R&D arm of the organization is for and where it is heading. It is pointless to install a QA-type ISO 9000 system in an organization that has no shared view of what will constitute success.

In summary, a sense of mission is:

- A statement of what the organization is to achieve—its core purpose
- The vision of where the organization is going to be in 10 to 20 years
- The guiding principles and shared values that need to be internalized by all employees
- *Not* a set of objectives or targets

Methods

Once the sense of mission has been agreed upon, QA systems compel the organization to document the methods by which things are to be done. It is usually fairly clear what tasks need to be done in an organization—design, develop, test, and prototype new products—although in new organizations even the list of tasks may be unclear. In more mature organizations, despite superficial order, there may be strongly conflicting views about how each task should be done and, in particular, who should do it. "No one told me I had to use a documentation system. I've always done it my own way."

Essentially the problems come down to a lack of agreement on:

- What needs to be done—*what*
- The method of doing it—*how*
- Who should do it—*who*
- When it will be done—*when*
- Why it was done and where it is documented—*why/where*

Interface Points

An additional concept in total quality is the interface point. According to quality theory, the critical point at which quality can effectively be assured is the interface between two functions: when person A hands a job over to person B. For example:

- A researcher delivers the first prototype to engineering
- Engineering develops working specifications and then delivers them to manufacturing
- Manufacturing delivers a product to the customer

An interface involves a preparer, a receiver, and a task, as illustrated in Figure 8.2. The receiver expects to carry out a particular stage of a process (e.g., develop test standards and product guidelines). He or she can only do this if someone else developed and refined customer requirements. One of the basic fundamentals of total quality is that clean handoffs at the interface points between departments or functions are necessary to ensure maximum quality and productivity.

This looks a bit abstract before considering what is expected to happen at an interface. The receiver expects that the preparer has done his or her job completely and in the agreed-upon manner, because the receiver can-

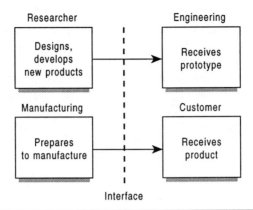

Figure 8.2 Interface Points. (Source: Freeman, Richard. *Quality Assurance in Training and Education*, London: Kogan Page, 1992.)

not do his or her job unless the preparer has done the same. Given that this handoff of work from preparer to receiver is so critical to doing a good job, the interface is often called a **critical interface**. By finding all the critical interfaces in an organization, fixing them, monitoring them, and continually improving them, a virtual total quality system is created. (In modern management total quality jargon, the receiver is often called an **internal customer** and the preparer an **internal supplier**. However, these terms have not been used here because they are generally disliked by R&D personnel.)

In practice, everyone is both a preparer and a receiver. Few tasks are initiated in isolation. Most involve carrying out the next stage in a sequence of processes.

Standards

As previously stated, the receiver expects that the task will be handed over in a completed state and in the agreed-upon form. No researcher is going to illegibly scribble the results of an experiment on the back of an old envelope. Thus, total quality systems assume that there are agreed-upon standards and/or formats for handing over tasks. For R&D, the researcher and company management might agree that:

- The specified requirements are clearly defined

- Interface points are agreed upon and communicated to all

- The flow of the design and development (research) process is documented

Meshing these standards is a critical part of setting up a R&D quality system. The process can often prove controversial, because opinions differ on how well tasks need to be done. One person might insist that customer requirements may be applied only to prototypes, while another could argue that customer requirements should drive the R&D process. These problems are easily resolved if there is general agreement to use the most common definition of quality: fitness for purpose and use. This means ensuring that all debates on quality are tested against customer expectations. The professional view of the R&D professional bows to the reality of what purchasing and management are willing to pay for.

The Building Blocks of an ISO 9000 System

As previously discussed, 12 of the 20 ISO 9000 modules, in addition to the use of statistics, are considered to be directly applicable to the field of R&D. The following is a brief synopsis of these items.

Module #1: Management Responsibility or Setting Quality Policy

Management responsibility is central to ISO 9000. If there is any suspicion that management—at all levels, including the highest—is not taking the total quality system seriously, then the ISO 9000 assessors will conclude that the system is not effective. This is summarized forcefully in the introduction to ISO 9000:

> The management of a company should develop and state its corporate quality policy. This policy should be consistent with other company policies. Management should take all necessary measures to ensure that its corporate quality policy is understood, implemented and maintained.

There is a very practical reason for this insistence on management involvement. Because total quality is itself a management system, and because an organization cannot run with two management systems, an ISO 9000 system can only work with total commitment from senior management.

A key management responsibility in setting up a quality system is defining a quality policy in a form that all R&D employees can use and understand. The policy documentation can be organized into four levels: (1) the basic policy statements, (2) the governing procedures, (3) the work instructions to be followed, and (4) the quality review. To be effective, they need to be clear and specific.

Policy Statement

A quality policy statement might cover:

- Who is responsible for setting up and running the R&D system
- How the system is to be monitored and reviewed by management
- For which functions/tasks defined procedures will be written
- How the implementation of those procedures will be monitored
- How failures to adhere to the procedures will be corrected
- A definition of quality as it relates to R&D

Procedures

Not everything R&D does can be subject to the full rigor of a quality system. To attempt to do so would be overwhelmingly time consuming. More practically, an organization identifies the functions or tasks where performance *critically affects* the service *as perceived by the users*. (In practice, ISO 9000 compels you to cover certain tasks, as will be explained later.) A procedure is then written for each of these. A procedure is a clear and systematic method that establishes how a function is to be carried out and who is responsible for each part.

Procedures should be written so that the user can clearly visualize the "flow" of the task. One useful tool for visualizing each task and decision criteria is the process flowchart. Flowcharts eliminate confusion by detailing each step and alternative action in the process.

Work Instructions

In order for procedures to be easily understood and followed, they must be short and must avoid unnecessary detail. Sometimes, however, more detail is needed to ensure that a job is done in a precise manner. Where this is the case, the extra detail is put into a work instruction. For example, a procedure might contain the paragraph:

Mini-vans for trips shall be ordered by the trip organizer at least seven days prior to any trip to a laboratory, using Form ABC99.

Form ABC99 then becomes the work instruction that tells the organizer exactly what details are needed and by whom.

The distinction between a procedure and a work instruction is defined as follows:

Procedure

- Refers to a process that includes many subtasks
- Outlines what needs to be done

Work instruction

- Refers to just one task
- Provides detailed guidance on how to complete the task

Procedures for R&D

All main functions that are to be controlled as part of the quality system have been identified in the quality policy. Because the policy statements are far too broad to be used by staff for day-to-day implementation, a procedure is written for each major R&D function. In operational terms, procedures are very important documents because they control most day-to-day actions and, even more important, identify who does what.

A procedure is set up for each major R&D function and includes the following:

- The main steps in that function with special emphasis on the critical interfaces
- Who is responsible for carrying out each function
- The quality standard to which each stage should be taken
- The form in which work is to be handed from one stage to another
- The quality records that must be retained to show that the work was performed according to the procedure

Once a procedure is written, employees should follow it as the agreed-upon way of working.

However well people know and understand the quality policy, their immediate reference will be one or more procedures. It is, therefore, critical that procedures satisfy a number of criteria:

- Accurately reflect how the research project should be done if the customer's requirements are to be met
- Be easily understood
- Clearly describe research activities in terms of what the outcome will be
- Clearly define responsibilities

For example, the following is poorly worded:

Researchers shall be tested regularly.

If you had to check on whether this wording had been followed, you would not know:

- How often constitutes "regularly"
- What evidence to accept to show that testing has been done
- Who should do the testing

The same sentence can be reworded with the kind of precision required in a procedure:

At least once a month, R&D managers shall test each of their researchers using one of the tests from the approved test bank. The results shall be recorded by the manager in the researcher's log.

From this statement it is clear:

- *When* the task is to be done—at least once a month
- *Who* carries out the task—the researcher's manager
- *What* the outcome is—a result recorded in the log

For every task, it should be easy to identify:

- What the outcome is
- Who does it
- When it is done

Anything that fails these three tests has to be rethought. (For additional information, see Abstract 8.1 at the end of this chapter.)

Work Instructions

Procedures should never describe *how* an experiment should be done. If that level of detail were allowed in procedures, they would become so cumbersome as to be useless. It is at this point that work instructions for the design and use of experiments should take over.

Work instructions can be very detailed—if necessary. Their function is to specify precise detail where needed. Creating a good work instruction is often a matter of considering who will use it and *how* it will be used. For example, consider the task of producing a product specification. A lengthy guide could be written to tell someone how to do the job. Would it be read? Probably not. Would it be followed? Even less likely. The solution is to turn the work instruction into a job-aid. This makes the user more likely to follow the work instruction since to do so makes the job easier. For these reasons, almost all work instructions are prepared in one of the following forms:

- A form to be filled in (e.g., an experiment entry form)

- A checklist of points (e.g., a list of points to check in preparing a research project)

- A list of headings (e.g., the headings under which to collect data for a product or experiment specification)

- A diagram to show how to conduct an experiment

Not only are such work instruction formats very easy to follow, but they are a natural part of the work. Wherever the ISO 9000 system can use natural documents and data, the better understood and received the system will be.

Quality Review

The final management role is the quality review, which is further emphasized by the self-adjusting nature of the R&D QA system. The management review is the engine for that process. At its simplest, the review needs to determine:

- What information is needed to be sufficiently certain that the quality policy is being implemented

- What information is needed to decide whether the policy needs amendment

- How frequently these data need to be collected

As ever, it is important to decide what is critical and genuinely indicative of the health of the organization. The more data management asks for, the less it will be able to make sense of. Also, the cost of data collection must be considered. The more management asks for data that are not automatically collected as part of day-to-day work, the more the cost of the quality system will rise. The efficient and economic way to resolve this is to scan the procedures once they have been written in order to identify data that exist in the system that will be of value in assessing the overall health of the system. There will, however, be two types of data:

- **Operational data**—product development cycle, product yields and rejection rates, product capability standards, etc.

- **Total quality system data**—percentage of R&D projects completed on time.

The management review should contain a sensible balance between the two. There should be enough data to convince management that nothing *critical* could go wrong, but no more.

The Quality System Loop

A final way to check on the role of management is to examine the quality loop and determine whether everything has been included. Figure 8.3 is a preliminary model to be used as a springboard for discussion.

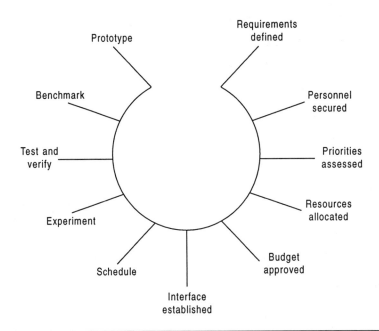

Figure 8.3   Quality System Loop for R&D. (Source: Freeman, Richard. *Quality Assurance in Training and Education*, London: Kogan Page, 1992.)

Module #2: The Quality System

It is one thing to have a policy, but quite another to turn it into a system that can deliver that policy. It is the responsibility of management to devise, promulgate, and monitor such a system. In one sense, everything that is done as part of the ISO 9000 system is part of the quality system, but here we are looking at the specification of that system and the documentation that goes with it.

Where does management start? It starts with the age-old question, "What kind of a business are we really in?" and then continues with the new question, "What is really critical?"

These two questions must be asked and carefully answered in order to (1) avoid a blind and inappropriate application of ISO 9000 (designed for manufacturing) to R&D and (2) prevent the system from tackling irrelevant detail. *For a total quality system to work well, it is essential that it concentrate on the things that make a difference.* What might these be? Each research facility is different, but the following areas might prove critical in most organizations:

- How market needs are identified

- How needs are turned into experiments and product specifications

- How researchers are recruited and counseled

- How researcher progress is monitored

- How achievement is assessed

- How staff are selected

- How staff are developed

- How products (rather than individual processes) are evaluated

Once such a list has been compiled (almost certainly by a bottom-up process involving staff and researchers at all levels), it is management's job to decide which items are critical and, therefore, those for which there will be a quality policy. Most organizations make this initial list too long.

Once a list of critical functions has been prepared, a policy is needed. This will set out, in broad terms, management's quality approach to each function. The policy for researcher recruitment and counseling might be:

> All prospective researchers shall receive written details of the products in which they have expressed interest. These details shall include: prior knowledge and skills assumed for the research, aims and objectives, learning time, methods of assessment, qualification awarded, and certifications available.

This is a policy statement and is, therefore, short on operational detail. Each critical function will be followed by a detailed operational procedure. Although it is acceptable to regularly review the quality policy, it should not be full of transient detail that requires frequent updating. The goal should be a balance between being a policy that is too vague to be meaningful and one that is too detailed to be considered a policy.

Module #3: Contract Review

The term *contract review* comes from BS 5750 and is a typical example of manufacturing terminology that is fairly simple to translate into R&D. In manufacturing, it is common for the manufacturer to make something that has been precisely commissioned by a customer, often another manufacturer or an assembly company. Hence, most of the work of manufacturers is dominated by contracts that specify what is to be produced and to what level of quality.

Contract review, as applied to an R&D operation, primarily involves the process and adequacy of defining and documenting customer requirements. The R&D organization must have input into test procedures, specifications, and special manufacturing or customer-handling requirements. By establishing the appropriate interfaces, R&D can provide input to the contract review process and assist in ensuring a complete quality system.

As with any part of ISO 9000, it is necessary to implement it only insofar as it is relevant to the nature of the organization and the needs of the customers.

Module #4: Design Control

In R&D, the design process involves the control and verification of the entire design and development process to meet specified requirements. As with contract review, customer requirements need to be completely defined. These requirements "drive" the design control process so that customers are assured that organizations will design the appropriate processes to ensure compliance. This section requires that plans exist for each design and development activity, including a listing of the individuals responsible for each activity in the process. The R&D organization, in conjunction with all defined "interfaces," must coordinate the requirements of this standard. Key elements of the ISO 9000 standard (ISO 9001:1994) for design control include:

- The assignment of qualified personnel, equipped with appropriate resources, to all specified design and development activities

- Procedures to resolve incomplete, ambiguous, or conflicting requirements

- Identify characteristics critical to the safe and proper functioning of the product
- Maintain documented procedures on design control
- Identification of responsibilities and qualifications of assigned personnel with all phases of the design and development process
- Plans that permit the design to evolve
- The removal of obsolete documents
- A definition and documentation of all information flow associated with design control
- A design review process
- Identification of appropriate inputs/outputs to the design
- Design verification at each stage of the design/development process

In summary, ISO 9000 identifies five aspects of design control:

1. Design and development planning—deciding who does what in the design system
2. Design input—making sure the designers know what the customers want
2. Design output—clarifying the final form the plans should take
4. Design verification—checking that the design solution is acceptable to the customer
4. Design changes—creating a system to ensure that any changes to the design are approved by the right people

Module #6: Purchasing

As with all ISO 9000 requirements, the purchasing of products/services must conform to specified requirements. Purchased materials include:

- All test and laboratory supplies/equipment necessary to ensure quality
- Consultants (academic/industry)
- Resource equipment (computers, technical services, etc.)

The R&D organization can request that suppliers demonstrate evidence that purchased product will meet all quality requirements. This permits the R&D organization to ensure that purchased items and services meet the needs of the department. The ISO 9000 standard requires that an approved supplier list be maintained and that qualification criteria be established for all critical purchased products directly related to quality requirements.

For each of the above, the organization needs to consider:

- The standard of performance required

- The selection process

- The records it will require suppliers to keep

- The resulting list of approved suppliers

Module #7: Purchaser-Supplied Product

The two general areas where this may apply are the supply of materials and the supply of equipment. Basically, the following tasks may apply:

- Ensuring that the correct items have been supplied on time and in usable condition

- Storing and retrieving items safely

- Reporting lost or damaged goods

Module #9: Process Control

The key to this module is to view research and product development from the customer's point of view. To apply this section to R&D, first it is necessary to identify what constitutes "process." The heart of process is everything normally associated with the design, development, test, prototyping, and evaluation/assessment. This comprises a wide range of activities, including:

- Definition of customer requirements

- Translation of customer requirements into design parameters

- Design plans and achievement milestones

- Developmental activities

- Research methodology

- Resource requirements

- Test and experimentation

- Evaluation and reformulation

- Operational parameters and safety limits

- Prototyping
- Product release

In other words, absolutely anything that researchers are expected to do during the experimentation process (as opposed to the preparation process or the evaluation stage) and that is critical to quality is covered by process control. In this context, a process control list for R&D would have to cover:

- Personnel (qualifications)
- Methodology
- Test, measurement, and verification

Additionally, a determination would have to be made as to which of the following processes need formal control:

- Research methods
- Adequacy of design/development planning and execution
- Documentation of research results
- Communication/interface process
- Test product integration
- Knowledge/information transfer
- Test result verification
- Product approval

In each case, what is being decided, in addition to whether to control that function at all, is:

- Do we need a work instruction for this function (e.g., documentation of experimental results)?
- Do we need to specify when/how often a function shall be executed (e.g., review management objectives monthly with R&D operational goals)?
- Do we need to specify the standard by which the organization judges success?

Module #13: Control of Nonconforming Product

Module #13 is designed to ensure that procedures and documentation exist to control product that does not conform to specified requirements and thus is prevented from use or installation. Of critical concern to a R&D organization is that no product, prior to formal approval, is used. This assumes that a formal product review process prevents the release of "experimental or test" product. In order to achieve compliance, a good interface between engineering, manufacturing, and R&D must be established, maintained, and periodically reviewed. Guidelines for releasing product from the R&D organization could include:

- Responsibility assignments for evaluation, review, and approval
- "Tagged" product that indicates state and intended use
- Preventive and corrective actions
- Disposition of nonconforming products

Without a formal process to release product from R&D, the organization jeopardizes the quality and integrity of the product.

Module #14: Corrective Action

Even auditing is not enough to ensure that a total quality system works. What happens if the auditing shows that some aspect of a procedure is being ignored? For example, suppose a procedure specifies that each researcher is to receive three copies of any change to the content of a test procedure before each experiment starts. Auditing reveals that (a) researchers receive only one copy and (b) the copies arrive a day before the experiment starts. The next step is corrective action, that is, rectifying what has been overlooked or done incorrectly. This can result in one of two actions:

1. In some cases, the audit simply reveals that the procedure is out of date. Perhaps the researchers no longer want three copies of the changes. In this case, the action is to amend the procedure.

2. In other cases, where there is agreement that the procedure is still the right way of doing things, the parties involved in the audit have to agree on how best to correct the discrepancies. If it is too late to correct the past action, then attention focuses on preventing the problem from recurring.

While everyone might hope that the audit will reveal complete compliance, noncompliances are not unusual, especially in a new system. The corrective action process is the means through which the noncompliance is straightened out. ISO 9000 requires a quality system to have a systematic method for corrective action.

Because there is no guarantee that the corrective action will have been taken at the end of the agreed-upon period, the quality system must have a means of acting on failure to implement corrective action. This would normally involve the auditor reporting the omission to someone higher up in the management chain.

Module #16: Quality Records

It is clear that successful auditing depends on evidence being available to demonstrate that the procedure has—or has not—been followed. Anything used to record compliance is called a **quality record**.

It is possible to introduce a total quality system that specifies numerous new and complex records that will have to be kept as quality records. However, this is not the way to introduce total quality. It results in deep resentment from the staff who have to run the system and fortifies the belief that ISO 9000 is just additional paperwork.

An efficient and successful quality system will seek every opportunity to use everyday working documents as quality records. Almost certainly, the existing document formats will need some revision in order to become quality records, but the important thing is that the number of documents is not increased.

Module #17: Internal Quality Audits

The quality policy and the procedures can be well prepared, but that does not provide any guarantee that they are being followed. Auditing is the means by which the organization checks that the procedures are really being implemented. Regular checks (audits) are made in a particular and systematic manner to identify whether or not the procedures are being adhered to. Inevitably this involves the potentially threatening process of interviewing the people doing the work. They can easily assume that they are being inspected, which is not the case at all. This impression has to be regularly dispelled by reminding everyone involved that it is the procedure that is being audited and not the person.

The entire management review system and the self-improvment nature of total quality systems demand that the system be continually under check to determine whether it is performing according to plan. This checking process is called **auditing** because the methods used are very similar to those in financial auditing.

Auditing is conducted by regularly checking each procedure to determine whether the work is being done as set out in the procedure. Any deviations are recorded as **noncompliances**, which then have to be corrected. The process of adjusting a noncompliance is called **corrective action**.

Through the quality management system, a timetable is drawn up which ensures that all procedures are audited on a regular basis. For example, the most important procedures might be audited once a year, while the less important ones are audited once every two or three years.

For each procedure, one or more auditors are appointed. When it is time to audit a procedure, the auditor visits the section using the procedure and, in an auditing meeting, works step by step through each statement in the procedure, checking the evidence that the step has been applied.

It is at this point that the difference between a good and bad procedure can often become apparent. In a bad procedure, precisely what evidence constitutes compliance may be very unclear. In a good procedure, the nature of evidence of compliance should be obvious. For example,

> The researcher shall perform experiments and tests to determine product acceptability

is vague because it does not state what constitutes evidence of agreement. The procedure can be reworded to remove this vagueness:

> Given specified requirements that define product acceptability, the researcher shall perform tests and experiments to verify these standards.

It is now clear that the auditor will be looking for the outcomes on the signed list. These clear-cut pieces of evidence are called **quality records**.

Module #18: Training

This is another section where R&D is no different than manufacturing or service. What ISO 9000 requires is that *for those activities affecting quality,* only properly trained staff be used. This probably includes all R&D staff, since R&D is only deliverable through skilled staff. For staff in critical areas or functions, a procedure must be set up for:

- Identifying the specific training needs of the staff

- Providing the training

- Keeping records of the training and R&D skill development

This does not mean that you will need to start carrying out extensive skills tests on all your staff. In R&D, almost all jobs are well defined, with clearly established standards or minimum qualifications. For example, a R&D organization may require that those persons responsible for managing a scientific experiment or test have an approved doctorate degree (Ph.D. or equivalent). If this is what is required to manage the experiment, then records for each person with a Ph.D. (or equivalent doctorate degree) need to show that they have these qualifications and that these are sufficient to meet the requirements.

Module #1 Revisited: Management Reviews

The ISO 9000 system begins and ends with management commitment, and the final part is the management review. A quality council composed of senior management holds regular review meetings to assess how well the system is meeting the needs of the organization and the customer and how well the system is being run. Such a review would receive summary reports on the system, which might document such areas as:

- Adherence to the audit schedule—Are audits being done on time?

- Implementation of corrective action—Are problems revealed by audits corrected in the agreed-upon manner and promptly?

- Procedure review—Are procedures regularly reviewed by their users and amended if needed?

- Mission—Is the mission statement still appropriate?

The overall approach is self-regulation and self-improvement, with heavy emphasis on documentation and audit, as previously discussed.

IMPLEMENTATION ISSUES FOR ISO 9000

Issues to Consider

Having identified and summarized the major components that constitute ISO 9000 for R&D, it is time to turn to the implementation issues. The following is a sample of those activities that should occur in order to fully implement the ISO 9000 quality system. Each activity is accompanied by an assigned responsibility. (See Table 8.1 for deployment details.)

Efforts needed to implement ISO 9000:

- Define, prioritize, and coordinate all ISO 9000 requirements with existing quality systems

- Create an ISO 9000 compliance "system benchmark" template

    Select a "shall" requirement of the ISO 9000 document and execute the following steps:

Table 8.1 Deployment Planning Matrix for Integration of
ISO 9000 and R&D

	Stage		
	Starting an ISO 9000 program	Operating a start-up ISO 9000 program	Sustaining an ISO 9000 program
Module #1: Management responsibility	• Learn the quality values and their implications for R&D • Develop personnel support mechanisms • Develop the overall corporate quality policy framework • Link to broad-based community movement focused on TQM • Provide resources	• Draft the corporate quality statement • Push the quality policy down to all levels every day • Communicate the quality policy, mission, and values to the public	• Lead consistently day to day; model behavior with staff; see things getting better • Perform quality reviews to ensure that quality policy is being implemented • Decide if policy needs modifying • Determine how frequently data need to be assessed
Module #2: Quality system	• Answer the questions, "What business are we in?"and "What is critical to success?" • Identify critical issues by involving R&D personnel • Decide upon items that need a quality policy	• Develop procedures for every process in R&D • Identify accountabilities and responsibilities • Define the quality standard and appropriate quality records that will be needed	• See an integration of QA in all major decisions • Decide where to pursue certification and choose a certification body • Experience a sense of personal transformation
Module #3: Contract review	• Identify areas where contract review is needed and appropriate • Define areas requiring review and ensure that documentation is available	• Review customer requirements to ensure that they are adequately defined • Ensure that changes have been accounted for • Allocate resources to fulfill the contract	• Check that the administrators and R&D staff have the proper skills • Follow up with certification body
Module #4: Design control	• Identify the product requirements • Identify the	• Prepare the design and development cycle • Design inputs	• Begin working with suppliers of test/lab equipment, consultants, and service

Table 8.1 (continued) Deployment Planning Matrix for Integration of ISO 9000 and R&D

	Stage		
	Starting an ISO 9000 program	Operating a start-up ISO 9000 program	Sustaining an ISO 9000 program
	research process to be followed • Ensure that customer requirements are being identified and captured	and outputs • Verify design and design changes with all customers • Establish a design review process in accord with quality requirements • Build in mechanism of continuous improvement	providers to ensure quality • Reexamine the entire R&D process from initial design to product release
Module #6: Purchasing	• Examine all supplies as purchased goods or services • Identify supplies as meeting specified requirements	• Identify the standard of performance required • Create a selection process for suppliers • Create a list of approved suppliers	• Evaluate the performance of suppliers • Assist suppliers with eliminating defective materials • Update approved bidder list
Module #7: Purchaser-supplied product	• Determine whether purchaser-supplied products are relevant	• Check to see if the products are correct • Report any loss or damage	• Eliminate unauthorized access to material and supplies • Create system to report any discrepancies
Module 9: Process control	• Identify processes that need to meet standards • Develop procedures that document process flow • Synthesize ongoing efforts • Develop measures to track effectiveness and improvement	• Design quality into research process • Examine "critical nodes"—are activities, responsibilities, and interfaces documented? • Develop preventive and corrective actions that support continuous improvement goals	• Consider "benchmarking" and "best practices" for R&D process • Reward the use of TQ principles in R&D practices • Apply continuous improvement tools and philosophy to every-day activities

Table 8.1 (continued) Deployment Planning Matrix for Integration of ISO 9000 and R&D

	Stage		
	Starting an ISO 9000 program	Operating a start-up ISO 9000 program	Sustaining an ISO 9000 program
Module #13: Control of nonconforming product	• Discuss, measure, and assess the cost of noncon-forming products	• Track costs of nonconformances • Develop pro-decures to dis-position non-conforming products	• Demonstrate a trend toward eliminating nonconforming product • Control costs of waste and rework
Module #14: Corrective action	• Specify the system for corrective action • Demonstrate how the system will function and how it will be monitored	• Take action decisively • Examine the actions that caused the need for correction • Establish feedback mechanism to prevent recurrence	• Review and revise procedures as a preventive measure • Use Plan-do-check-act cycle • Develop a consistent response for corrective actions
Module #16: Quality records	• Identify require-ments and verifi-cation mechanism for quality records • Use benchmarking as a method of establishing "needs requirements" for quality records	• Document the use of all records that affect quality requirements • Review pro-cedures, revise when inapprop-riate or do not serve quality requirements • Benchmark for standardization • Make decisions based on quality	• Ask if need for record exists on an ongoing basis • Check to determine if records can be substantiated • Monitor and review the document process • Use data to drive decisions
Module #17: Internal quality audits	• Appoint or train internal personnel to complete audits • Create the audit plan • Assign priorities to process for audit	• Develop and execute audit schedule • Review results and follow-up activities • Ensure the proper audit records are maintained	• Implement audit recommendations • Modify audit plan to adjust for quality system changes or modifications • Build in evolutionary approach to audit improvement

Table 8.1 (continued) Deployment Planning Matrix for Integration of ISO 9000 and R&D

	Stage		
	Starting an ISO 9000 program	Operating a start-up ISO 9000 program	Sustaining an ISO 9000 program
Module #18: Training	• Orient all employees to ISO 9000 standards • Discuss and demonstrate the benefits of ISO 9000 to employees • Develop a "simplified" but comprehensive training program for all R&D employees	• Develop a training and development plan for all employees • Foster professionalism through training and participation with technical and trade associations • Obtain feedback on training effectiveness	• Experiment with training methods that produce desired results • Institute ongoing improvement in training that enhances quality system requirements

Source: Based on the deployment planning matrix concept developed by Randy Schenkat.

1. Requirements definition (i.e., what does the "shall" state?)
2. List the critical "nodes" (i.e., critical elements in the process that directly relate to the quality requirements):
   o Actions (steps) taken to meet requirements
   o Responsibilities (who, what, where, when)—show interconnectivity of responsibility
   o Effect of actions taken (action–reaction, i.e., if...then)
   o Continuity of actions/responsibilities
   o Verification of actions (measurement)
   o Follow-through to next activity
   o Audit trail identifier (traceability)
3. Verify that all critical nodes were completed and meet quality requirements
- Review all documentation/traceability for ISO 9000 requirements
- Apply ISO 9000 compliance (system benchmark) template

- Align and coordinate quality systems and responsibilities
- Create (modify) verification system
- Link all documented practices/requirements for traceability
- Audit in-house systems to ISO 9000 compliance
- Modify practices and documentation
- Implement ISO 9000 quality system

Management Reviews and Responsibilities for Implementation

Day in and day out, employees will be carrying out tasks and functions according to the agreed-upon procedures and work instructions. At regular intervals (perhaps once a month), some part of the procedures will be under audit. The entire process becomes an integral part of how work is done and how it is managed. However, just as any process or system needs to be evaluated from time to time, so does any ISO 9000 quality system. This evaluation process is called **management review**.

Management review should be second nature to researchers and scientists since it follows the basic principles of evaluating any ongoing R&D system. In quality system language, we would say:

- Are we meeting our objectives?
- If not, what action do we need to take?
- Do our objectives need to be changed?

For additional information, see Abstract 8.2 at the end of this chapter.

Management must share in the responsibility for implementing ISO 9000. In general, management responsibilities for implementing ISO 9000 can be summarized as follows:

- Assist in creating a quality mission statement that reflects the intent, purpose, and commitment to ISO 9000 standards.

- Participate in creating an ISO 9000 "system benchmark" that acts as a framework from which all departments/functions can develop their quality systems.

- Accept ISO 9000 as a "requirement for doing business in a competitive global marketplace" and operate within its broad framework.

- Maintain the ISO 9000 system by using the structure as a performance measure. Look at the alignment and efficiency of all departments/functions to the quality standard. Give subordinates clear directives to maximize efficiency and effectiveness through ISO 9000.

- Periodically review the progress of the ISO 9000 implementation. Keep rewards and benefits clear and focused.

- Sustain the effort and benefits of the ISO 9000 quality system by obtaining certification.

The management review follows a similar format:

- Are we implementing the procedures?

- If not, what action do we need to take?

- Do our procedures need to be changed?

As with any evaluation system, if steps are not taken early to collect the data as work proceeds, it may be difficult, expensive, or even impossible to collect the data later. That is particularly important because if compliance with procedures cannot be proven, noncompliance is assumed. No news is bad news in ISO 9000. This means that management must be explicit about the data to be evaluated in its reviews. Data will tend to be of two types: (1) routine statistical data and (2) ad hoc surveys. The types of routine statistical data that management might seek include:

- Percentage of audits carried out within one week of target date

- Number of noncompliances detected per audit

- Percentage of corrective actions carried out within the time period agreed upon between auditor and auditee

- Percentage of total noncompliances that belong to each procedure

- Average length of time since each procedure was last reviewed

- Number of procedures not reviewed in the last twelve months

All these types of data are easily plotted on time graphs so that management can see the trend in performance.

The other category of data that a management review group might seek is ad hoc reports. For example, the group might want to review:

- Trainers' views on how well the quality system supports them in their day-to-day work

- Suppliers' views of the quality system

- A sample of quality systems in similar establishments

Obtaining ISO 9000 Certification

Whether or not to seek external recognition of the total quality system is a matter of choice. If the decision is made in favor of external recognition, then the system must be assessed against either the ISO 9000 standards or another quality standard such as the Malcolm Baldrige Award.

The British Standards Institute (BSI) issues the 5750 standard in the United Kingdom. A number of separate bodies are approved to assess organizations against BS 5750 (ISO 9000). These are called certification bodies. Currently there are about fifteen such bodies in the United Kingdom. The role of a certification body is to conduct an in-depth assessment of the quality system in order to determine whether it meets the standards set out in BS 5750. The certification body requires a fee, which is negotiated according to the size of the organization and the complexity of the quality system. A quality manual and procedures must be submitted, but otherwise documentation is kept very simple. The certifying body then:

- Reviews documentation

- Visits the premises to interview quality staff and other employees and to generally see the total quality system in practice

- Produces a report which either confirms that the standard has been met or indicates the changes needed in the system to meet the standard

Including the certification process alongside the other steps in this chapter, the full sequence for obtaining ISO 9000 is as follows:

1. Obtain the necessary parts of ISO 9000

2. Design the system as set out in this chapter (in practice, the assistance of an external consultant will probably be required for this step)

3. Choose a certification body

4. Schedule certification body visit

5. Receive certification or amend the system

For additional information, see Abstract 8.3 at the end of this chapter.

Choosing a Certification Body

A list of certification bodies can be obtained from BSI or the National Accreditation Council for Certification Bodies (NACCB). In choosing a certification body, it is best to identify one with plenty of experience in working with R&D organizations. The more the certification body understands this type of business, the better it will be able to understand the subtleties of adapting ISO 9000. It is also a good idea to check with other similar organizations and determine which certifying body they used (if any) and what their experience was. If a certifying body with a poor track record is chosen, difficulties can be expected as it adapts to the specific needs of total quality in R&D.

PROFILE ON THE ADAPTATION OF THE JAPANESE QA SYSTEM TO THE R&D ENVIRONMENT[7]

The following principles are based on the work of Tetsuichi Asaka and Kazuo Ozeki, as originally documented in the JUSE research materials and writings.[8]

Make Quality Your Top Priority

Putting quality first is fundamental to the long-term survival of a R&D organization. Those organizations that neglect QA in favor of delivering a product first in a competitive market later discover defects and suffer for it in the long run. Many companies have failed for this reason. In the 21st century, the same will be said of research organizations.

Build in Quality

It should be understood that inspections and examinations do not create quality; quality is built in during the product development process. R&D administrators need to create improvement targets to build quality into the experimentation process. The administrator might set the target at 133% or more of the current process capability and then work with researchers, scientists, and other employees to create and implement a quality improvement plan.

Problems Are Opportunities to Improve the Quality Assurance System

Administrators should see claims and quality problems as opportunities to improve organization and attitudes and to make reforms. The fundamental principle of quality control is to identify the root cause of a problem so it will not recur. If the administrator does not search for the root cause and strive to prevent the recurrence of the problem, his or her work becomes haphazard.[9] Thoroughly search for the root cause.

Quality Assurance Checkpoints for the Lab

1. Motivating for quality consciousness

   - Are the philosophy and general policies of the R&D area and top management easy to understand and have they been thoroughly implemented?

   - Have you made your researchers aware of the damages the organization suffers due to poorly prepared experiments and customer complaints (loss of customer confidence, loss of image, and so on)?

   - Have you provided concrete examples to your researchers showing the importance of quality as a shortcut to lower costs, higher customer confidence, and a great sense of achievement in working?

   - Have you helped your staff and researchers to understand the role that quality plays in their work?

2. Objectives and planning

   - Are laboratory quality targets clear and understood?

   - Is the QA improvement theme clear?

   - Did each individual receive instructions for his or her part in the plan for carrying out the product development and research improvement themes that will achieve these targets?

   - Are the plans related to these targets and improvement themes clear?

3. Education

   - Are you improving your chances for achieving the goals and plans through education, exchanges with other labs, and participation in experiments outside the organization?

   - Have you explained the functions that make the offerings useful to the market and the current extent of the product's use in the market?

   - If a problem arises, do you take charge, give proper instructions for solving the problem, and direct the improvement activities?

4. Practical work and its improvement

   - Do you thoroughly carry out tasks related to the quality characteristics?

   - Have you used a handbook summarizing work procedures to teach your researchers how to do their jobs?

   - Have you taught research workers how to use computers, instruments, and tools and to make revisions and adjustments to the experiments?

- Do you check to see if the experimental work methods are performed properly?

- Do you encourage your workers to upgrade their technical knowledge and skills? How much time is spent each year per employee?

5. Problem solving and team activities

- When problems or accidents occur, do you guide your workers in solving the problem?

- When on-the-spot emergency firefighting must be done, do you go on to find the root cause of the problem to make sure it does not recur?

- Do you direct the R&D project team to work together to solve a problem?

- Do you use effective and rational problem-solving methods, such as the seven quality control tools?

- If improvements and reforms are needed in experiments, systems, or standards to prevent a problem from recurring, do you work with the researchers and other employees involved to take the necessary actions?

- Do you consider carefully whether your laboratory workplace culture is the problem and take appropriate measures to change the situation?[9]

EPILOGUE: ISO 9000—THE DRIVING FORCE BEHIND TQM

Total quality began in those markets where Japan and the United States were in direct competition. It has continued to spread wherever markets are characterized by an ever-increasing demand for quality and reliability combined with a reduction in price in real terms. Thus, TQM is particularly common in automotile manufacturing, process industries, and electronics, areas where today's products are far more reliable than those of a decade or two ago.[10] Accordingly, as the worldwide trend toward privatization continues, it is likely that R&D will become more competitive. Particularly with the aid of high-tech media, internal customers will less and less frequently automatically turn to their corporate R&D providers. It is, therefore, reasonable to expect that R&D providers will increasingly find themselves competing in terms of quality, satisfaction, and price. Mandatory total quality and ISO 9000 could well be on the way.[11] Today's choice may be tomorrow's mandate. (For additional information, see Abstract 8.4 at the end of this chapter.)

Overall, the goals of an integrated ISO 9000 based total quality system for R&D can be summarized as:[12]

- Listen to the voice of the customer

- Focus on the needs of the market

- Achieve top quality performance in all areas of research, not just in the product or service

- Establish simple procedures for performing experiments

- Continually review processes and experiments to eliminate waste

- Develop measures of performance

- Understand the competition and develop a competitive strategy

- Ensure effective communication

- Seek never-ending improvement

When comparing QA-based ISO 9000 programs to total quality, the most significant difference is that total quality adds customer focus and cost to the quality debate. QA essentially ignores cost (or money in any form), whereas total quality uses cost as a critical performance measure.

It is not the intent here to draw any firm conclusions as to the merits of ISO 9000 versus TQM. Indeed, there is too little evidence of the application of either method in R&D to validate conclusions. What can be said, however, is that R&D cannot expect to escape the current drive toward higher quality and being more answerable to the customer. Therefore, a more sensitive measure of performance will be required, as well as a means of improving on past performance. However, in phrasing such a need, it points toward some form of QA. Perhaps ISO 9000 will fit that need. Perhaps TQM will, or a combination of the two. If neither does, some other approach will soon be required.

ENDNOTES

1. Freeman, Richard. *Quality Assurance in Training and Education,* London: Kogan Page, 1992, pp. 9–12.
2. Partnerships between industry and educational institutions are also helping to promote quality improvement in R&D. For example, the TQM

University Challenge, first proposed by Robert W. Galvin, chairman of the executive committee of the board of directors of Motorola, is intended to foster the integration of TQM principles into existing business and engineering curricula and into administrative processes that support curricula development. To help accomplish this, the university representatives will complete a week of on-site education at their host companies. A pilot program, the TQM University Challenge, pairs Motorola with Purdue University, Proctor & Gamble with the University of Wisconsin-Madison and Tuskegee University, Xerox with Carnegie Mellon University, Milliken & Company with North Carolina State University and the Georgia Institute of Technology, and IBM with the Massachusetts Institute of Technology and the Rochester Institute of Technology. (Source: Axland, Suzanne. "A Higher Degree of Quality." *Quality Progress*, p. 42, October 1992.)

3. Sprow, Eugene. "Insights into ISO 9000." *Manufacturing Engineering*, p. 73, September 1992.

4. Freeman, Richard. *Quality Assurance in Training and Education*, London: Kogan Page, 1992, pp. 10, 14.

5. Spizizen, Gary. "The ISO 9000 Standards: Creating a Level Playing Field for International Quality." *National Productivity Review*, pp. 331–346, Summer 1992.

6. Note on traditional quality control: Quality control is a much more widely known term than QA, but the distinction between the two is not always well drawn. Quality control is essentially a method of inspecting for, and rejecting, defective work (although some of its statistical methods can be used to prevent defective work from occurring). In R&D training and education, a quality control system might measure the number of R&D projects completed (as well as the time taken to complete the projects) and then penalize those projects which would have taken longer to complete if following quality principles. In such an approach, there is no concept of preventing the problem in the first place. QA is essentially *preventive*, as the word assurance implies. It means preventing errors, not correcting them time after time.

7. Voehl, Frank. "ISO 9000 Adapted to Various Businesses & Industries" (unpublished manuscript), Coral Springs, FL: Strategy Associates, 1993.

8. Ozeki, Kazuo and Asaka, Tetsuichi. *Handbook of Quality Tools: The Japanese Approach*, Cambridge, MA: Productivity Press, 1990.

9. According to Dr. Asaka of JUSE, most problems can be classified as follows: (a) problems related to worker skills or attitudes: pure mistakes, not following the experimental procedure, skills not yet adequate, and concern for quality not strong enough; (b) problems related to the R&D quality assurance system: the quality characteristic to be assured is not well defined, operating standards incomplete, management points unclear, casual about QA methods, and quality control process chart not yet complete; (c) lack of motivation to solve the administrator's problem:

no desire to delve deeply into the problem and solve it, and administrator's leadership in setting improvement goals and in making improvements is inadequate; (d) problems in the lab culture: never delving deeply into problems, and blaming the lab custom; (e) problems originating in another department: design error, and error in determining customer specifications. Asaka believes that if problems are solved in a haphazard manner, a problem might mistakenly be identified as a recurring worker error when the true cause is the R&D training and quality control education being provided to the researchers and support workers. Try to create an atmosphere in which everyone is motivated to want to build quality into their experiments and projects. A lab administrator should look for the root cause of any problem that occurs, consider if he or she (not others) is causing the problem, and implement the basic policies needed to correct it.

10. Total quality is based on the assumption that suppliers will only prosper in their markets if they are able to both improve quality and reduce costs. While this concept is not novel in manufacturing, it is perhaps revolutionary in R&D. We frequently read of researchers asking for more resources so that they can improve quality. Total quality says that you must improve quality with fewer resources, because if you don't, your competitor will.

11. Total quality assumes that there is a hidden source of fat in any organization (Freeman, 1992). That source is the cost of quality, also known as the price of nonconformance (PONC) or the cost of not doing things right the first time. In R&D training and education, the cost of quality includes: (a) planning a course for ten researchers, but running it for eight because the time did not suit two people or for twelve because of scheduling problems; (b) learners starting courses for which they were not ready and dropping out without completion; (c) researchers having to rework experiments because the initial scheme was not adequately standardized; and (d) researchers failing to execute experiment properly because of substandard training.

12. Jackson, Susan. "What You Should Know about ISO 9000." *Training*, pp. 48–52, May 1992.

ABSTRACTS

ABSTRACT 8.1
QUALITY SHOULD BE DOCUMENTED, NEVER DICTATED

Larson, Bruce
Intech, May 1992, pp. 26–28

How can a company build employee ownership through the ISO 9000 documentation process? The author suggests ways to expand ownership of the quality system at each step:

- **The management policy.** The first step is for the top management to buy in to the process and to state its commitment as a policy.

- **The quality manual.** The author suggests starting with the existing processes to encourage "buy in" by employees. He also recommends using a cross-functional team to write the manual after they are trained on the standard.

- **The internal self-assessment.** This provides a record of how well the company is implementing its quality system. The author suggests that the team performing the assessment should also write the procedures comprising the second tier of the documentation. He recommends flow-charting as an integral part of the process. Also, communication must be improved between different functional groups during documentation. Employees will then see the benefits of the system and commit themselves to it, according to the author.

- **Employee training.** Training based on the newly created documentation aids in developing ownership of the procedures. The author urges establishing a change system that allows any employee to send a recommendation to change a document of the quality system. There should also be a continuous review through internal audits.

A sidebar by Wes Chase offers seven steps for documenting what the company has already implemented. Another sidebar by Chase lists the advantages of using an ISO documentation specialist. (*©Quality Abstracts*)

ABSTRACT 8.2
ISO 9000: AN IMPLEMENTATION GUIDE FOR SMALL TO MID-SIZED BUSINESSES

Voehl, Frank, Jackson, Peter, and Ashton, David
St. Lucie Press, Delray Beach, Fla., 1994

The *1995 Quality Yearbook* calls this book a most welcome addition to the literature, especially in light of the fact that most books on ISO 9000 focus on the large enterprises. Increasingly, more and more small businesses are focusing on the certification process and are experiencing different issues than the large companies are facing. This book is an attempt to deal with those issues, with a particular focus on implementation.

This book is written specifically for the small to mid-sized business organization that is interested in the implementation of ISO 9000 as one of the building blocks of its quality system. It is also written for those organizations that want a do-it-yourself as much as possible approach. However, since ISO 9000 is also an accepted standard for quality, we need in this first chapter to understand what quality means in a business environment and how it can be achieved.

During the past three years, there has been an explosion of books in the field of total quality and ISO 9000. Yet in all of the hundreds of books and millions of words written on the subject, there is an absence of good working models and comprehensive yet concise overviews, according to the authors. The promise of this book is to offer a clear and simple systems model of ISO 9000 which can be used for certification (registration). The how-to approach offered in this book comes complete with sample procedures and forms, where appropriate. Its intent is to demystify the ISO 9000 standards and to demonstrate their appropriateness for improving day-to-day business operations. A detailed ISO 9000 master plan is included, along with an integrated case study of an organization that achieved certification in nine months, using a worker-empowered approach. Profiles and supplements provide additional insight into the subject.

ABSTRACT 8.3
ISO 9001 CERTIFICATION AT LOGITECH:
STAN SALOT CREDITS ISO 9000 AS THE BASIS FOR
LOGITECH'S SUCCESSFUL QUALITY-IMPROVEMENT EFFORTS

Johnston, Christopher E.
Quality Digest, September 1992, pp. 28–36

Logitech, a Fremont, California-based manufacturer of computer mice and hand-held scanners, chose to seek ISO 9001 certification since 40% of its business is in Europe and Asia, says the author, and this certification would eventually be required to do business there. ISO 9001 registration also became the foundation of Logitech's quality improvement process. The author describes the process.

1. Logitech assessed its quality assurance systems and established a 120-day time frame to complete certification.

2. They chose not to bring in external consultants and selected the National Standards Authority of Ireland to serve as their third-party register.

3. The project manager for quality standards attended a 2-week training program, and he subsequently trained a 20-person cross-functional ISO team.

4. Each team member performed audits within his or her own department, reviewing procedures, policies, and documentation. They focused on identifying who their suppliers and customers were, and they made sure that policies, procedures, and documentation addressed those elements.

5. Corrective action programs were set in place.

6. The ISO team prepared a formal quality assurance manual.

7. Logitech requested a formal audit and submitted their documentation to the third-party register.

8. Two auditors arrived and spent 4-1/2 days auditing the plant, after which they compiled a list of nonconformances and gave a conditional certification based on the assumed correction of the cited infractions.

9. Four weeks later, an auditor returned to validate the corrected nonconformances.

10. Logitech received its official certification on November 18, 1991.

11. Each quarter, the company trains an additional ten people in internal auditing procedures, both their own employees and supplier employees.

12. In June 1992, the company received its first surveillance audit.

The author notes some confusion between European and U.S. terminology, and he describes how Logitech had to overcome initial resistance to the sets of rules within the ISO program. (©*Quality Abstracts*)

ABSTRACT 8.4
YOU CAN EARN ISO 9002 APPROVAL IN LESS THAN A YEAR

Gasko, Helen M.
Journal for Quality and Participation, March 1992, pp. 14–19

Union Carbide's Taft, Louisiana plant—its Ethyleneamines Business (EA Business)—used a multi-functional team to help it gain ISO 9002 approval after only four months, reports the author. Since a large portion of the company's products are sold outside the U.S., ISO registration was needed to compete in European Community member countries. A steering committee was formed to remove obstacles to progress, while day-to-day activities were left to accountable individuals. A preliminary evaluation and specific gap analysis was conducted, highlighting areas which needed correction. Then a three-tiered document system was adopted—with each document assigned to a different individual to write in parallel rather than sequentially—(a) a "Quality Systems Manual," which included a broad policy statement, (b) a "Facilities Quality Manual," which defined specific activities and assigned accountabilities to various plant functions, and (c) "Procedures and Systems," which detailed the standard operating practices for day-to-day operations. Since the writers kept in continual contact, nothing was written with which another could not comply. Some of the other insights the company gained concerning the completion of the ISO criteria were:

• Adapt, don't re-invent. Where different names are used for the ISO requirements, use your own jargon where you already comply.

• Entrust individuals with seeing their portion of ISO compliance through to completion without management interference.

• Use the people on the compliance team as quality auditors.

- Set an aggressive time frame to act as a catalyst.

- Allow each functional team to do whatever works for its particular area without bureaucratic rigidity.

- "Don't study it to death—just do it," became the motto.

"At Taft, we were able to do this because EA Business was already partially in compliance, and we recognized that we could adapt many procedures in place," says the author. "A more realistic target would be to aim for approval in less than a year." The article includes two sidebars: a brief description of each of the elements of the ISO 9000 series and the elements of the ISO 9002 standards dealing with production and installation. (©*Quality Abstracts*)

CHAPTER 9

CASE STUDY: TOTAL QUALITY AT CORNING'S RD&E

INTRODUCTION

Corning, Inc. has an established relationship with customers that dates back to 1879 when Thomas Edison requested that Corning craftsman manufacture the first glass bulb.[1] This emphasis on meeting customer needs has been the hallmark of Corning, Inc.'s success. In order to maintain lasting customer satisfaction and strengthen business objectives, Corning Inc. embarked on a total quality effort in 1983. Four specific quality principles drove the Corning effort:

1. Meet the requirements of the customer

2. Promote "error-free" work

3. Manage by prevention

4. Measure the cost of quality[1]

These principles were accomplished through ten actions involving education, recognition, corrective action, teams, cost of quality, events, communication, goals, measures/display, and management/corporate commitment.[1] These actions provide a successful strategy for implementing total quality and are as applicable today as they were when introduced in 1983.[2]

Total quality principles continue to be integrated into the entire organization. With a diverse group of scientists (26%), engineers (26%), unionized hourly workers (20%), and technical support staff (28%), total quality was undertaken in the RD&E (Research, Development, and Engineering) division.[1] The true success of this effort is the fact that the total quality effort was implemented in spite of what would seem to be difficult odds, especially in an R&D division. Some typical difficulties faced by the RD&E division included an independent history, a multi-functional work force, a strong "corporate culture," and internalized systems and procedures. Effort, determination, and strong commitment from the entire corporation to implement total quality yielded a substantial benefit (over $21 million) to the RD&E organization.[1]

RD&E DEPARTMENT OVERVIEW

Twenty departments are actively involved in the total quality process within the RD&E group. Quality Improvement Teams (QITs) have been formed throughout each of the twenty departments. The responsibility of each team is to examine and improve its processes. The Malcolm Baldrige Self-Assessment criteria are used to evaluate each department. Teams search for where improvement is needed and where the biggest impact can be made through the application of total quality principles and practices. Each team chooses three to four potential projects, called the "Vital Few," and then begins to devise a methodology for improvement. Teams design measures for each process they intend to improve. These metrics indicate how well the teams are accomplishing their tasks. Measures are assigned to both process characteristics and results-oriented indicators. These measures serve as "Key-Results Indicators" which gauge quality improvement as well as demonstrate tangible benefits.

Each team is unique, and these differences may extend to the team's organization, goals, methodology, structure, and overall purpose. Each team within RD&E has its own personality. According to Dr. Eve Menger, "Quality is a line function," with each team taking its own responsibility to achieve success.

Teams and total quality activities are monitored through the "World Class Quality" (WCQ) committee which reports directly to the vice-president's staff. WCQ provides a framework from which to measure success by using a template that examines what, how, and why total quality principles were used to solve a problem or identify/implement an opportunity. The WCQ committee's responsibilities include review and feedback. The committee uses customer satisfaction as a measure of the team's progress and its overall effectiveness. The WCQ committee measures how well the team accomplished its task, met its objectives, and the benefits obtained from such an effort. From these extensive reviews, five to six teams are selected for their contribution to developing "best practices." "Best practices" are then identified and freely shared with the entire organization. Corning, Inc. has encouraged its employees and managers to "steal shamelessly" from the successful teams and adapt these "best practices" to meet a particular set of needs.

Overall, according to Dr. Eve Menger, the system is working well. Numerous insights have been gained by using the total quality process. RD&E seriously considers its customers—both internal and external. The division has become very attentive to its customers, and the results of customer satisfaction surveys verify this assertion. Both technically and managerially, the organization has benefited from the implementation of total quality principles.

AN EVOLUTIONARY APPROACH

As with the implementation of any new cultural change, skeptics existed within RD&E from the beginning. The company initiated the total quality approach with the announcement by Chairman of the Board James Houghton in 1983 that quality would become a key component of the Corning approach. Corning created the "Quality Initiative" and began to implement the process using a top-down approach.

Within the RD&E division, Dr. Jack Hutchins was assigned the task of integrating quality principles into the organization.[3] A traditional approach was initially applied (using factory-type concepts of problem solving and application of tools). This traditional approach was phased out when it became obvious that a customized, flexible effort was needed to involve employees into the total quality process. Traditional quality approaches, used in industry, serve plant employees well but were never accepted globally by the RD&E division. Therefore, process "ownership" was transferred to the division, where it continues to be successfully implemented.

Changes that did occur focused mainly in the human component of total quality. Early in the process (1983–85) simple successes won over employees.[4] The total quality approach emphasized better equipment,[4] more efficient procedures, and more concern for executing experiments in a controlled manner. That is, total quality emphasized a certain "logic" for how to successfully execute an experiment.[4] The "logic" comprised the principles of total quality that emphasize meeting customer requirements, teamwork, effective tools, and a rational (process-oriented) approach. As time progressed, the keys to Corning's program (see the Introduction) have become the cornerstone of success. At present, the philosophy of total quality has become institutionalized within the organization. Buy-in among employees is strong, given that the vision and values of total quality have remained consistent. Recognition and rewards have facilitated the process of cultural change. The application of total quality principles continues, although proceeding at different rates within the division.

KEY ELEMENTS OF THE CHANGE PROCESS

The most critical change in the culture at Corning's RD&E division was the focus placed on the internal and external customer. The division now sees itself as both a customer and supplier of products and services. "Total quality principles have given RD&E a dialogue (common language) with their customers."[4] That is, the division no longer operates in isolation but rather addresses customer requirements as a way of doing business. The notion of customers and their requirements (needs, wants, and desires) has been a major paradigm shift for the division. There is a sense of "interconnectivity" within the organization and outside of RD&E with its customers.

As mentioned previously, the method used to experiment and conduct research has changed within the RD&E division. Mistakes are seen as learning experiences. What matters is that the scientist or engineer learns from his or her mistakes rather than the frequency of errors. Total quality has infused the organization with the desire to do scientific research using "best practices." The definition of failure and mistakes has changed over time.[4] The division now sees errors such as inventing a product that does not meet customer requirements or not following established scientific procedures as negatives. Employees are empowered to use those practices and methods that support the objectives of the customer and the division (corporation). If RD&E brings a product to market that does not meet customer needs, then quality principles have been violated. This commitment to customer satisfaction challenges the traditional paradigm by creating a new culture dedicated to meeting the needs of the division's customers.

Another element of the Corning success story is that the division found ways to make innovation move faster.[3] By implementing the "Innovation Process" "scientists and engineers can now use their technical skills faster and better with more cost efficiency."[3] The innovation model has become a hallmark of the Corning RD&E total quality program. Five key stages define the "Innovation Process":

1. Build knowledge

2. Determine feasibility

3. Test practicality

4. Prove profitability

5. Commercialize[2]

This "team-driven process provides incremental steps to reduce development time, increase the success rate for projects and identify less promising projects early in their development."[2] The process provides employees with a method of using skills and expertise to accomplish objectives and goals in an efficient and effective manner. Through the use of quality principles, innovation has accelerated within the division. Total quality has created an environment for a better model of innovation to emerge by outlining a successful path for employees to follow.

Changing economic conditions have caused Corning to reexamine operations and personnel. Total quality has assisted in restructuring the organization. An example of this is as follows:

> The division has assembled a redesign team to facilitate the transition to a more effective and efficient organization. Rather than using a top-down approach, the division has selected employees throughout the organization to offer creative solutions. The redesign team is composed of both exempt and non-exempt employees, representing a diagonal slice through the organization.

This team continues to provide management with creative recommendations concerning issues such as consolidation, capital budgeting, cost containment, etc. As a result of using total quality principles, employees continue to maintain a positive attitude and feel good about the suggestions they make. In essence, employees are shaping the "bottom line" and reshaping their organization for the future.[3] Accordingly, "if people are treated well, they will keep an interest and passion in their job and will make things better."[3]

BENEFITS OF TOTAL QUALITY

Total quality has assisted in bringing "breakthroughs" into the corporation. Employees are empowered to seek their greatest potential. By working in teams and communicating with customers, products have been brought to market at a more efficient pace with fewer errors and within projected costs. An example of this ongoing effort is the following:

Scientists and engineers had to request certain trades organizations to set up equipment and experimental apparatus before conducting a scientific experiment. Requests for equipment were made through a supervisor. Trades organizations that assemble experimental apparatus and equipment formed a high performance team to facilitate this process. The purpose of this team was to provide scientists and engineers with apparatus to conduct experiments in a timely manner. The team at first was resisted by scientists since the technical people would have to deal directly with the trades (hourly) individuals rather than requesting the equipment from a supervisor. Some scientists felt a loss of control. However upon implementing the improvement, mistakes and errors significantly decreased. Scientists can now complete their experiments in a straightforward manner. A feeling of connectivity now exists between the trades people and the scientists. That is, both groups share a similar goal (purpose) for working together. This is total quality at work in Corning's RD&E division.[4]

Another striking benefit of implementing total quality is the self-awareness that employees now have concerning their quality of work (i.e., the tasks they perform). As a result of ongoing global quality requirements (e.g., ISO 9000), the Analytical Lab is now certified for established tests and fully accredited. Prior to total quality, many employees would have questioned the need for an outside accreditation agency to approve the ongoing work within the laboratories. Total quality has influenced the method employees and management use to evaluate the quality and excellence of work. This accreditation has also assisted the bottom line by increasing the level of performance and enabling Corning to enter commercial ventures that supplement the income of the lab.[3] That is, business has grown with assessment and evaluation...two key principles of total quality.

Work groups (teams) as well as individuals are now empowered within RD&E. The integration of teams into the RD&E culture has been significant. Employees are conscious of working as a team.[3] For example:

Employees want to know how well they are performing. Departments within the division are involved in an ongoing audit process to check the quality of their output. This is a complete reversal of traditional policies that suggest that frequent evaluation destroys the "creative process." Now employees can be open and honest concerning their work, not protective or secretive. Employees want to know "how well they are doing" and are actively involved in the evaluation and continuous improvement process.[3]

Employees experience the benefits of teams when working on technical projects, especially when new methods are being developed or the team is problem solving.

During the present series of economic changes underway at Corning, the total quality initiative has allowed open communications during the restructuring process.[3] Morale would certainly be lower if the company was not at its present level of integration in the restructuring process. Much of the success is due to the efforts of the many QIT teams which have facilitated more open and honest communications among and between management and employees. Employees can ask challenging questions of management that are answered truthfully.[3] In addition, Corning RD&E employees are now actively involved in cross-training within and between departments to facilitate this ongoing economic challenge.[3]

APPLICATION TO THE TOTAL QUALITY MODEL

In terms of the total quality model, the largest change in RD&E occurred in the human systems.[4] Early on in the process, people felt that total quality was improving their work and indeed felt better about themselves. This is one reason why teams were successful and why the process continues today. Although human systems changed most, management systems benefited the most. The largest paradigm shift is continuing to occur within management as the total quality evolution progresses. Managers are redefining their role as employees become more empowered. Changing management systems also present the biggest obstacle to total quality, given that many managers are well vested in the old system. Managers need to see the rewards and benefits of total quality, and they need to become more integrated into the process. According to Mark Mitchell, managers need to be better understood and valued for their contribution. Threatening managers and supervisor places an adverse burden on these individuals and discourages total quality. Evolutionary change within management continues to be the largest challenge to implementing total quality.[4]

Technical systems have also changed with the implementation of total quality. For Wes Strzegowski of the Analytical Lab, technical system changes have accounted for up to 50% of total quality implementation. Technical system changes have increased and enhanced creativity and innovation, continuing to facilitate the total quality process.

LESSONS LEARNED

The most difficult aspect of total quality for R&D divisions/departments appears to be that of metrics. Quality metrics are often difficult to quantify. Measures such as cost of quality are more applicable for manufacturing divisions where the bottom line is easily quantified. Corning's RD&E division has taken a unique approach which has worked well. A description of this approach follows and represents a valuable lesson learned for implementing total quality.

Like many R&D organizations, Corning RD&E has struggled with measuring quality used to track improvements. Many traditional measurements of quality are manufacturing related, where the outcome (results) is readily quantifiable. The difficulty for R&D arises in calculating measures that are "in the line of sight of the people who use them."[4] That is, measures must gauge the activity and pertain to the work in which the individual is involved. For RD&E, these measurements were difficult to obtain. Corning as a company used the percent of total sales that resulted from new products as a measure of the RD&E effort. Although this has worked in selected applications, new products are difficult to define and the "line of sight is poor."[4] Measures must be "local," i.e., pertain to the specific task and developed within the work group. These measures must come from the work group, with its input and buy in. Therefore, measures must be unique to the function and task.

Due to the unique nature of R&D, two global measures were chosen to gauge improvement. The first of these is customer satisfaction. This information comes from both internal and external customers. Customer satisfaction is measured with traditional instruments such as surveys, forums, and one-on-one personal interviews.[3,4] In order to interpret these data, a gap analysis is performed between the rating a customer would assign and that recorded by the department or RD&E individual. A gap analysis is the difference between what you expect and what your customer scores you on for a particular characteristic. For RD&E, these gaps constitute specific areas that require improvement. Thus, RD&E can assess its customer's response and identify specific characteristics of the service (or product) that require improvement. For example:

> RD&E sells its services to Corning plants and divisions. The price
> is fixed for the time/effort of an engineer or scientist. Occasionally, plants have complained that "new" engineers or scientists
> cost the same as experienced professionals. In order to satisfy the
> customer and insure the reputation of the division, a certification
> program was developed to assure customers of the knowledge
> and experience potential of an engineer or scientist. That is, a
> certified individual would possess the knowledge needed to meet
> the specific customer requirement. In this way customers could
> be assured of the quality they received from the division.[4]

The above example demonstrates the ability of the RD&E division to implement total quality principles by "listening to the customer."

The second critical measure of excellence adopted by the division is employee satisfaction The focus of this measure is to "pay attention to employees needs."[4] As an example:

> Many engineers and scientists have expended long hours traveling to and from plant sites. Given the concern of these employees, the division has decided to relocate those employees who wish to be closer to their work site.

By relocating workers and their families for the duration of the project, engineers and scientists can expend more energy on completing their respective tasks. Satisfying employees meets the critical needs of internal customers and underscores the importance of the human component in total quality.

CONCLUSION

Corning's RD&E division's total quality effort has evolved over the last ten years. A continuous improvement mindset has been embraced by the corporation. The pace and timing of changes have been accomplished by both employees and managers working together. Incremental movement toward total quality has been achieved. Changes that have occurred are the result of a process that has evaluated the social, management, and technical systems. Successes are well publicized, employees are recognized and rewarded, and there has been time to celebrate achievements made throughout the organization. Mistakes and errors have been used as a learning rather than a disciplinary tool. There has been time for employees and managers to acclimate to the process and adapt. There has not been a "one way—only way" approach to total quality. The individual's talents and abilities have been incorporated into the process. Total quality may have begun as a top-down mandate, but the results in the 1990s involve employees and managers who know the goals and objectives of the organization.

Corning's RD&E division serves as a model organization for total quality implementation, yet its approach has been "individualized" to meet the needs of internal and external customers. The success of Corning's efforts lie mainly with its employees and their "enlightened" management practices and policies. Any organization can follow the Corning model by implementing total quality principles in an evolutionary rather than revolutionary manner. The secret of Corning's success lies within the organization, its employees, and its management systems.

REFERENCES

1. Seward, E. (1992). "Quality in R&D: It All Began with a Customer's Request." *Research-Technology Management*, 35(5), pp. 28–34.
2. Corning, Inc. (1994). *Corning Total Quality Digest*, Corning, NY: Corning, Inc.
3. Strzegowski, W. (August 1994). Personal Conversation.
4. Mitchell, M. (August 1994). Personal Conversation.
5. Menger, E. (July 1994). Personal Conversation.

BIBLIOGRAPHY

Davis, D.C. (1994). "QA in the R&D Environment." *Defense Electronics*, 26(2), p. 30

Davis, T.R. (1994). "Benchmarks of Customer Satisfaction Measurement: Honeywell, Toyota, and Corning." *Planning Review*, 22(3), pp. 38–41.

Morone, J.G. (1993). "Technology and Competitive Advantage—The Role of General Management." *Research-Technology Management*, 36(2), pp. 16–25.

Wrubel, R. (1992). "Joint Ventures and Alliances." *Financial World*, 161(19), p. 4.

ACKNOWLEDGMENTS

The author would like to thank Dr. Eve Menger, Mr. Mark Mitchell, Mr. Wes Strzegowski, and Mr. Mark Spetseris of the Corning RD&E division for their assistance in preparing this case study. These individuals provided exceptional information that enabled the author to complete this project. Their assistance and cooperation are greatly appreciated.

GLOSSARY

Abnormal variation: Changes in process performance that cannot be accounted for by typical day-to-day variation. Also referred to as nonrandom variation.

Acceptable quality (AQL): The maximum number of parts that do not comply with quality standards.

Activity: The tasks performed to change inputs into outputs.

Adaptable: An adaptable process is designed to maintain effectiveness and efficiency as requirements change. The process is deemed adaptable when there is agreement among suppliers, owners, and customers that the process will meet requirements throughout the strategic period.

Appraisal cost: The cost incurred to determine defects.

Benchmarking: A tool used to improve products, services, or management processes by analyzing the best practices of other companies to determine standards of performance and how to achieve them in order to increase customer satisfaction.

Business objectives: Specific objectives which, if achieved, will ensure that the operating objectives of the organization are in alignment with the vision, values, and strategic direction. They are generally high level and timeless.

Business process: Organization of people, equipment, energy, procedures, and material into measurable, value-added activities needed to produce a specified end result.

Business process analysis (BPA): Review and documentation (mapping) of a key business process to understand how it currently functions and to establish measures.

Competitive: A process is considered to be competitive when its overall performance is judged to be as good as that of comparable processes. Competitiveness is based on a set of performance characteristics (defects, costs, inventory turnaround, etc.) that are monitored and tracked against comparable processes within the corporation, the industry, and/or the general business community.

Competitive benchmarking: Comparing and rating the practices, processes, and products of an organization against the competition. Comparisons are confined to the same industry.

Conformance: Affirmative indication or judgment that a product or service

241

has met specified requirements, contracts, or regulations. The state of meeting the requirements.

Continuous improvement: This is a principle used by W. Edwards Deming to examine improvement of product and service. It involves searching unceasingly for ever-higher levels of quality by isolating sources of defects. It is called *kaizen* in Japan, where the goal is zero defects. Quality management and improvement is a never-ending activity.

Control: The state of stability, or normal variation and predictability. It is the process of regulating and guiding operations and processes using quantitative data. Control mechanisms are also used to detect and avoid potential adverse effects of change.

Control charts: Statistical plots derived from measuring a process. Control charts help detect and determine deviations before a defect results. Inherent variations in manufacturing and non-manufacturing processes can be spotted and accounted for by designers.

Corrective action: The implementation of effective solutions that result in the elimination of identified product, service, and process problems.

Cost of quality: The sum of prevention, appraisal, and failure costs, usually expressed as a percentage of total cost or revenue.

Critical success factors (CSFs): Areas in which results, if satisfactory, will ensure successful corporate performance. They ensure that the company will meet its business objectives. CSFs are focused, fluctuate, and are conducive to short-term plans.

Cross-functional: A term used to describe individuals from different business units or functions who are part of a team to solve problems, plan, and develop solutions for process-related actions affecting the organization as a system.

Cross-functional focus: The effort to define the flow of work products in a business process as determined by their sequence of activities, rather than by functional or organizational boundaries.

Culture (also vision): The pattern of shared beliefs and values that provides members of an organization rules of behavior or accepted norms for conducting operational business.

Customer: The recipient or beneficiary of the outputs of work efforts or the purchaser of products and services. May be either internal or external to the company.

Customer, internal: Organizations have both external and internal customers. Many functions and activities are not directly involved with external customer satisfaction, but their outputs provide inputs to other functions and activities within the organization. Data processing, for example, must provide an acceptable quality level for many internal customers.

Customer requirements (also called valid requirements): The statement of needs or expectations that a product or service must satisfy. Requirements must be specific, measurable, negotiated, agreed to, documented, and communicated.

Customer/supplier model: The model is generally represented using three interconnected triangles to depict inputs flowing into a work process that, in turn, adds value and produces outputs that are delivered to a customer. Throughout the process, requirements and feedback are fed from the customer to the supplier to ensure that customer quality requirements are met.

Cycle time: The elapsed time between the commencement and completion of a task. In manufacturing, it is calculated as the number of units of work-in-process inventory divided by the number of units processed in a specific period. In order processing it can be the time between receipt and delivery of an order. Overall cycle time can mean the time from concept of a new product or service until it is brought to market.

Defect: Something that does not conform to requirements.

Document of understanding (DOU): A formal agreement defining the roles, responsibilities, and objectives of all the parties to that agreement. The degree of detail is dictated by the nature of the agreement, but it should always clearly address the requirements of the work product in question.

Effective: An effective process produces output that conforms to customer requirements. The lack of process effectiveness is measured by the degree to which the process output does not conform to customer requirements (that is, by the level of defect of the output).

Effectiveness: The state of having produced a decided or desired effect; the state of achieving customer satisfaction.

Efficiency: A measure of performance that compares output production with cost or resource utilization (as in number of units per employee per hour or per dollar).

Efficient: An efficient process produces the required output at the lowest possible (minimum) cost. That is, the process avoids waste or loss of resources in producing the required output. Process efficiency is measured by the ratio of required output to the cost of producing that output. This cost is expressed in units of applied resource (dollars, hours, energy, etc.).

Employee involvement (EI): Promotions and mechanisms to achieve employee contributions, individually and in groups, to quality and company performance objectives. Cross-functional teams, task forces, quality circles, or other vehicles for involvement are used.

Employee well-being and morale: Maintenance of work environment conducive to well-being and growth of all employees. Factors include health, safety, satisfaction, work environment, training, and special services such as counseling assistance, recreational, or cultural.

Executive Quality Service Council (EQSC): Comprised of members of executive management and union leadership who oversee the quality effort from a corporate view and set strategic direction.

Facilitator: Responsible for guiding the team through analysis of the process. Also concerned with how well the team works together.

Failure cost: The cost resulting from the occurrence of defects (such as scrap, rework/redo, replacement, etc.).

Functional organization: An organization responsible for one of the major corporate business functions such as marketing, sales, design, manufacturing, or distribution.

Human resource management: Development of plans and practices that realize the full potential of the work force to pursue the quality and performance objectives of the organization. Includes (1) education and training, (2) recruitment, (3) involvement, (4) empowerment, and (5) recognition.

Implementer: An individual working within the process and who is responsible for carrying out specific job tasks.

Indicators: Benchmarks, targets, standards, or other measures used to evaluate how well quality values and programs are integrated.

Information system: A database of information used for planning day-to-day management and control of quality. Types of data should include (1) customer related, (2) internal operations, (3) company performance, and (4) cost and financial.

Inputs: Products or services obtained from others (suppliers) in order to perform job tasks. Material or information required to complete the activities necessary for a specified end result.

Involved managers: Managers who have responsibility for the day-to-day activities and tasks within the process.

Just-in-time (JIT): The delivery of parts and materials by a supplier at the moment a factory needs them, thus eliminating costly inventories. Quality is paramount because a faulty part delivered at the last moment will not be detected.

Kaizen: See Continuous improvement

Leadership: The category of the Baldrige Award that examines personal leadership and involvement of executives in creating and sustaining a customer focus and clear and visible quality values.

Management for quality: The translation of customer focus and quality values into implementation plans for all levels of management and supervision.

Measurable outcomes: Specific results that determine, corporately, how well critical success factors and business objectives are being achieved. They are concrete, specific, and measurable.

Measurement: The methods used to achieve and maintain conformance to customer requirements. Measurement determines the current status of the process and whether the process requires change or improvement.

Mission: The core purpose of being for an organization. Usually expressed in the form of a statement 25 to 50 words in length.

Operating plans: Specific, actionable plans which, if carried out successfully, ensure that critical success factors are met, which in turn ensures that corporate business objectives are met. They are tied to critical success factors, are detailed, and contain measurements of success.

Operating Quality Service Council (OQSC): Comprised of activity management and their direct reports, and many include union and staff representation. The council oversees the quality effort within an activity and ensures that quality strategies support the corporate strategic direction.

Organization for quality: Structuring organizational activities to effectively accomplish the company's objectives.

Outputs: The specified end result, materials, or information provided to others (internal or external customers).

Pareto analysis (or Pareto chart): A statistical method of measurement to identify the most important problems through different measuring scales (for example, frequency, cost, etc.). Usually displayed by a bar graph that ranks causes of process variation by the degree of impact on quality (sometimes called the 80/20 rule).

Prevention activity: Elements of prevention activity include (1) education in process quality management and (2) process management (ownership, documentation/analysis, requirements activity, measurements including statistical techniques, and corrective action on the process).

Prevention cost: Costs incurred to reduce the total cost of quality.

Process: The organization of people, equipment, energy, procedures, and material into the work activities needed to produce a specified end result (work product). A sequence of repeatable activities characterized as having measurable inputs, value-added activities, and measurable outputs. It is a set of interrelated work activities characterized by a set of specific inputs and value-added tasks that produce a set of specific outputs.

Process analysis: The systematic examination of a process model to establish a comprehensive understanding of the process itself. The intent of the examination should include consideration of simplification, elimination of unneeded or redundant elements, and improvement.

Process capability: The level of effectiveness and efficiency at which the process will perform. This level may be determined through the use of statistical control charts. Long-term performance level after the process has been brought under control.

Process control: The activity necessary to ensure that the process is performing as designed. Achieved through the use of statistical techniques, such as control charts, so that appropriate actions can be taken to achieve and maintain a state of statistical control.

Process elements: A process is comprised of activities and tasks. A process may also be referred to as a subprocess when it is subordinate to, but part of, a larger process. A subprocess can also be defined as a group of activities within a process that comprise a definable component.

Process management: The disciplined management approach of applying prevention methodologies to the implementation, improvement, and change of work processes to achieve effectiveness, efficiency, and adaptability. Critical to the success of process management is the concept of cross-functional focus.

Process model: A detailed representation of the process (graphic, textual, mathematical) as it currently exists.

Process owner: Coordinates the various functions and work activities at all levels of a process, has the authority or ability to make changes in the process as required, and manages the process end-to-end so as to ensure optimal overall performance.

Process performance quality: A measure of how effectively and efficiently a process satisfies customer requirements. The ability of a product or service to meet and exceed the expectations of customers.

Process review: An objective assessment of how well the methodology has been applied to the process. Emphasizes the potential for long-term process results rather than the actual results achieved.

Quality function deployment (QFD): A system that pays special attention to customer needs and integrates them into the marketing, design, manufacturing, and service processes. Activities that do not contribute to customer needs are considered wasteful.

Quality Improvement Team (QIT): A group of people brought together to resolve a specific problem or issue identified by a business process analysis, individual employees, or the Operating Quality Service Council. A group of individuals charged with the task of planning and implementing process quality improvement. The three major roles in this task force are the team leader, team facilitator, and team members.

Quality management: The management of a process to maximize customer satisfaction at the lowest overall cost to the company.

Quality management system: The collective plans, activities, and events established to ensure that a product, process, or service will satisfy given needs. The infrastructure supporting the operational process management and improvement methodology.

Quality planning: The process of developing the quality master to link together all of the planning systems of the organization. The objective is to follow all areas of achievement of the vision, mission, and business objectives and to operationalize the strategy by identifying the requirements to achieve leadership in the market segments chosen. Includes key requirements and performance indicators and the resources committed for these requirements.

Quality tool: Instrument or technique that supports the activities of process quality management and improvement.

Requirements: What is expected in providing a product or service. The *it* in "do it right the first time." Specific and

measurable customer needs with an associated performance standard.

Resource allocation: A decision to allocate resources, capital, and people to support specific operating plans, tied to the budget process.

Results: Results are, quite simply, a measurement of how well corporate business objectives are being met. Results require that standards and goals for performance are set and the results of processes and performance tracked.

Robust design: Making product designs "production-proof" by building in tolerances for manufacturing variables that are known to be unavoidable.

Root cause: Original reason for nonconformance within a process. When the root cause is removed or corrected, the nonconformance will be eliminated.

Six-sigma: A statistical term that indicates a defect level. One-sigma means 68% of products are acceptable, three-sigma means 99.75, and six-sigma means 99.999997% perfect or 3.4 defects per million parts.

Sponsor: Advocate for the team who provides resources and helps define mission and scope to set limits.

Stakeholder: Individual or department who either has an effect on the process or is affected by it.

Statistical process control (SPC): The use of statistical techniques, such as control charts, to analyze a work process or its outputs. The data can be used to identify deviations so that appropriate action can be taken to maintain a state of statistical control (predetermined upper and lower limits) and to improve the capability of the process.

Statistical quality control (SQC): A method of analyzing measured deviations in manufactured materials, parts, and products.

Strategic quality planning: Development of strategic and operational plans that incorporate quality as product or service differentiation and the load bearing structure of the planning process. Includes (1) definition of customer requirements, (2) projections of the industry and competitive environment for identification of opportunities and risks, (3) comparison of opportunities and risks against company resources and capabilities, (4) employee involvement, and (5) supplier capabilities.

Subprocesses: The internal processes that make up a process.

Suppliers: Individuals or groups who provide input. Suppliers can be internal or external to a company, group, or organization.

Taguchi methods: Statistical techniques developed by Genichi Taguchi, a Japanese consultant, for optimizing design and production.

Task: The basic work element of a process activity.

Total quality management (TQM): The application of quality principles for the integration of all functions and processes of the organization. The ultimate goal is customer satisfaction. The way to achieve it is through continuous improvement.

Variation: The degree to which a product, service, or element deviates from the specification or requirements. Quality in service organizations deals with identifying, measuring, and adjusting to variability resulting from interactions with customers, while manufacturing organizations are focused on bringing product variability under control.

Vision: The long-term future desired state of an organization, usually expressed in a 7- to 20-year time frame. Often included in the vision statement are the areas that the organization needs to care about in order to succeed. The vision should inspire and motivate.

INDEX

T